Home Sanctuary

Home Sanctuary

Practical Ways to Create a Spiritually Fulfilling Environment

Nicole Marcelis

Foreword by Denise Linn

Illustrations by Vicki Holt
Photography by Don Mason

CB

CONTEMPORARY BOOKS

Library of Congress Cataloging-in-Publication Data

Marcelis, Nicole.
    Home sanctuary : practical ways to create a spiritually fulfilling
environment / Nicole Marcelis ; foreword by Denise Linn.
      p.   cm.
    ISBN 0-8092-2489-5
    1. Home—Religious aspects.   2. Spiritual life.   I. Title.

BL588.M37   2000
643—dc21   00-24043
                                      CIP

I dedicate this first book to my first-born, Dominic William Carrico, whose tremendous heart and expansive spirit grant me permission each day to be all I am meant to be. I am grateful.

Cover design by Monica Baziuk
Cover illustration copyright © Helen D'Souza
Interior design by Jeanette Wojtyla
Interior illustrations copyright © Vicki Holt
Interior photographs copyright © Don Mason

Published by Contemporary Books
A division of NTC/Contemporary Publishing Group, Inc.
4255 West Touhy Avenue, Lincolnwood (Chicago), Illinois 60712-1975 U.S.A.
Copyright © 2001 by Nicole Marcelis
Printed in the United States of America
International Standard Book Number: 0-8092-2489-5

01 02 03 04 05 06 ML 19 18 17 16 15 14 13 12 11 10 9 8 7 6 5 4 3 2 1

Contents

SECTION THREE *Home Templates*

Foreword

*I*t was a perfect summer evening in the Cascade Mountains of the Northwest. A golden haze from the afternoon's lingering rays of light gently sifted through the trees. The air was rich with the smells of August. As I walked down a country road with Nicole, she told me about her intent to write *Home Sanctuary*. I was excited to hear about her ideas and felt certain that the book would bring value and understanding to many people.

A year and more has passed since that lovely evening. It's a blustery December day in Seattle. I have just finished reading *Home Sanctuary* and feel as though I've just finished a splendid meal, accompanied by a glass of fine aged wine and great conversation with good friends. I feel so full and satisfied.

What a wonderful book! It is full of practical information, ancient wisdom, and inspiring ideas. Nicole has successfully melded information she has gathered from the world of Feng Shui and her own deep experience with the spaces we occupy. She has done this in a way that is at once pleasing and deeply insightful. I feel richer for having read this book, and I look forward, in a future August, to swinging lazily in my hammock strung between two old apple trees, rereading this gem of a book.

—Denise Linn, author of
Space Clearing: How to Purify
and Create Harmony in Your Home

Acknowledgments

This book is the product of knowledge acquired through workshops and lectures, reading, colleagues, and experience. My intuitive sense of space and placement and my sensitivity to energy patterns also contributed greatly to this book.

I am grateful to my teacher, Denise Linn, who opened my eyes to the layers of pattern and metaphor present everywhere. Her powerful teaching style and passion for her work are inspiring.

I thank everyone at NTC/Contemporary Publishing Group for their assistance and dedication in completing this project. I am especially fortunate to have worked with Erika Lieberman, whose confidence in my idea encouraged me tremendously. I appreciate the technical expertise of Vicki Holt, who spent many hours reviewing my work. Some of her beautiful artwork graces the pages of this book, as does the masterful photography of Don Mason, neighbor, friend, and consultant. Thanks to all.

The unwavering support of my family helped me balance all of my commitments and gave me more reason to forge ahead with my writing. Special thanks to Dominic and Eva, who inspire me.

I thank God for my gifts, and for the opportunity to share them through the pages of this book.

How to Use This Book

*T*his book is a guidance system for manifesting specific results in your life through the platform we affectionately call Home, and will benefit each reader according to need and belief. My purpose is not to plant ideas in your mind, but rather to assist the unfolding of your own ideas. You will find many suggestions throughout the book that will help you raise your consciousness to the limitless ways our homes can be sanctuary.

I recommend reading through the book once without any predetermined ideas about how you want your home to look or feel. Spend extra time on whatever subject matter seems to flag your attention. Once you have done this, reread Chapter 2, "Getting Clear About Home," performing the exercises as you go. Take all the time you need to complete each exercise. Dismiss any linear thinking about the benefits of this type of creative work, for linear thinking has little to do with the flow of creativity or the needs of the soul. If you are a skeptic, you will be pleasantly surprised by your results, and perhaps even amazed by the transformative power behind creative intention.

When I speak of creative intention I refer to acting in alignment with our higher selves. We are multifaceted and multidimensional beings. When we circumvent our cluttered, logical minds and excavate information about what our souls need, we allow creative thought to flow through us. When we direct the flow of creative thinking, our lives are transformed intentionally—adding great power to what we do—and in alignment with the universe and the agreements we hold in spirit.

If you are orderly to the point that it restrains your joy and that of others around you, resist the temptation to read this book paragraph by paragraph taking notes to orchestrate a critical path for the development and enrichment of your home environment. Focus on balance. Put your feelers out and examine those ideas that elicit a positive response from your gut. Focus on big, not little, first. On the other hand, if your home and life can be loosely classified as messy, it may benefit you to be a little more structured in your approach to producing the life you truly desire and need. We are part of an orderly universe in which even chaos is nothing but layer upon layer of pattern. Again, intuitive guidance is key to getting the most of the material presented here.

This book is divided into three sections. Section One provides introductory information about creating a home sanctuary, including information on decluttering and space clearing. The essentials introduced here are prerequisite to creating sanctuary. The exercises presented in Chapter 2 will help you develop a filter through which to run the information encountered in the remainder of the book. Ideas in alignment with your newly excavated sense of Home should be noted and incorporated into your life.

Section Two, "Components of Home" (Chapters 4 through 14), is an overview of the components used to articulate the home templates discussed in Section Three. Your interest level should ultimately drive how much time you devote to each component. While these chapters are concise, I have brought forward the essence of each topic so that you will acquire an instinctive, full-spectrum understanding of the components that make a home.

Section Three is the heart of the book and encompasses Chapters 15 through 24. Each of these chapters represents a home environment theme. I refer to these themes generically as *home templates*. These templates are examples of how information presented in Section Two can be compiled to create thematic sanctuaries. A creative mind will immediately detect that the combinations of components that may be used to create specialized environments are actually endless, and that the really powerful thing is your level of awareness of all you do at Home, all you are at Home, and all Home does and is for you. A solid grasp of the concepts presented will allow you to continuously make adjustments in your home environment to support you as you evolve through life.

At Home, may wisdom and beauty reign, may peace and contemplation await, may festivity be conducted with creativity and accompanied by friends new and old, may nurturance and safety provide shelter, and may love be the driving power behind Home always.

The material in this book regarding the use of essential oils and flower essences is not meant to take the place of diagnosis and treatment by a qualified medical practitioner. All recommendations made are believed to be effective, but since the actual use of these products is beyond the author's control, no expressed or implied guarantee as to the effects of their use can be given nor liability taken.

Introduction to Home

CHAPTER ONE

Creating Sanctuary

Creating Home is one of the most significant things human beings do. Home is the repository of all we do to satisfy our nesting instinct, which is arguably one of the strongest drives we possess. Home is the canvas upon which the essence of our lives is most brilliantly and definitively captured and depicted. Within the walls of our homes we love and nurture; we contemplate and evolve; we rest, rejuvenate, and celebrate. At home we wrestle with knowing and being ourselves. Home is where we really matter, and where we are absolutely transparent. The consequences of all we say and do become etched upon this truly sacred space in some way or another. No other place extends us the arena and safety net for exploring the vastness of life in this manner.

If our homes are sufficiently nurturing, the world is enhanced simply through our presence. The more refined, loving, and vibrant we are, the more our world is. It follows, then, that it is far from a selfish endeavor to focus our attention on our homes and home life. By creating a home sanctuary we give to the world a precious gift: a balanced, well-loved, and loving individual.

Perhaps most meaningful to us individually is that when our home environment is aligned with a purposeful inner life, our outer life—what the world sees—reflects the highest and truest vision we hold for ourselves. When all aspects of our lives are aligned to a distinct purpose, we are powerful. That we unfold from a place of love and genuine confidence, rather than from shame, uncertainty, or inner conflict, grants others permission to shine as vibrantly as we do. The serenity we embody seeds the world with peace as we move through it.

There are many reasons for coordinating our living environments with our dreams. Whether we live in a tiny flat on the twelfth floor in the inner city, a log cabin nestled in a stand of old-growth trees, or a clean-lined tract home in the suburbs, we benefit from an awareness that our homes are integral to the quality of our own lives and those of our lineage. Therefore, creating Home needs and deserves a considerable amount of our attention and priority status in our hearts. The love vibrations we foster within the walls of our homes are contagious.

Home should be a place of nourishment, a place where we become physically, mentally, and spiritually refreshed: a sanctuary. A home sparkling with love and intention provides these things. It becomes the perfect backdrop for entertaining and playing, romancing and cradling, dreaming and overcoming. A home sanctuary inspires and grounds us, stimulates and soothes us, draws us inward and releases us—more aware—into the arms of our loved ones and the world. It is a treasure and a blessing to all those who dwell within its walls and a wellspring of joy to all who visit.

For many of us, the thought of being without Home is one of the scariest imaginable. Our homes are our friends; they protect us from the elements and much more. Home provides us with a place to run to when we feel lonely, off-center, struck by misfortune or tragedy, or otherwise compelled to go deep within. Whenever we are out of sync with the cosmos we still have our homes—places to hide while we work it all out.

Our homes, no matter how grand or humble, owned or rented, belong to us, and we are free to choose who and what enters. There is very little that any external force can dictate to us in connection with our home life. Allow your free choice to serve you well. Recognize the preciousness of your domain and be selective about everyone and everything brought into it. Whatever you bring to Home will be reflected back to you, and this is very powerful. Our minds operate on many different levels and know much more in any given moment than we ever consciously realize. Become wise to the messages transmitted to you through your home's energy field.

You have chosen this book because you love your home and all who find support and comfort within its hallowed walls. Resist the temptation to merely decorate it. For a home adorned without thorough consideration for its own soul and those of its occupants is not a home; it is a house and it will not be authentic or loved. A beautifully appointed house, no matter how stylistically resonant with modern culture or any other particular era, will only temporarily appease us unless it is filled with love and the accompanying memories of a life well lived. A house is capable only of displaying our material wealth and status. A home displays what lives in our hearts: our dreams, our values, our priorities, and, hopefully, our purposeful evolution.

Modern Home Culture

There is no doubt that our modern frame of reference for Home differs greatly from that of native and ancient cultures. People used to live communally and with great allowance for their spirituality. This manner of living is nearly obsolete in industrially mature cultures. The information age has descended indiscriminately upon us, inundating us with distraction. Most of us lead such crazed existences these days that there is little time to contemplate how we can be better supported in accomplishing our dreams. All this busyness can put us dangerously close to allowing the nurturing warmth of Home to fall away completely. In the blink of a cursor we could forget the lore, the love, the luxury of Home.

The sterility and spiritual disintegration of modern life are reflected in our homes in many ways, and often quite poignantly. Homes are frequently either cold in appearance and feeling, or a disheveled, unsightly mess as a result of complete neglect. Of course there exists every imaginable home environment in between. In general, modern design culture seems to over-focus on the form and function of a neatly orchestrated palette of objects—leaving hearts and souls out of the picture. If we cannot entrust our care into the refined sensibilities of a soulful home, it is likely our dwelling place will exhibit a certain empty, isolating quality. A healthy dose of awareness and love facilitates the connection between our souls and our homes.

Quite opposed to the form-and-function approach, a home sanctuary honors the beings dwelling within it by embracing them as its frame of reference. The stylistic elements of Home, namely color, texture, finishes, objects of affection, and placement, evolve from loving consideration of the dreams of the occupants. Embrace these elements as sacred and something magical occurs.

A sanctuary not only reflects our dreams but inspires and nurtures them. The more distressing symptoms of modernistic thought with regard to Home deserve to be immediately remedied if we are to truly become an advanced civilization wherein every dream of every soul is deemed significant and supported. Ideally, and most effectively, our dreams are born and fed primarily within the walls of Home.

Home as Mirror

Home mirrors all we fill it with, in ways both overt and subtle. This is because we have relationships with our homes. As is the case with any relationship, a certain amount of our self is revealed to us through the law of attraction: we draw to us that which is similar to us in order to come face to face with those parts of ourselves that are prime for growth and development. These parts of ourselves may be displayed physically, through the components we've assembled within our homes, which are representative of our feelings and emotions, states of mind, priorities and values. To discover whether we are on the pathway to a fulfilled, inspired, meaningful life, we can look at the effects present in it—in this case, the home environment it yields. A metaphor for our inner life, Home provides clues about what may be amiss, and any positive and intentional adjustments made to Home will assist and support us in manifesting our dreams.

There are many reasons why this works. Such adjustments arouse in us a higher level of awareness. When we see the direct and immediate responses of the universe to the slightest of our actions as we conduct our home lives, we realize that what we are seeing is cause and effect on a divine scale. We begin to see the correlation between our actions and their consequences everywhere, not only in our home lives, but also in relationships, in the workplace, within ourselves, and in the common thread running through seemingly isolated events.

Making constructive adjustments requires that we become more invested and responsible. Once we enter that higher realm of awareness we understand at all levels of our being that we are the sole creators of everything that occurs in our lives. This awareness simply will never fade. Every thought, word, and act is important and contributes to our destiny.

When we really live in our homes and conduct our home lives with intention, we invoke a powerful, ancient, and loving collective consciousness that brings tremendous meaning into our lives. As a result, activities previously viewed as mundane or bothersome become propelled by a certain amount of enchantment. We then begin to experience the profuse richness of purposeful living.

The Living Home

For each of us, the very idea of Home brings back memories of an entire lifetime of activities, events, festive occasions, feelings, and emotional milestones. Add to this the genetic matter of Home—its history, lore, and the meaning people have assigned to it through the ages—and Home suddenly commands a higher place in our hearts and minds.

Whatever the image we hold, one thing is true: Home is far more than a mere structure; it lives. Our homes live because we live, and we live most openly at home. Our energy fields and those of our homes are enmeshed. It certainly pays to think about our own energetic pulsation. If we are sorrowful victims, dictators of chaos, unforgiving tyrants, uncompassionate beings, or in general choose to behave negatively, our homes will absorb and hold the same kind of harmful energy. However, if we live as loving, caring, compassionate, and positive beings, our homes will embrace the love circulating within their walls, radiating goodness back to us. This exchange of positive vibratory energy between us and Home will be there to draw upon during challenging times.

Yet, Home has a rather imposing consciousness, for it is difficult to show ourselves to be anything other than our very essence while at home. Home squelches any dramatic attempt to impress. Our worldly persona seems to melt away as we step through the front door. But just as assuredly as it detects and reveals a fake, Home also lovingly supports and sustains any right evolutionary growth we undertake within its walls—especially when given the proper tools.

Sanctuary

When we find and use the right tools for our personal growth, when we surround ourselves with whatever inspires us, with whatever stirs our souls, when there is no conflict between our inner reality and who we show ourselves to be in our most sacred space—Home—the result is sanctuary. When whatever delights all of our senses is taken into account, when whatever makes us feel complete, balanced, and peaceful inside is present, when the energy swirling gently around us is about love and nurturance of our dreams, Home becomes sanctuary. When ancient and native wisdom is resuscitated within our living space, blended with the elements of nature, and laced into a delicately balanced sensorial palette, we experience sanctuary.

The posture of Home and all it represents plays powerfully into our psyches. An intentional home environment is the foundation on which we build our lives and support our endeavors. In an environment that assumes a certain thematic posture, it is nearly impossible to feel otherwise. For instance, it would be difficult to feel lethargic for very long when the environment exuded optimism in all of its components.

There are a couple of prerequisites to creating a home sanctuary. The first is that we must know what we want in life before we can be supported in it by our home (or by anything else for that matter). This knowing must come from our gut, be fully sensed, and should have its origins in pure love—not fear. We must be able to articulate what we want. The second prerequisite is that we must act. However, we must keep in mind that, ultimately, it is not merely physical effort that will produce the desired outcome, but an act of faith. Rest assured that once we proclaim our dream, our very first step in sync with that dream releases it into the universe. Once this is done we cannot hang on to or worry over our aspiration because doing so may only sabotage it. While keeping the dream in clear focus, simply let it go. Every ensuing step toward this goal, then, becomes a leap of faith.

The universe responds because it has to. This is no different than cultivating a lovely rosebush. Once planted in fertile soil, it has no choice but to respond to mineral content, sunlight, and rain. It grows and it blossoms. This universal law is applied in like measure to us. Once we understand that thinking and intent cause definitive and sometimes immediate response from the universe, our entire perception of how life works shifts dramatically. Perceiving the intricate web of oneness we all weave together, we can also then see how a shift in one person's life elevates the condition of all human beings. The role of Home in all of this is huge, given that real change is fostered within its privacy.

It can be daunting to look upon the effects in our lives and ask, "What is it I have planted?" Fortunately, Home is the great mirror *and* workstation. In this book you will learn to identify ways your home can aid you in harvesting your life's objectives. You will clarify, strengthen, and augment your understanding of Home. You will then be guided in making the appropriate adjustments to your environment—both concrete and metaphysical—that will create a personalized sanctuary.

Part of creating sanctuary involves infusing the home environment with a certain amount of mysticism. That does not mean spending inordinate amounts of energy on the traditional props of mysticism, such as burning incense, meditating, using crystals, and having paranormal encounters—although these things may be a part of an individual's experience. In this book mysticism simply implies an air of enchantment borne of the inherent spiritual meaning of an action or object brought into higher awareness. Washing the dishes becomes much less mundane when we begin to see it as a purification ritual and we undertake the task with love. Wash them alone by candlelight and a feeling of tranquillity will grace your being.

Home Symbolism

To produce an environment glistening with magic, it is helpful to understand that our consciousness is powerfully steeped in the very idea of Home. Each component of Home and every activity, from the everyday to the very festive, conducted within Home is exquisitely significant. Understanding this is key to unleashing the intense life force behind all aspects of Home. So, leave behind any linear thoughts of form and function and allow yourself to become bewitched by the symbolic power of Home.

The common reference to Home as "four walls" is conceptually striking when we consider that the number four represents stability and security, order and organization. Four also represents wholeness and completeness. How magnificent it is that our roofs are pointed, following a logic similar to that behind the pyramid: to acknowledge our position in relation to heaven.

Climbing stairs becomes much more meaningful when we become aware that they represent ascension to a higher plane, that they are a metaphorical bridge between two levels of understanding. Stairs also represent success; we've all heard the phrase "climbing the ladder" and instinctively understand its meaning.

Thresholds are magical points of suspended transition. While crossing a threshold, time seems to stand still. Doors represent opportunity. The Romans even acknowledged a god of passageways and doors: Janus, who has two faces, one representing the past, the other the future, or one looking inward, the other outward. Some say an invisible third face is the most illusive point along our linear concept of time: the present. We can accentuate the magic of thresholds by decorating them, as many cultures have done and continue to do. One traditional symbol is the pentacle, or five-pointed star, which signifies good health and knowledge. In the Middle Ages it was used to discourage demons and witches from entering. Any threshold marker carrying personal meaning will suffice if it is hung with crystalline intention.

Allow yourself to become enchanted next time you walk through a hall-way, knowing they, like pathways, symbolize spiritual awakening. What is your soul awakening to? What does it yearn to more fully express?

Let the symbolism of the element of fire enter your consciousness each time you engage your stove. Keep it sparkling clean and use all burners routinely. Honor the element of fire by embellishing the cooking area as the shrine to health and prosperity it really is, for food equals abundance. Display objects that represent the sun: anything red, a sun-shaped mirror, or perhaps a cross to keep away maleficent influences.

Treat mealtimes as sacred events. If you are part of a family, eat together as often as possible; this is a powerful bonding experience. Light candles, say a blessing, and recognize that your very lives are being sustained and extended, all compliments of a repast conceived and executed with love.

Notice that every step in the cooking process has a corresponding spiritual metaphor and you will never again view cooking as drudgery. Allow this imagery and the sinuous dance of yin and yang in all cooking-related activities to render the cooking process a meditation of love and gratitude.

The fireplace, or hearth, symbolizing the vital or creative center of Home, deserves to be an exalted and sacred area. Fire is purifying, and as anyone who has sat around a campfire knows, it bonds people socially—making it the ideal spot for family gatherings. The goddess Hestia was associated with the hearth and represented the organizational energy of the home. Her presence was felt by focusing on the glowing embers of the fire. We can honor that energy by fashioning our mantel into a sort of family altar. During stretches of inclement weather, find reasons to lounge around the fireplace, mesmerized by the patterned flicker of the flames. If your home does not have a fireplace, create a symbolic one with a forest of candles wherever you feel the center of your home is.

Nothing is more reviving to the spirit than an elegantly spare and natural bathroom. No matter what our setup, we can find solace in our own sacred purification ritual, for cleansing honors not only our bodies but our souls as well—it is both practical and poetic.

Bedrooms are perhaps the most emotionally charged spaces of our homes. Something critical yet beyond our conscious grasp hangs in the air.

The lively dance of our souls during dream time leaves its mark as a feeling of otherworldliness, of a huge open universe. In these rooms tender vows of commitment are whispered and expressions of passion are released into the care of a sacred relationship. We sense all this, for when the world becomes a bigger challenge than we feel up to, we often retreat to this room. Do we escape our physical world of effects when we dream, or does the essence of life and who we really are escape us during our waking hours and return during sleep? Allow yourself to be cradled in expansiveness in your own room.

Closets contain the power of secret information, of things beyond physical vision. There is a time to hold back information from others: when giving it away means giving your power to someone or something not supportive of your evolutionary growth. Each time you open your closet doors, query yourself or the universe about whether you have withheld information now ripe for dispersion. Make it a routine and your psyche will be free and clear of "skeletons."

By infusing our home with love and conscious attention, and by honoring the power Home has gathered through the ages, we create a sanctuary for our soul—a place from which to draw vital energy and creativity for every activity life leads us to, and a beautiful backdrop so powerful that it brands a lifetime's memories into our heart.

CHAPTER TWO

Getting Clear About Home

*T*he cleaner and more energetically clear your home is, the easier it will be to craft an environment that truly supports you. It's like beginning with a blank slate. Getting clear about Home involves purging your environment of all things that are psychically, emotionally, and practically meaningless or obsolete and then physically cleaning and energetically clearing your home, which is referred to as space clearing.

Decluttering

Vital to getting clear about Home and creating sanctuary is one simple truth: to become clear you must completely declutter your environment. In America especially, where vigorous consumerism is typical, people own a lot of stuff. It is not uncommon for people to rent storage units for their excess things, or live in large houses to accommodate it all. This kind of accumulation is not only a financial drain, but also a drain on energy and spirit.

Understanding energy flow is key to creating a home sanctuary. If your home is filled up wall to wall, top to bottom with clutter, you effectively block the flow of spirit, life force, Chi-energy, and the cycles of nature. Once you dismiss unwanted or unused items from your home, leaving only useful and cherished things, it and you will feel lighter and closer to the metered whisperings of all life.

When you have created a clear, pure, and organized domain, the exercises for exploring your understanding of Home and the ensuing challenge of developing a new vision of your home based on your objective becomes much more facile. If the mere thought of sorting through books, paperwork, clothing, toys, tools, garden miscellany, kitchenware, craft and hobby supplies, photos, furniture, and household embellishments is intimidating to you, allow yourself to go into that feeling and explore your true reasons. Is it because the task is genuinely huge? Is it because you overly identify yourself with your material possessions? Do your possessions bring you comfort? Why? Are you fortifying yourself against some imagined future state of poverty?

Once you have come face to face with the beliefs that enslave you to your belongings, affirm the truth to yourself. You are not your things. You are part of the abundant flow of the universe. You love yourself and are fully capable of proper self-care. Acknowledging the truth about yourself in this manner, thoughtfully and with a heart full of love for yourself and your home, will begin to rewire your thinking. Say your affirmations daily, several times a day. Write them over and over in your journal. Soon, when a counter-thought or -belief comes into your mind, you will be aware of it. Automatically you will chase these remnants of old programming out of your head, and you will center yourself in what you know deep inside to be the truth. When change begins to erupt inside and you begin to feel lighter, freer, like the limitless being you are, begin the decluttering process.

Removing Clutter

First, remove anything from your home that elicits a negative emotional response. This will facilitate the presence of uplifting and joyful energy. Negative items not only block your energy, they draw it away from you. It is best to remove these things as opposed to simply storing them away, because you will, in fact, be aware of their presence lurking somewhere in your home. Some of these energy traps are easy to identify—such as photos from a previous marriage. A little more consideration may be needed to deduce that leaving your son's not-so-good report card laying around may be the equivalent of an affirmation for lackluster academic performance. Be thoughtful and thorough.

Any item you feel indifferent about should also be eliminated. What is not loved or held in high esteem will detract from or interfere with the relationships you have with things in your home you do love. When something is unneeded or unloved it may also evoke a feeling of sadness. Always, it is to your greatest advantage to permanently eliminate from your home objects of ambiguity.

Hanging on to things believing someday you will rediscover a use for them carries the imprint of many detrimental energy patterns. In this sense, a cluttered environment is a breeding ground for fear. You may treasure and continue to display your teenage daughter's doll collection, but if she has outgrown her dolls it may truly feel to her that you are unaccepting of her passage into adulthood. Keeping clothes you wore when you were twenty pounds heavier "just in case" speaks to your distrust of your own ability to maintain your weight and care for yourself, potentially creating an actual need for the larger sizes.

Keeping a fleet of similar objects, thinking you will have a working one if the front-line machine should break down when you can't afford to buy another, is an affirmation for struggle. It displays a lack of faith in the abundance of the universe to provide everything you need when you need it.

The way to go about decluttering is not necessarily to have a detailed plan, just a set amount of time to work on it regularly. If you feel a little timid and prefer not to jump in with both feet, commit to decluttering one room at a time. Assign each room a calendar date or dates for clearing and schedule your other activities around these times. Sort through everything—leave no stone unturned. Even if you choose not to discard things, it is crucial to become familiar with them, to reconnect with them. You will know again where they are, remember why they are significant, and put them to use or in a place where they are most meaningful. Go to task with an assortment of boxes. I suggest one for garbage and recycling, one for each of your favorite charities or for a garage sale, one for things that need to be relocated within your home, and one for disbursement to family and friends. For things you wish to give away to loved ones, make piles or use bags to keep them together. Then, so that you don't add clutter to their lives, give your friends and family members the courtesy of a phone call, tell them what you've set aside for them, and ask whether they would like those items. If the answer is yes, make arrangements to bring the gifts to them—so they are not put back into storage for an indefinite period until their new owner claims them.

In your decluttering you are bound to confront large items that haven't been doing much but taking up space for years. These things may have monetary value and you may wish to sell them. But if you are sentimentally attached to a particular item or fond of it in some way, receiving money in exchange for the object may feel uncomfortable. In this case, I encourage you to find someone who really needs or wants and will care for your piano or 1950s dining room set or ping-pong table and cannot afford to purchase one, and give it to him or her. It feels better than a few dollars in your pocket.

Clearing Out Gifts

Most of us regularly face the question of what to do with gifts that don't mesh with our lifestyle. I have neither heard nor read of a satisfactory solution. Based on what I know about relationship dynamics and the flow of energy, my first effort is to prevent getting them in the first place. Here are a few suggestions.

For gifts you receive out of someone's sense of obligation or misinterpretation of your taste and lifestyle, why not explain that there is nothing you really need or desire to accumulate and you prefer to get together for dinner and a movie, or have a contribution made to a favorite charity, nonprofit organization, or your spiritual community instead? Simply let these individuals know you are clearing things out, and that they would be honoring your process by not giving material gifts at this time. You might suggest that gift certificates for haircuts, massages, and so forth would be lovely and very welcome. Be sure, of course, to casually drop the name of your practitioner. Be very specific, and always sensitive, always gentle, and full of love whenever you direct people in this way.

If you already have in your care unwanted gifts that need to make their way out your door, just do it with love and be prepared to offer an honest answer if the givers should inquire about them. Know in advance what you will tell them if they ask. Frame it in such a way that they can feel good about it: "I'm so glad you asked because I learned that my son's school really needed one of those. Since my kids had outgrown it, I saw giving it to the school as a way to continue to honor your thoughtfulness."

Continue on with your decluttering until every drawer of every room and every closet has been cleared and cleaned. You will feel invigorated, inspired, and ready to begin transforming your life into one in which you are a fully present, active participant. To guard against creeping clutter in the future, lighten your home by at least one item each time a new one arrives.

Cleaning and Maintenance

When something is orderly and clean its essence shines radiantly, a deep glow seems to spring forth from it. I've often heard people say they think better when their desk is clean, or their car seems to run better when it's clean inside and out. It is no different for Home. Cleanliness improves our ability to appreciate and connect with our possessions and our home. From improved connections with our belongings emerges a sense of order, which generates efficiency. It is difficult to lose a possession in a well-loved, orderly space. Connectedness, whether it be to Home, to nature, to spirit, or to family, releases us from the isolation of our own thoughts. Home is a relationship—a frame of reference for self-discovery.

Cleaning is an ideal way to establish this connection with Home. However much time cleaning consumes, the results reward in like measure. Cleaning is an excellent way to release pent up stress. Although it pays to be mindful while cleaning, its repetitive motions are perfect for clearing the mind, allowing it to run free or be still. While our mind heals through our surrender to task, our home is also healed. Previously imprisoned beauty emerges while we scrub and polish, releasing its magic into our environment.

Sadly, cleaning seems to be denigrated in our culture. Cleaning professionals are not usually highly paid or respected. Yet a sense of ownership, honor, and healthy pride comes from cleaning and maintaining the things we give our love to. Cleaning is purifying of Home and heart. And the happy ending is that we, our families, and our guests are more comfortable, joyous, and free to be who we are at Home.

The key to making cleaning a powerful and joyful experience is to do it with love. Focus on how much you appreciate your sacred space and the loved ones who dwell in it. If I am folding clothes I think of my baby as I fold her things, of how beautiful she looks in them. When we build love into all activities they become purposeful and worth doing. Furthermore, everything we engage in deserves our full attention. It is worthwhile to stop ranking activities we regularly perform based on how much fun they are. The important stuff of life is rationed out to us through experiences grandiose and humble, exciting and mundane, dramatic and quaint. Know that cleaning is an offering of gratitude to spirit, for beautiful and necessary things living in your home are ritualistically exalted when you clean them.

Try transforming the area you are cleaning by eliminating artificial light. Open the curtains wide and let the daylight in. Even if it's wintertime, crack the windows while you are cleaning and let the fresh air filter through. The energizing effect of the sun and fresh air produces joy and clarity and is the perfect companion during an intense cleaning session. At night, consider operating by the kinetic light of candles.

As a practical matter, clean with environmentally friendly products only. Yes, they cost more, but they will not taint the love you hold for Home and family with toxins. Environmentally sound or homemade cleaning products also smell authentic and truly clean—free of the perfumey, invasive aroma that masks more toxic products. It is fairly easy to locate safe, unscented cleaning products, and to these you can add a few drops of a chosen essential oil if you wish.

Being practical about furnishings makes cleaning easier. Light-colored rugs where your children play will quickly become an eyesore and a continual source of irritation. Placing fragile glass figurines within reach of small children demands your constant supervision if not the sweeping up of the broken pieces.

In honoring Home, you may wish to ask family members—and perhaps even visitors—to remove their shoes. Obviously, no shoes inside means less dirt and less cleaning. This simple act also serves to establish a certain level of intimacy between Home and occupant: nothing feels quite so grounding as hardwood flooring or the texture of a wool rug underfoot. Keep in mind, however, that some people are uncomfortable or unsteady without their shoes. For this reason you may want to be flexible about a no-shoes rule.

Set aside time to clean regularly. Once each quarter, around the time of the winter and summer solstices and the spring and fall equinoxes, do a more in-depth cleaning in preparation for the change of season. A powerful collective consciousness has evolved around the idea of spring cleaning, which originally signified and welcomed the fertility and rebirth associated with the season. If you are too busy to clean as often as you would like, hire someone to help if you can. But when you feel your home needs your attention, make the time to clean it yourself.

The premise of this book—that Home is an expression of our inner lives—dictates that everything about our homes should be in good working order. Doors that cannot fully open, light fixtures that blink on and off, plumbing that frequently backs up: any of these things could signal that life is trying to get a message through. Keeping windows clean allows clarity of vision, literally and metaphorically speaking. Always make necessary home repairs as soon as you are able.

Space Clearing

After decluttering and cleaning is the perfect time to perform a thorough space clearing. See Chapter 3, "Space Clearing," for information on how to perform your own space clearing. Such techniques are used in native and ancient cultures around the world to discharge stagnant energy from the environment. The space clearing is fueled by the power of your intention. In other words, its effectiveness is dependent on how clear your objectives are and how focused your being is on ridding your home of the blocked energy.

Having released an inordinate amount of emotionally charged energy into the space of your home while sorting through your personal possessions, you will most likely need to make several passes through your home using a different space clearing tool each time. Begin with the most powerful tool available to you, such as a drum or gong. On the next pass, clap your hands. On the last round, use a tool providing a finishing touch that feels right and sacred in connection with your dream for Home. This could be chimes, or a bell, or a sprinkling of aromatic water.

Bless and dedicate your home to whatever it is that stirs your heart. Is it peace and harmony, trust and integrity, honor and commitment, or unconditional world-changing love? Say it out loud into the presence of your angels, guides, and spirits, to the oneness of the universe. Your words will produce a ripple effect and all life will be touched by them. A simple blessing I crafted for our home reads:

> *Spirit, bless our home, who supports us with love,*
> *cradles us in peace and comfort, evokes wisdom,*
> *attracts prosperity, and wraps us in beauty.*
> *Amen.*

Exercises for Getting Clear About Home

I introduce here a banquet of exercises for bringing forward and assimilating what it is you need from Home to align it with your life's objectives. Ideally you will choose to perform them all, because each exercise renders its own form of truth and allows you to see your desires from differing perspectives. You may not resonate with every exercise presented. Perhaps my exercises will help you birth your own method of connecting with your concept of the ideal abode. Go with your instinct in selecting which exercises to perform and how to best use the information.

EXERCISE ONE • MENTAL TOUR

This is a visualization exercise that you should allow yourself thirty to forty-five minutes to complete. Read through these instructions once, then delve beneath the layers of your mind to discover the home your soul desires. You will need a relaxing setting, uninterrupted peace and quiet for the duration of the exercise, and a pen and notebook or journal. Turn your telephone ringer off. Sit on a cushion on the floor, or on a favorite chair with your feet touching the floor, while performing this exercise.

Close your eyes. Take about six deep, slow breaths, consciously casting out the worries and concerns of the day each time you exhale. Then allow your breathing to return to normal, sitting quietly until you feel very calm.

Allow a mental picture of your dream home to come into your mind. This abode could be the one you currently reside in, or simply what you consider ideal—you may never have actually beheld this home. You are touring this home. Take mental note of all you see and experience during this tour.

See this home first from overhead, as if you are hovering above it in a hot-air balloon. Notice the shape of it and the plantings of its garden, if it has one. Now come closer and view it as if you were standing at the street. Notice architectural details and its entrance. Make your way to the door, and when you feel ready, enter.

Moving counterclockwise on first the main floor of the house and then on any other floors it may have, examine every detail. Observe how the light plays upon its walls; note the colors and how the light interacts with them. Notice the furnishings and fixtures of each room. Feel the textures and finishes. Note the function of each room; imagine the activities conducted therein. See any symbols and decorative embellishments. Stand in the center of each room taking in the unique energy it individually possesses.

Take all the time you need to finish your mental tour. When you feel complete and have soaked into your consciousness as much detail as possible, slowly open your eyes and come back to the here and now.

Now use whatever techniques make sense to capture the essence and fine detail of your home on paper. You may wish to draw a floor plan and then write in a journal the details of each room. Pay attention to symbols and themes, for these may be indicators of life qualities that would benefit you in your current objectives. Did you see a dove, or was the color green present in every room? Perhaps, then, you should adopt peace as your guiding principle.

Once you are finished writing, date your notes. Keep them handy for review during the unfurling of your sacred space. The images that presented themselves to you during the visualization may be so vivid that you will not need to refer to the notes, but they will be there in case you ever do.

EXERCISE TWO • TREASURE MAP

A treasure map is a collage. You need glue, scissors, poster board, and magazine photos that embody the elements you would like to introduce into your home. The key to empowering the map is to mount it on a wall in your bedroom where it will be the first thing you see in the morning and the last thing you see at night, day in and day out.

I like to do treasure mapping on New Year's Eve and fill my collage with the things I want the new year to bring to me. This year's collage was filled with photographs of writing instruments—symbolizing my desire to write and publish this book; pastels—representing my interest in resurrecting art in my life; and a new kitchen—something I really wanted but felt there was no way I could accomplish for at least two years. Within weeks I had my book contract; after purchasing a set of pastels, I found out I was surprisingly good for never having really used the medium; and my new kitchen became a reality!

So, be selective about what you glue to that poster board. Gather a wide variety of shots. Be sure that color, lighting, and scent—things that evoke the desired mood or feeling—are somehow depicted. Pay attention to what instinct tells you, and to what is fresh in your mind from the visualization exercise. What is joyful to one individual may be completely abrasive and intolerable to another. There is no right or wrong.

Because you are going to look at this collage many times each day, make it as beautiful as you possibly can, in a style you can relate to. Is your personal style eclectic? Or is it well ordered and traditional? Reflect these traits in the layout of your collage. Order your collage according to priority. Do you rank painting the bathroom a new color this spring over embellishing the side yard with a birdbath? If so, place the picture representing the painting at the top of the page, and the birdbath elsewhere on the page. Be thorough and thoughtful. Once your collage graces your bedroom wall, observe the miracle of dreams unfolding.

Treasure mapping is unexpectedly powerful. Approach this activity with a healthy caution because what you include in your map will most likely find its way into your life.

EXERCISE THREE • TALK TO YOUR HOUSE

After you get over feeling ridiculous about it, you will rest in great comfort knowing you actually consider Home to be real. We tend to mutter things out loud to the four walls when we're upset—which, when you really consider it, is probably crazier than speaking to your home purposefully and with kindness. Do you want to know what you most need to transform in order to feel comfortable in your living room? Ask your house. Then imagine the response. Do not dismiss this idea, for the line between our imaginations and our intuition is an imperceptible one, if there is one at all. There really is nothing new under the sun. Our imaginations are that part of us that connects with whatever higher level of wisdom and understanding exists beyond our rational thinking. There are many ways of receiving information from the universe, and imagination is a powerful one.

Use this exercise when you are contemplating a question whose answer has eluded you thus far. Does the room want to be rose or mauve? Know that glimpse of instantaneous information is perfect. It is like following gut instinct.

EXERCISE FOUR • LISTING

There are those among us who cannot manage without a list. Listing is quite helpful and, in this case, a very good way of tying all your excavated information together. Make the following lists without pondering your responses at all. Work on each list for as long as you would like. When one list feels complete, move on to the next.

List 1: Things I believe to be beautiful.
List 2: Things that would make my home more functional.
List 3: Things that would make my home more comfortable.
List 4: Activities I conduct, or wish to conduct, at home.
List 5: How I want my *living room* to feel. (Make a list for each room).
List 6: Descriptions and examples of my personal style.
List 7: Qualities that describe myself.

With all of this information about yourself, you are ready to find out what makes Home a sanctuary, a safe and lovely haven, a temple to your dreams.

CHAPTER THREE

Space Clearing

Once you expose yourself to the sacred experience of clearing the energy in your home, you will be forever more acutely attuned to energy fields. Space clearing is really about moving stagnant energy, diffusing or disintegrating negative energy, and instilling the desired energetic essence into Home. Many ancient and native cultures have subscribed to some type of space clearing or purification ritual, for good reason.

The word *ritual* is important, for it implies distinction, ceremony, the designation of a sacred event. While it is possible to perform space clearing in an informal, casual manner, its effectiveness will be limited to resuscitating stale energy. When we mark something as sacred, formal, and distinctive, more of our energy is channeled and directed with tremendous intent into specific results. The more present we are, the more powerful the outcome.

The results of a thorough, formal space clearing are palpable. Once it is complete your home will sparkle. Colors will appear brighter and clearer, your home will feel more comfortable and open, and sounds will be more crisp. The notes and nuances of the thematic spin you give your space clearing will add richness and depth to the environment.

It is crucial to know what outcome you wish to create prior to conducting your clearing. Outcome can mean anything; preferably it will encompass layers of wishes and dreams. Perhaps it is your overall intention to create stability in your life. From your perspective this stability becomes concrete when you are financially comfortable. You envision this financial independence coming through the purchase of a business you have had your eye on for a while. The essence of the experience you wish to create then almost seems the polar opposite of stability: freedom. You could say, then, that your overall intention for your home is that it help stabilize your life. You specifically want to attract whatever resources are necessary to acquire the business you've been contemplating. In the long term you desire complete financial freedom. The point is you must know, in very specific terms, what it is you wish to create overall, specifically, and in the next two to five years.

Let me emphasize that space clearing is an art form. Space clearing professionals are available for hire. Most of these individuals have extensive training and experience in performing space clearings and are very sensitive to energy fields. But they cannot feel for you. In other words, someone else's energy may not resonate with the energy of the antique sofa you absolutely love and find comfort in. On the other hand, a little objectivity is quite often beneficial. Should you decide to hire a professional to perform your space clearing, make sure you let her know any strong feelings—positive or negative—you hold for your furnishings.

Tools for Space Clearing

Once you've established your objectives, if you're performing your own clearing, you must decide which tools to use. Your choice of tools will be driven by your overall intention for the clearing and your individual personality type. Following are some examples of space clearing tools, categorized. As you read through the list, notice any tools that capture your attention. The most powerful tool is not listed, and that is your mind. It is possible to create a clear environment just by projecting the proper thoughts into it.

Tools That Sound

Anything that makes a sound is useful for space clearing. I will mention only the more common ones here. The most important criterion for choosing tools for space clearing is that you love the tool you are working with.

Your Hands One of the most effective space clearing methods is clapping. The clapping should become louder as the environment is cleared.

Bells There are various types of metal and crystal bells. Bells vary greatly in size and tone. The undulating satin sound of bronze bells makes them excellent for grounding. Brass bells are yang by nature and will help reverse energy patterns in a home where individuals have been too inward. Copper bells are medium in tone and encourage a more active flow of energy. Silver bells are soft and very yin, inviting introspection. Crystal bells have a highly refined energy, good for polishing an environment. If you love bells, you could perform the clearing with several, beginning with a bell that makes a big, deep sound and progressing toward a bell with a light, silvery sound. With all bells, each ring will produce an increasingly lingering sound as the energy in the room lifts.

Gongs If you have a large room to clear, or the environment you are clearing contains lots of negative psychic debris, you may opt to begin with a gong. They produce a powerful, earthy effect.

Singing Bowls Made from several different metals or even crystal, singing bowls create a whirlpool of energy that progressively builds momentum. A mallet or stick is used to continually massage the rim of the bowl, thus building the sound. Bowls typically symbolize receptiveness, and in this case, the singing bowl is poised to receive the goodness you've set your sights on.

Chimes Chime bars, which come in various sizes, discharge a mystical energy into the atmosphere. The beauty of their sound and the energy they invite is almost surreal.

Drums The sound of a drum carries our wishes and dreams to Spirit, and at the same time it is grounding. I've noticed that when I strike my drum, I feel its reverberations inside my chest, creating a feeling similar to my own heartbeat. In this way drums become bearers of comfort. Drums are perfect for balancing an environment, the drum representing the feminine, or yin, element, and the drumstick the masculine, or yang, element.

Other sound-making tools for space clearing include cymbals, rattles, click sticks, chiming balls, and noisemakers. You can even use your own voice by singing, toning, or chanting. If any of these appeal to you, be sure to include them in your ceremony.

Water

Water is perhaps the most common purification tool. Water cleanses and washes away, blesses, anoints, initiates. It has an air of innocence and at the same time carries with it the great feminine mystique of our emotions.

To create water that is the most energetically potent and pure, it is necessary to charge it, preparing your own holy water. To charge your water in preparation for space clearing, choose one of the following methods. If you feel the need to develop a ritual around any of these procedures, please do so. This may include a blessing, bell ringing, or incense burning. Whatever your heart tells you to do to make the process meaningful and reverent is exactly what should be done.

⚛ Fill a glass bowl with water and allow it to absorb the rays of the sun for three to four hours. The water will take on the sun's energy, which is that of clarity, vision, joy, and physical energy.

- Fill a glass bowl and charge your water in the pale light of the moon. This water's energy is feminine and more mystical. It is an excellent choice for anyone wanting to go deep inside themselves or to create a more restful environment that is more conducive to dreaming.
- Follow either of the above procedures, except place a meaningful stone or crystal in the bowl of water. The water will absorb the subtle energy of the stone.
- Channel universal love and purity into the water by placing your hand over the bowl, fingertips curved slightly toward the water. In your mind's eye, conduct pure, vibrant, white or rainbow light, allowing it to enter through the top of your head and pass through your fingertips into the water. Your intuition will tell you when the process is complete.

Tree Branch Method

The tree branch method is a very nice way to perform a space clearing. Because the effect is fairly refined, this may be a good choice for a clear environment that simply needs a little refreshing, or as the last pass in a space clearing involving several passes through your home utilizing a different tool each time. Simply soak a small tree branch or herb sprig in your charged water for a few minutes. The water will absorb the characteristics of the tree from which the branch came. Then use the branch to flick water throughout the house.

Pine is disinfecting and is incredibly lifting of despondent energy; it is also said to encourage fertility. Cedar is symbolically more spiritually lifting and represents stamina. Oak is strong. The energy of ash is stabilizing. Olive stimulates the intellect and increases vitality. Peach and mulberry are said to protect against maleficent forces. Pear tree limbs invite passion. Alternatively, use a sprig of a disinfecting aromatic herb such as lavender to flick the water. To add a touch of beauty, use a flower head. There cannot be a more symbolically beautiful clearing to make the way for romance than to use a red rose in this manner. Allow your creative thinking to guide you.

Misting

To gently wash the atmosphere of Home with love, mist it with a very fine mist of charged water. To reinforce the intentions set for your space clearing, mist your home in between clearings for maintenance. Add to the water a few drops of your favorite essential oil or one that is aligned with the intent of your clearing.

Salt

Salt is a mighty purifier. While there are several ways to use salt in a space clearing, I have found that perhaps the most useful way is to sprinkle it in problem areas, such as corners and closets, where energy tends to pool and stagnate. Salt possesses a protective spirit, and so can be sprinkled across doorways and window sills, as traditionally done, to keep out unwanted entities and energies. Use sea salt, and if you desire a finer consistency, grind it using a mortar and pestle. Dead Sea salt is perhaps the most sacred and ceremonial salt available.

Smudging

Smudging is quite purifying and adds a Native American flavor to the clearing. The most sacred herb to smudge with is sage. It may be best to smudge after lots of negative energy has been discharged by a thorough clearing using a powerful tool, such as a gong or drum. Individual objects and pieces of furniture can be cleansed through smudging. A feather is typically used to propel and direct the smoke to the specific area or object to be cleansed. Holding the feather in your dominant hand, use a somewhat staccato motion—as if you were slicing the air—for the most effective treatment.

When to Perform Space Clearing

To optimize the mystical and practical benefits of space clearing, you might wish to develop a schedule. One idea is to perform a clearing with each change of season. Twice a year may suffice for your home, once at the onset of the holiday season and once in the late spring. Perhaps you would like to coordinate your clearings with the moon's cycle. Always clear the air after the release of strong negative emotions, or after an unwelcome visitor leaves. Space clearing is definitely in order whenever you enter a new phase of life or face a new beginning in some way. Allow your intuitive guidance system to tell you when a clearing ritual is needed.

How to Perform a Basic Space Clearing

Step-by-step directions for performing a basic space clearing follow. Each of the space clearings in the home template chapters in Section Three uses these steps as a general guide. Please use your imagination to customize your clearing so that it is especially meaningful to you.

Preparation

Eat lightly, or even fast, for twenty-four hours prior to commencing your space clearing. During that time, choose the tools you will use, crystallize your intention for the space clearing, and choose special clothing and sun it for a few hours, if possible, to purify it. To maximize the effectiveness of the clearing, clean your home, or have it cleaned, thoroughly. At bedtime, ask Spirit for direction in guiding the space clearing. Recognize yourself as an instrument and beneficiary of the outcome. Accept and acknowledge that this is for your good, and because it is for your good it is also of great importance to the entire planet.

If possible, perform your space clearing early the following morning. Ensure the house is quiet and there are no disturbances. Turn the phone ringer off. Bathe or shower; allow yourself to feel cleansed and renewed just prior to your clearing. Avoid wearing metal jewelry because it can interfere with the energetic outcome of the space clearing. Perform your ritual barefoot, wherever practical. Bare feet connect you with the grounding energy of the earth and will increase your sensitivity to the energy you are working with. Open the windows and doors of your home just enough to allow energy to move through your home without creating a wind tunnel effect. A caressing breeze will kiss your home atmosphere with a revitalizing freshness. Your hands are energy sensors, and for some people, like myself, so are the insides of the forearms, from the wrist almost to the elbow. If your forearms are very sensitive, roll up your sleeves. Always wash your hands just prior to performing any space clearing.

Right before your clearing, light a candle in each room to be cleared, and one in each connecting passageway. As you light each candle, dedicate that candle to your overall intention for the house, and to a specific objective for that individual room. For example, as you light a candle in your bedroom you could say: "I dedicate this candle to the spirit of peace and harmony. In this room I accept restful sleep, sweet dreams, the gentle touch of my angels and those who love me." The color of the candles you choose can be aligned with your overall intention for your home. But I have found that white candles produce the most incredible results in space clearing. They are thought to burn up negative energy.

Another nice touch is to set out an offering in each of your home's main rooms. This offering can be whatever your intuition tells you it should be. However, it empowers your clearing if the theme of the offering is aligned with the overall theme you are creating for your home. If you are creating romance, float some red, velvety rose petals in a crystal bowl of water, along with some white floating candles. If your theme is clarity or excellence, arrange an abundant display of sunflowers around a golden pillar candle.

Once the candles are lit and you have made sure they are burning safely, and any offerings are in place, it is time to begin the space clearing ritual.

Projecting Your Intention

Standing in the doorway of the main entrance and facing the interior of your home, take as much time as you need to connect with its energy. This is best facilitated by pressing the palm of your dominant hand or both palms against the doorjamb. As you do this, invoke the protective embrace of your angels, guides, or helpers in whatever words bring your spirit in alignment with their presence. My experience has led me to believe that the key to successful space clearing is to hold the feeling of connection you encountered when your palm physically rested against the doorjamb throughout the entire clearing.

Next, focus intently on the desired result. Project or radiate the essence, the basic form, of that objective into your home. Imagine your home being filled with peace and harmony, romantic adventure, solid self-knowing and self-intimacy, or whatever it is your heart desires. Once you've visualized your experience-to-be and infused every corner of your home with it, proceed with the actual space clearing.

Space Clearing

Beginning with your first tool, which is quite often your own hands, and from your position at your home's entry, begin to move and to employ your tool in whichever direction and in whatever way you feel called to. Move counterclockwise or clockwise around the room, being very thorough in corners and closets as you encounter them. Generally, it is most effective to clap (or ring, or chime, etc.) beginning closer to the floor and moving upward in each particular spot.

Use your tool in any meaningful or comfortable way to work with the energy. For instance, if you are working in a small, high-traffic area where the sofa resides and you are using a bell, you may wish to ring it a couple of times, then use your other hand to move the energy all around and almost into the sofa. Use your intuition to guide your movements. The enjoyment comes from making your movements a very individualized expression of your personality. If you are flamboyant and love to dance, you may wish to engage your entire body to move the energy. If you're an artist or musician and you work with your hands a lot, you may wish to use intricate hand movements.

A very effective technique that I use is to unify with the energy in the room, to become the energy. As you breathe in and out, imagine breathing in the new, light feeling of your space, breathing out the old, unuseful energy. Imagine yourself an instrument of divine light: see and feel that light filling you up through the crown of your head and dispensing itself through your fingertips into your now radiant environment. Many people see this light as white. For me this light is always pinkish-gold.

If clapping, you will notice that initially the sound is very dull. Stay with the clapping in each particular area until the sound becomes more clear. The same holds true for any sound maker you have chosen. Other methods or tools, such as smudging or misting, will require you to tune in to your deeper feelings about the space.

If you are using one tool, you must seal off each room once you feel it is complete, before moving into the next room. Stand at the doorway of the room, facing it, and draw the sign of infinity in the air. As you do this send your love into the space. If your space clearing plan involves multiple passes through the house using a different tool or method each time, it is not necessary to seal off the room until the final pass in that room is complete.

If your home has a basement, enter the basement and clear it when you encounter its doorway during your pass of the main floor. If there is no basement, just continue clearing the rooms on the main floor as you come to them. Then, if there is a second floor, move on to it next, clearing it exactly as you did the first floor.

Your space clearing is now complete. From this day forward, vow to honor the sacred bond you have established with Home. The way to do this is to acknowledge Home's aliveness and honor the fact that it has needs. When the needs of Home are met, it can in turn meet your needs in abundance. So talk to your home, just as you would your spouse, your neighbor, your car, your plant, or your computer. To keep everything in your life running as smoothly as possible, however, it is imperative that your words are always filled with kindness and love. The sacred secrets of life will no doubt reveal themselves to you through the walls of your well-loved, blessed home.

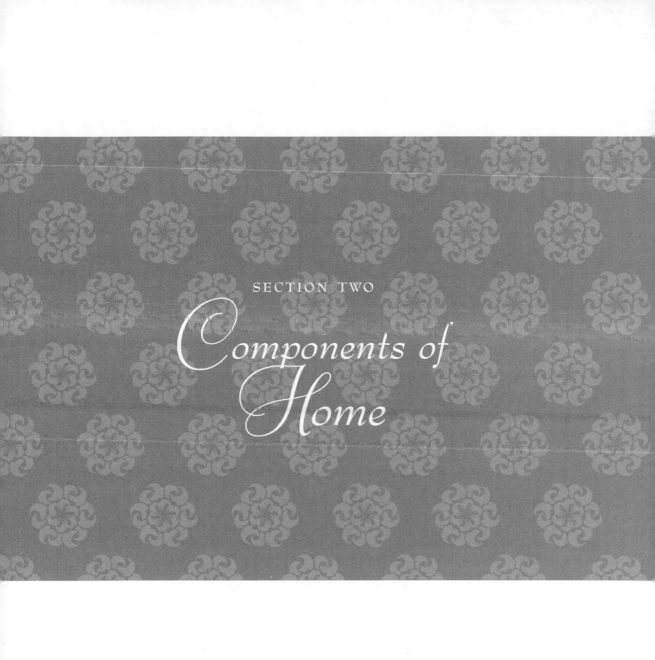

SECTION TWO

Components of Home

CHAPTER FOUR

Energetic Design

$\mathcal{E}$nergetic design is a design philosophy that brings into physical form what is intuitively comfortable and nourishing to the soul. This is easily stated, yet this type of design is driven by many subtleties that almost defy articulation. Still, any step toward the unveiling of your true being is an honorable endeavor and is never lost ground.

Energetic design is at once a road map to our life's objectives and a mirror of how we are living our objectives. It is wound around several ideas: that we have a heart connection with every possession in our domain; that we must take into account the needs of our spiritual self; that everything is alive, if not in the breathing sense then in the sense that our love and awareness enlivens it; that the unseen has a magical presence at home; and that our intention creates our world.

Following your own design instinct may be frightening to those of you who do not trust your taste—yourself, really—enough to display it deliberately. To put your heart completely and creatively to work is so intimate it may seem an unimaginable feat. However, basic design principles can be learned. You can also trust that love is the most powerful unifier. If love can bring divided countries together and heal deep wounds, it can certainly restore energetic balance to your home. What you create from your heart is bound to be pleasing to your soul.

If you have decluttered your home as discussed in Chapter 2, you probably already know about having a heart connection with all your possessions. You have, hopefully, picked up every belonging and actually considered it. You have remembered how you obtained it—whether as a gift, an inheritance, or by purchasing it yourself—and you have decided whether to keep it. You have relived many vignettes of your life and in the sorting process have expelled previously dormant emotions, some precious, some painful. Your home is now occupied by kept things, things retained based on your love for them or your reliance on their function. It is inescapable, then, that your belongings bring you joy and therefore are energizing and soothing, uplifting and comforting all at once, for they were chosen to live in your space. They belong to no one's portfolio but yours. The act of choosing is a form of gratitude, for embedded in it is appreciation, which helps to seed your world with kindness and synchronicity.

Home should reflect your spiritual essence and accommodate your life purpose because your soul, like anything else, needs attention to evolve and thrive. Most people go out of their way to feed their physical bodies daily. Our souls also need regular feeding. Some individuals nourish their souls primarily through their spiritual community. Some have developed their own sacred rituals. Some do creative work. Some perform acts of service. Some people love whatever it is they do so much they shine brilliantly—granting others permission to follow their own dreams. Home can also nourish our souls and refortify us so we can continue on in the work of our souls. Sadly, many of us are so busy and so wrapped up in a technocratic society created to produce income and signs of affluence that we have actually quit listening to the deep yearnings and subtle prompts our souls emit. Once we define what our souls long for, we can design for it and allow Home to support us in it. For example, if you believe one of your gifts is cooking and you absolutely love to cook, your soul will respond with complete delight to a lovely kitchen, whatever that means to you. Your spirit will lift each and every time you have the chance to work there.

Knowing that every component of Home is truly alive and doing everything within your power to make Home feel as alive as possible will change your relationship to your belongings forever. Everything consists of matter—it only differs in its exact expression. Be sensitive to all that lives with you at Home, and you will see the truth in this. Is there a piece of furniture you are especially drawn to or seem to avoid? Pay attention: your possessions contain life.

When my husband and I first set up house, he had a set of antique chairs. He likes to build furniture and work with wood, and to his craftsman's eyes, these chairs were especially interesting. I, on the other hand, could not be around those chairs for more than a few seconds without feeling uncomfortable, though I could not put my finger on why. The chairs had been used by slaves, it turned out, and for me the energy was thick and oppressive. When my feelings became salient to me, I spoke to my husband about it and out went the chairs. Instantly my sense of comfort in my home was enhanced.

Do you have something beautiful that you use a lot, so down on the floor or into a convenient chair it goes? I have a handmade Native American drum I acquired on a family vacation in Santa Fe, and I just love it. It used to reside on the floor in my office, where I could easily have access to it whenever I felt the need to clear my mind or break up the energy there. One day I had the idea to hang it on the wall, and as I held it in place to see what it looked like the entire energy in the room became more elevated. When you love something and seek to honor it by assigning it a place of respect, the energy in your home will respond.

Know that you will benefit immensely by simply caring for your things in a way that acknowledges and honors their aliveness. When you are lying in bed, what feels best, most restful: leaving the closet doors open with everything inside the closet in complete disarray; closet doors closed but knowing everything inside is in complete disarray; or closet doors closed knowing everything inside is tidy? The latter, no doubt. Love—no matter how it is expressed—is soothing.

Increasing aliveness is simple: introduce sound and movement and living things. Our plants, our pets, the voices of those who share our living space—these living things add vitality to our home landscape. Make Home even homier and more alive by introducing an aquarium full of bright fish, by growing herbs on the window sill, or filling the air with glorious symphonic music.

Inviting the magic of the unseen into our lives is easy and fun. Give play to your imagination. Your imagination knows, and is itself evidence, that not everything takes expression in physical form. Acknowledge the unseen by bookmarking it, if you will, in your life. That is to say, give yourself a physical reminder of the existence of other realms. In your garden, what can you do that would attract a fairy? Try adding things that move, such as small windmills or wind socks; things that delicately chime; a water garden or birdbath; things that invite whimsy, such as a miniature table and chairs placed under the protective refuge of a shrub, a gazing ball.

Indoors, find ways to invite the Divine to interact with you and your family. Your home is a stage and with the addition of the very best props, can be a powerhouse with psychic symbolism and down-home comforts peacefully coexisting. What makes you feel divine? Is it your dog-eared book of prayers upon the end table next to your favorite chair; the cross worn daily around your neck; the well-worn deck of tarot cards; the pair of candles lit each night to remind yourself of your most sacred relationship; the lions flanking your front door—protective and noble elements; the angel peering down over your entryway? All of these things are signs of your humble submission to and high regard for an otherworldly presence. Ask any child—symbols bring in magic through your association with them. The magic is there and real and felt by all who enter your home.

I have said that intention creates our world. That's a big statement, for it places sole responsibility for what happens in your life on you. You are an individuation of something immense and powerful. In fact you are what you think; your thoughts are your future. It's the law of attention: what you focus on is drawn on some level into your life, whether you are aware of it or not. It pays to be aware. This powerful law is easily recognizable when applied destructively. We all know lethargic people whose lives and homes are just as sad and sleepy; we see how not caring enough can lead to family disintegration; we witness how those who try to control too much are brought, at some point, to their knees.

Many people have recognized this law and applied it to their advantage. They have learned that to attain a dream you first begin living it in thought, by visualizing the dream in full-blown form. This is a constructive, gentle maneuver that allows the universe to begin unfolding in favor of your dream. The universe responds immediately, sending opportunities. At first they might seem small, but the process always plays out to be layered and complex, a laying of the seeds of possibility.

Visualize the life your soul is yearning for. See yourself supported in your home. Then, deliberately and with keen focus on the dream you wish to manifest, create your home sanctuary. With every change you make to your home, take one moment in which you are completely present to see the end result and bless the change. From that point on, seeing what you have put in place becomes a silent yet dramatic affirmation for whatever it is you wish to attract.

Getting Started

How do we begin to create such a lush, intentional, and symbolic home landscape? How do we give audience to our higher selves? In what form is our higher self best expressed? One way to discover where to start is to ask yourself "What is it I most love about this space?" The answer can be anything: the way the sun bathes the sofa with light in the afternoon; the Madonna bookends; the generations-old wardrobe coated with seven layers of paint; the needlepoint rug acquired at a garage sale; the exact positioning and style of the little gothic window in your breakfast nook. Find what you love most about your home, whatever fuels your vision of Home, and let it all begin there.

Just as a room's monochromatic color scheme sets you apart from the space, pure style can do the same. Imagine entering your living room with the newspaper on a Sunday morning. You have on your sweatpants and an old, worn T-shirt, and you sprawl out on a sofa resembling a bench with a scant black leather pad covering it, in a room with two other pieces of skimpy furniture, bleached oak floors, and white walls. The room is true to its minimalist intentions, perhaps, but probably not to your soul—even if you were the patron saint of minimalist design. A concept applied in pure form is often misapplied.

So scrap the cramping nature of pure style and focus only on the thing you find most irresistible; allow it to inspire your dream of Home. For me, this is very often a color. Several years ago I came across an inexpensive glass vase in a luminous, earthy shade of pinky-orange. I had no idea that, by bringing that vase home and placing it on top of the wardrobe in my bedroom, I would soon find a floral duvet cover with the same glowing color in it. And in it some other colors: sage green, which attracted a wicker chair with a similarly colored cushion and two matching wicker nightstands; a deep brown-garnet, which beckoned a sisal rug and another vase; and a creamy beige that inspired the color on the walls. An angel plaque pulls all of the colors together again and hovers overhead to protect me in my sleep. Five years have passed since it all came together, and I have not tired of it even a little. And it continues. I began to love a coppery-red tone so much that when a pair of handblown candlesticks in that color surfaced at an art gallery I grabbed them up. They became the inspiration for the tribal rug in my dining room (which also contained a nice shade of gold-green), which in turn inspired the raffia-colored paint on the dining room walls. When illumed by the sun, the walls glisten like straw.

So, if you really love something, let it command a high place in your design scheme. Inspiration can also be found by flipping through the pages of a magazine, checking the colors of your wardrobe, referring to your notes from Chapter 2, and so forth. It does not matter from where the inspiration comes.

Arrange your possessions artfully and in a manner, generally, that causes them to flow into each other. Respect shape whether you are arranging objects atop your piano or furniture within a room the size of a dance hall. Allow the large, rounded arms of your sofa to accentuate the domed glass in the light fixture above it. You can carry on this theme of roundness by framing the sofa with two large plants with big, curvaceous leaves. Grace your mantle with the imposing presence of a team of candlesticks, each with a pronounced roundness.

Group objects in meaningful ways. If you love to collect something, display the collection in the room that makes the most sense. An eclectic ensemble of teapots will feel most at home wherever the act of serving tea most often takes place, probably in your kitchen. Group them in numbers carrying symbolic importance (see Chapter 10) or in ways that please the eye. For example, the eye tends to like groups of three.

Arrange objects based on color or another similar attribute. An assortment of cobalt blue glass could take up the middle shelves in your glass-faced kitchen cabinets for a striking effect. A wooden bowl, a small wooden box, a pair of wooden candlesticks, and a small wooden doll can feel as if they belong together even though their shapes and finishes differ.

Unusual collections command notice and become energizers when loved and used. For example, old sheet music scented with lavender or rose water could line your dresser drawers, or a grouping of outdoor thermometers from various decades could be strategically placed outside the kitchen window. Not only do collections of things give you the latitude for stylish energetic design themes, but they reveal another dimension of your personality and animate your environment.

Energetic design also demands that all space is well used. The risk otherwise is that energy may accumulate and stagnate, and the space will begin to feel lifeless and dull. Some typical energy traps are spare bedrooms, dining rooms, and basements. Rather than allow energy to pool in these places, convert the space into a meditation retreat, office, or workout room. Or consciously use the room for its intended purpose: insist on Sunday dinners in the dining room. These efforts will make your home life richer and keep your living space feeling vibrant. If you do convert a room to another use, however, really convert it. Your workout room will still feel like a bedroom with that pink-rose wallpaper engulfing it, and then the room will feel sad, as though it has failed its mission. If your five children have moved out, leaving you with more room than you can possibly use, you might even consider a less expansive home in order to energetically occupy it.

For comfort and balance between family members, make every effort to ensure that everyone has a personal retreat. A retreat is where we feel most empowered, closest to our essence, and in the emotional or mental space we long for. This monument to respite could be an entire room, an intimate corner of the living room where the piano stands, an entire room devoted to the piano, or maybe even just a telephone table and chair placed under the stairwell where Sunday afternoons are spent chatting away with loved ones.

Energetic design dictates that you make any functional space homey. Though you love your modern, streamlined, stainless steel–clad kitchen, introduce the quaintness of home in some way, even if unexpected. Add an old black and white photo of your great grandmother working the cotton fields, a baby on one hip; place a lace doily under a potted plant; or hang a plate rack holding four plates hand-painted by each family member. Touches like these make an otherwise sterile place human and delightful, creating an atmosphere poised for memory making.

Find the energetic center of your home and pay tribute to it in some way. Some experts suggest this is the exact center of the house. I believe the energetic center is wherever the essence of your home is so thick it is palpable. The energetic center is where people congregate. This could be the family room, the kitchen table, or in front of the fireplace. Mark or anchor this area somehow. Something heavy works best, be it your favorite houseplant, a rock or crystal dedicated to Home (see Chapter 11), or statuary. Add love by writing down a blessing and placing it underneath your marker.

Never allow the television or any other piece of electronic equipment to occupy the energetic center of your home. This might indicate that reprioritizing is in order. In fact, pay special attention to where electronic equipment is placed. It should not be the first thing you see in the morning or last thing you set eyes on at night—keep all of it out of the bedroom. The reason for keeping television sets and other electronics out of the bedroom is that they have electromagnetic fields that have been shown to alter brain waves. If you have an electronic clock, place it no closer than four feet from your head. As for where to put the television, make sure the spot it occupies is sufficiently comfortable for moderate amounts of viewing time and perhaps off the beaten path. No television should be seen upon entering your home through its main entrance. Some people advocate covering television sets when they are not in use, sometimes with a nice piece of fabric. The only time I personally do this is when I'm in a hotel room, because covering something with fabric seems impermanent. Impermanence makes most people feel insecure. Keep the television closed up in a cabinet if possible.

A home sanctuary crafted using energetic design tools will always make the best use of natural light. Human beings need sunlight physically and emotionally. Consider light based on room function. Your home might have two bedrooms upstairs, one that receives lots of late afternoon light, and one that receives little light during that time. If you would like to make one of them into a playroom for your toddler and use the other as her bedroom, the obvious choice for the playroom would be the one receiving the golden light of afternoon. That choice will undoubtedly encourage many happy hours of play without need of artificial lighting. The other room would make a very soothing bedroom, especially during the summer.

Allow yourself to experience natural lighting without the intervention of artificial light more often. We turn on overhead lights without thinking about it. Not only is this wasteful, it also partially cuts us off from the refreshment and nourishment of the sun and the cyclic breathing of nature. I am particularly sensitive to the intrusion of artificial light, especially in the morning. If your bathroom enjoys a moderate or better amount of natural light, try showering in the morning without artificial light. You may find that you feel an increased sense of peace and well-being, a stronger experience of being one with all life.

It is especially helpful during the long, dark months of winter to use full spectrum lighting (bulbs producing light similar to natural light) wherever possible. For those of us who become depressed without enough natural light, full spectrum lighting is an environmental energizer. Avoid the harsh green cast of ordinary fluorescent lighting. In addition to making you appear sick, many people find it uncomfortable and irritating.

Keep your windows clear of furniture and anything else that would block light or your view. Obscuring your windows interferes with your vision not only literally, but metaphorically. It can be quite irritating. Adorn your windows only with the most fitting treatment based on the activities conducted in each room. Always keep your windows—hence your vision—clean.

Firelight creates instant sanctuary. A flickering flame, be it from a roaring fire or a single candle, melts away worry and fear and disperses peace, sacredness, a deep sense that all is well. Fire is purifying, and is therefore extensively used in ritual and ceremony. Lighting a candle consecrates time. It gathers people to it and hence together; somehow it defuses differences.

Feng Shui

The ancient Chinese art of Feng Shui folds into this energetic design philosophy in that it is concerned with intuiting placement and spatial relationships. It also helps you focus your intention to create certain outcomes in life through the platform of your home or property. Feng Shui, in a nutshell, is about energetically appropriate placement.

As with all things cross-cultural, something usually gets lost in the translation. The commercialization of Feng Shui as a practice in this country seems to focus on obtaining results through the use of Feng Shui cures and the application of its basic concepts. Secondary emphasis is placed on why it brings results. Its premise is similar to that of this book: our thinking—both collectively and individually—powers our outcomes; we are energetic channels whose thinking creates the world we experience.

As I see it, Feng Shui is a tool for stepping up your awareness and sense of space. Though its roots extend back probably more than three thousand years, its essence can be captured and applied by anyone with even a cursory knowledge of it. What I find especially useful are Feng Shui's treatment of Chi—the energy—and its emphasis on balancing. It is popular to use a *bagua map*, explained later in this chapter, for determining placement. Some basic and intrinsically beautiful cures that meld nicely with the home environment themes presented in this book require reference to the bagua.

While it would be offensive to imply that only a few Feng Shui tips are worth mentioning, the basics I've written about in this chapter and throughout the template chapters will definitely enhance your understanding of energy flow—an idea energetic design philosophy and Feng Shui share.

Releasing Chi

Chi is life force, vital energy. As with anything vital, it is best that it circulates. Conjure up an image of Chi meandering freely through your home. What will it encounter? Here are some common obstacles or challenges to the harmonious flow of Chi.

Stuck or Blocked Windows or Doors If they don't open correctly or all the way, this hinders your home's potential for attracting Chi. Things stacked behind doors, preventing the doors' complete opening, are especially unlucky. Make sure all your doors and windows fully extend.

Sharp or Pointed Edges, Corners, or Objects Chi moves more easily around smooth, rounded shapes. Rather than encouraging Chi to flow, sharp or pointed edges propel it away from them. Anyone in the path of this energy will feel directed away from the area—not exactly a welcome for visitors. If you are exposed to this type of Chi for long periods—such as while working at your desk or sleeping in your bed—it can adversely affect your health. Soften architectural corners by placing a round-leafed plant in front of them. When purchasing new furniture, choose designs sporting more rounded shapes, or at least softer edges.

Squareness Arrange your furniture so that inside corners are softer. I have a very large wardrobe in my bedroom. Originally it was placed along the wall opposite the door. The room never felt inviting, even though the colors were lovely, and the room was a nice size with lots of natural light and a pleasant water and mountain view. As soon as I turned the wardrobe, placing it diagonally in that corner and flanking each side with a beautiful plant, the room felt much more comfortable.

Stagnant Corners Energy tends to collect and stagnate in corners, and something living, such as a plant, fish, or bird, can not only soften but enliven corners. You can also try works of art such as statuary or pottery. If you are reworking a room architecturally, choose softer moldings or ask your wall finisher to do rounded corners.

Long, Narrow Hallways and Staircases Long hallways can have the effect of pressurizing Chi so that it shoots through rapidly, instead of meandering. This is especially true if there is a window at the end of the hall. The Chi may shoot down the hallway and right out the window—leaving your household bereft of its benefits. Simply introduce something to slow it down. If the hallway is wide enough this could be a plant, statue, or small table (preferably a half-moon shape). You can also try hanging something from the ceiling, such as a pendant light fixture or artful banner. Staircases cause problems when they directly face a door. You can imagine how Chi might come tumbling down them and straight out of the house through the door. If this is a problem for you, again, hang something overhead to slow the Chi. If the stairs have a landing, you can place a plant there to help sustain the Chi.

Balancing the Five Elements

Home environments that have sensory balance are more comfortable to live in. Feng Shui accomplishes balance primarily by ensuring that all five elements—Earth, Metal, Water, Wood, and Fire—are present in every room or component of Home. When you begin making changes to your environment to balance the five elements, you will find the shift in beneficial energy quite pronounced.

You can transport the element of Earth indoors with materials born of the earth: brick, tile, adobe, or sand, for example. Surprisingly, stone and rock are considered Metal elements. Earthenware and ceramic objects such as pottery are Earth materials. Earth is also exalted by squarish shapes and patterns, as well as flat surfaces—common design components of many home furnishings, such as dining and coffee tables. A palette of browns and yellows underscores the essence of Earth, as does any type of art depicting earthy themes. Desert landscapes are especially good because of the strong earth-toned colors typically present.

Metal can be introduced, of course, with metal objects: copper, bronze, gold, stainless steel, aluminum, silver, and iron. Natural rock and stone are also Metal conductors. Metal is expressed metaphorically through round shapes and archways. Whites and pastels represent Metal. You can see how powerful it would be to have an arched river-rock fireplace, or a creamy yellow round table in your breakfast nook.

Bring the soothing and mystical music of Water into your home with features like indoor fountains and aquariums, and into your garden via birdbaths, fountains, pools, streams, and waterfalls. Water magic is also invoked through the reflective surfaces of mirrors, crystal, and glass. Softly flowing shapes accentuate the spirit of Water, as do the colors of the midnight sky. Cobalt blue drinking glasses become conductors of Water magic with your new awareness.

Most of us enjoy ample amounts of the element of Wood in our homes, through our furnishings and flooring. Wood floors help to make us feel grounded and strong. Houseplants and flowers, including natural silk, and dried arrangements, are also Wood elements. Fabrics spun of cotton and hemp are of plants and so accentuate Wood. Floral patterns in textiles and wall coverings also symbolize Wood. And columnar shapes, resembling tree trunks, are elementally Wood. These include beams, columns, stripes, and pedestals. The harmonizing colors of green and blue bring Wood to life. A wooden plant stand with a distressed green paint finish and adorned with a flowering plant emphasizes the Wood element.

Fire is found in lighting of any kind, including and especially sunlight. The energy of Fire is also emulated by things of animal origin, such as leather, bone, feathers, wool, and silk. Triangular shapes, including pyramids, play up the presence of Fire. The seductive power of Fire is fueled by the color red.

An environment is balanced when all five elements are present and are somewhat equally represented. Inventory the items in a room, classifying them according to the element they most distinctly represent. In an eminently comfortable room you will almost assuredly find the presence of all five elements. If you find you have a room dominated by one element, you can quickly correct that imbalance by introducing its controlling element:

- ❀   Wood is controlled by Metal.
- ❀   Metal is controlled by Fire.

- Fire is controlled by Water.
- Water is controlled by Earth.
- Earth is controlled by Wood.

So, if you have a predominantly Wood environment—very common—you can quickly achieve greater balance by introducing Metal. Further work can refine the balance between all of the room's components. Add in other elements as you feel they are needed.

To continue with the previous example, the next step may be to choose Metal's nourishing element from the following list. In this way you can strengthen Metal's balancing effect.

- Water is nourished by Metal.
- Metal is nourished by Earth.
- Earth is nourished by Fire.
- Fire is nourished by Wood.
- Wood is nourished by Water.

Introducing Earth elements will strengthen the Metal elements and further diminish the dominance of the Wood energy.

This five-element approach to balancing a room can be used on a smaller scale, for instance, to balance the items on display in a cabinet or on a table-top. This sounds very detailed, but you should stretch your efforts out over time to give yourself a variety of Home projects that will keep you constantly engaged in creating a home sanctuary.

Some readers may be prone to extremes in creating a balanced environment. Resist any temptation to be perfect or rigid in achieving this kind of balance in your home. There are many things to balance: color, light, patterns, textures, the natural elements, and the elements of style. The bottom line is that your home is sanctuary when it feels great to you. Any thought that helps you bring balance to your environment is really just helping you achieve another level of awareness of life and how Home plays into it. Perhaps this awareness will give you some tangible explanation to back up feelings you already had about what your soul longs for and what makes you comfortable in your earthly endeavors.

The Bagua

The bagua map is essentially a grid system with its roots in the *I Ching*, a sacred Chinese text concerned with divination. When this map is overlaid on a footprint of your home or an individual room, nine different energetic centers will align with various parts of your house. There is a bagua map at the end of this chapter for reference. Align your front door along the lower edge of the map. It will fall into either the self-knowledge/education, career, or helpful people/travel energy centers. In your mind or on paper, enlarge this map to encompass your entire home. The other six energy centers include health/family, center (Tai Chi), creativity/children, wealth, reputation/fame, and relationships/marriage.

You will find that if your house is U-shaped or L-shaped—anything other than a square or rectangle—it will not fit neatly into the bagua map. A uniquely shaped home will have an area or areas considered either a projection of the home or a missing area. A projection is any extension of interior space, exceeding the otherwise square or rectangular shape of your home, with a length less than half of the width of the front of the house. A missing area is any extension of interior space with a length greater than half of the width of the front of the house.

A projection can be lucky, for it augments the energetic center of the bagua area from which it extends, but it can also cause an imbalance. For instance, according to the bagua map, a small projection off the right front side of your home is an extension of helpful people/travel. This is said to accentuate this type of energy in your life, so perhaps travel would be a more dominant theme in that opportunities for travel would frequently arise. Or you might extend yourself to others in need. The possibility of overextending yourself would always be there, so in such a scenario you would probably take steps to make sure you did not.

A missing area could be unlucky. Perhaps you discover a missing area in your relationships/marriage sector. It could be that you are experiencing a love relationship in decline, or that you are having difficulty finding a partner. In this case you could metaphorically incorporate and strengthen this area in your life by making this part of your dwelling space beautiful and lighting it well.

Bagua Area	Color(s)	Element
Helpful people/travel	Grey, white, black	
Career	Black, dark colors	Water
Self-knowledge/education	Blue, green, black	
Creativity/children	White, pastels	Metal
Center (Tai Chi)	Yellow, earth tones	Earth
Family/health	Green, blue	Wood
Relationships/marriage	Pink, red, white	
Reputation/fame	Red	Fire
Wealth	Blue, red, purple	

Each area of the bagua has colors associated with it, and some of these areas also have direct associations with elements. These areas are emphasized when the elemental characteristics are brought forward in the decorating scheme.

Although color selection in a strictly Feng Shui approach seems limiting, keep in mind the tonal variety of each color listed. Purple can be interpreted in shades ranging from the frostiest lavender to the richest, most earthy plum. I find it freeing to have guidelines that whittle down the overwhelming number of color choices available. Lots of creativity can be expressed even within this particular approach.

For example, my kitchen is located in my relationships/marriage area. During remodeling, I chose to have my cabinets made. I selected a lighter wood with an interesting grain and had it stained a rich shade of mahogany red—which respects and uplifts the relationships/marriage energy this area signifies, and also represents the element of Fire. I also chose beech floors, which, combined with the wood cabinets, produced a lot of Wood energy. To balance the room, Metal energy in the way of stainless steel appliances and backsplashes were installed. Earth is represented by the tiles in the counter top, Water by the horizontally ribbed glass that the upper cabinets frame. I like to imagine the ribbing as rippling water.

Before going on, I would like to briefly clarify each bagua area and what it represents.

Helpful People/Travel Helpful people are those individuals and entities who you believe support you in life. They are your friends, special family members, good neighbors, community groups you feel especially attached to, and your angels and guides or helpers. Travel is actual travel: adventures, excursions, pilgrimages. This particular area is also associated with fathers and brothers, causing it to carry a lot of male energy. Men might find it difficult to live in a house missing this area. In addition to decorating with its associative colors, you can intensify the energy of this area with photos or keepsakes of your helpful people, or figurines of entities you rely on, such as saints. If you wish to travel to certain destinations, photos of or artifacts from these places will bring power to your travel plans and serve as a daily affirmation of your goal.

Career This area represents your secular career as well as your life's path. If you wish to create movement in your career—presumably upward movement—place in this area of your home things that move or simply symbolize movement. Moving water, such as a water fountain, is an excellent choice because moving water attracts prosperity, and its soothing sounds are welcome to all who reside at Home as well as to visitors. A work of art depicting movement, such as a butterfly in flight, is especially powerful if you are attracted to butterfly magic. The power of this area can be further amplified through the use of crystal prisms, for crystals are powerful intention magnifiers (see Chapter 11, "Stones and Minerals").

Self-Knowledge/Education This energetic center concerns itself with your soul's development via introspection, meditation, guidance. It also represents education and study in the traditional sense. I've noticed that when I want to rest or just be quiet I tend to place myself in this particular area on either floor of my home.

Creativity/Children Bearing children is the ultimate creative endeavor, combining the projectile, scattering energy of yang with the receptive, nourishing energy of yin. Hence creativity and children are generated by similar energetic forces. If you wish to conceive children, this is an excellent part of Home in which to place your bed. If this is not possible, overlay the bagua map on a map of your bedroom. Perhaps you can place your bed in the creativity/children area of your bedroom. To increase creativity, enliven this area with flowers or something meaningful in your creative work.

Center (Tai Chi) This area is the still point where all other areas of the bagua map connect. All life flows harmoniously around the center. This is an excellent space for an altar or meditation retreat. When all other areas of your home and life are beautiful and peaceful, this area is strengthened. The Earth energy of this area makes it an especially grounding spot.

Family/Health This area is energetically connected with your immediate family, your parents, your ancestors, and your general health and vitality. The *I Ching*'s wisdom is that if we are emotionally and physically fit, we are poised to act when opportunity comes our way. If this area of your home and life is in order, you are in an outstanding position for growth and expansion. This is an excellent place to pay tribute to your relatives and your immediate family by displaying photos of them or evidence of their individual triumphs, such as trophies and certificates.

Relationships/Marriage Relationships, especially between your spouse or partner and yourself, are the domain of this particular place. Wherever we truly love, a strong commitment to the individual and the relationship thrives, and yet we also accept the other's experience as we allow it to unfold. It is the dance of authentic support, knowing when to push forward and when to retreat by holding high consciousness for the other's earthly escapades. To move into a greater experience in relationship with others and yourself, prime this area with icons of love, whether a souvenir of a spellbound evening or a pair of candles to light each night. Look out for problem symbols here: the litter box, trash bin, or other such things could spell big trouble.

Reputation/Fame This is where the energy in our home connects with the labels we acquire through the circles we move in, be they professional or community-based. Perhaps you've heard people boast that they do not care what others think of them. The wisdom of the *I Ching* responds that maintaining a good position amidst our peers lights our way with goodwill, generating assistance from others. In this area of the home place objects that metaphorically indulge your dreams of how you wish others to perceive you. Do you wish to be known for your generous heart? Say it symbolically here. Placing rose quartz hearts in your potted plants to help your love for others grow in recognition. In a tiny heart box, place affirmations for a reputation for loving kindness.

Wealth In addition to wealth, this area relates to abundance, good fortune, happiness, and blessings. If this area is missing due to a projection of the reputation/fame area, there could be a draining away of financial resources, or your work might not yield its worth in income. This area can be enhanced by a water feature, such as a fountain or aquarium. Adorn your wealth area with beautiful objects of excellent quality.

Bagua Map

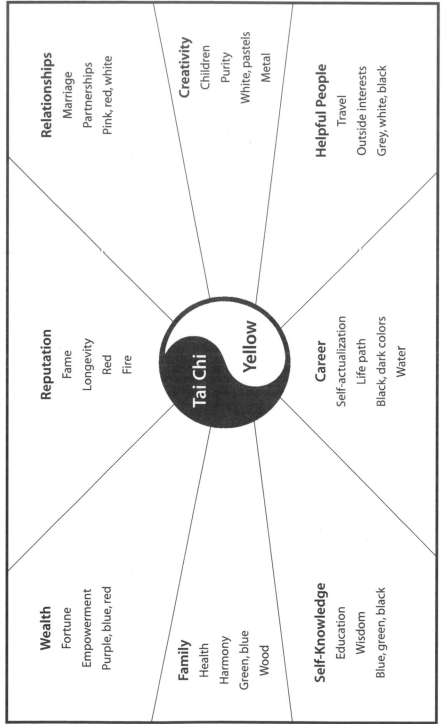

Relationships
Marriage
Partnerships
Pink, red, white

Creativity
Children
Purity
White, pastels
Metal

Helpful People
Travel
Outside interests
Grey, white, black

Reputation
Fame
Longevity
Red
Fire

Tai Chi

Yellow

Career
Self-actualization
Life path
Black, dark colors
Water

Wealth
Fortune
Empowerment
Purple, blue, red

Family
Health
Harmony
Green, blue
Wood

Self-Knowledge
Education
Wisdom
Blue, green, black

CHAPTER FIVE

Altars

*A*ltars are three-dimensional treasure maps. They are places where the divine intersects with the everyday, places to deposit and process our deepest wounds and fondest memories. Whether or not you have a conscious altar established in your home, it is highly probable you have several unconscious ones: the photos and mementos encircling your computer monitor; the bulletin board adorned with swim meet ribbons and certificates of achievement; tassels and crystals hanging from the rearview mirror of your car; the eclectic collage of refrigerator miscellany. Bringing consciousness to altar building creates a powerful resonance capable of harnessing, aligning, and funneling universal creative energy to your path.

Altars are places to be still and know the truth of yourself. They help you hold your highest vision of yourself. They are places where you can simply reflect and process your day. Altars can honor your heritage or ancestral line. They can keep you focused on what is important and precious in your life. Altars can be an endearing expression of self. If there is something you wish to salute—be it an event, person, or something evolving inside of you—an altar provides a creative outlet and power supply for all of these things and more. Because keeping altars is so richly and deeply embedded in our collective psyches, altars are powerful tools for self-exploration and for recognizing the synchronicity and patterning expressed through all life. They help us find meaning and purpose.

An altar need not be elaborate—unless you truly like elaborate things. Although some people say you can place one upon just about anything, I believe much attention needs to be given to placement of the altar itself. A bookcase shelf, for example, could suffice. But every book on that bookcase possesses its own energy: words are mighty and the creative process behind them is intense. A dedicated tabletop, cabinet, or shelf is better. It is recommended that altars be placed along interior walls.

Altars are extremely personal. Just as you would probably prefer not to impose your private space upon your visitors, it is usually undesirable to have the energy imprints of your visitors impressed upon your sacred space. Consider keeping your altar in a place that you pass by frequently, but others do not. Some of you may have an extra room that can serve as your personal retreat and altar space—a spare bedroom or den perhaps—or maybe even a meditation room. Don't despair if this luxury is not yours; few persons have one. A hallway off the beaten path, a small nook underneath the stairs, or even a corner in the formal dining room will work just fine.

You may wish to consider the four directions in siting your altar. While some attributes of the four directions are virtually universal, use your intuition as the ultimate placement guide. North is more yin: cool, receptive, mysterious. South is the direct opposite, more yang: warm, passionate, assertive. East, from where the sun rises, can symbolize potentiality, beginnings, and enlightenment. West, to where the sun sets, can represent completion, fullness, resolution. Undoubtedly one of these directions will strike a chord based on your current objectives.

Wherever you keep your altar, let it be a place where tears can be wept freely, where secrets are revealed and spoken, where lives are celebrated and mourned—where your attempts to articulate a fledgling direction are properly introduced to the physical world of effects.

This book is intended to reveal to you the power in creating a physical representation of your aspirations and needs: in this case, Home. See your blessed altar (and every other element of Home) as a physical microcosm of Home—a place aligned with your dreams. Altars modeled with emphasis on an overriding theme, yet balanced in their presentation, are best.

The ancient Chinese art of Feng Shui, the principles of which are discussed in Chapter 4, can aid you in deciding exact placement of your altar adornments. This art form is based on the bagua map, the grid system pre scribing appropriate placement for maximum Chi, or energy flow, that is derived from the *I Ching*. After assembling your altar ingredients, refer to Chapter 4 and the bagua map located at the very end of that chapter.

What are altars made of? Allow your intuition to guide you in the specifics. This list, however, may provide a starting point:

An image representing Divinity or a universal being
Things of nature
Gemstones
Photographs
Statuary
Rosary beads, medallions, crosses
Boxes, bowls
Prayer wheels
Candles, incense, misting water infused with essential oils, smudging
   or aromatic herbs
Cloth, lace
Prayer books
Written affirmations and blessings
Bells, chimes, rattles

Any meaningful object can be used on an altar. Some items conjure their own magical meanings. For instance, a lone robin's egg found while on a quiet walk during which you received a message about your life's direction has double significance. That egg becomes a powerful reminder of the message you received, while eggs represent life and generation—adding yet another layer of meaning to your altar icon. Every physical form has a spiritual and metaphorical counterpart. The fabric, fragrance, lore, and essence of every item of your altar should be considered. When this is not immediately possible, rely on your intuition. If something feels right to you, it is right. What may be missing is an awareness of why it feels right. Make sure you understand the meaning behind each object you enlist in the creation of your altar.

Visiting your altar daily, or perhaps weekly as part of a Sabbath tradition, introduces another ritual into your life. You might wonder why doing the same thing repetitively is beneficial. It is similar to listening to a story over and over, or seeing a meaningful movie over and over: each time we observe or participate, another truth bubbles up to the surface, into our awareness, and is thus revealed. Ritual also adds shape to and imposes pattern over our existence. The confines of an altar space are freeing to the extent that our full attention on one matter releases otherwise scattered, and thus wasted, energy. This concept is illustrated in the playing of a musical instrument. The focused energy required to play a piano concerto is tremendous, yet relaxing; it demands complete mental, emotional, physical, and spiritual presence—none of which is wasted on anything that does not contribute to the music.

Energize your altar during your visits with sound, fragrance, water, or fire. Sounding a chime or bell will help clear the energy and signal the onset of a sacred ritual. Fragrance, through smudging or the use of essential oils, sets the tone for the session depending on the energy carried by the scent or device used. Smudging is an act of purification and is steeped in Native American wisdom. Water, symbolizing life, abundance, and emotions, can be placed in a decorative bowl. In it you may want to float some beautiful flowers as a love offering to Spirit, or to display some river rocks found at a favorite beach you visited with your spouse, allowing them to appear before you as they glistened that day.

Say a prayer, meditate, count your blessings, or just be mindful for a few moments. Release your fears. A rhythm will eventually emerge, and a ritual will be born.

CHAPTER SIX

Aromatherapy

*T*he strength of aromatherapy lies not merely in its intrinsic ability to lift our spirits with the lovely scents many of the essential oils release. Though a mighty mood inducer, its real power rests in its healing properties. Aromatherapy is medicine—the oldest medicine our species has to call upon.

Aromatherapy is also a fascinating science that is equally interesting as an art. Perhaps this is because essential oils affect humans on many different levels. Aromatherapy is more akin to homeopathy than to the westernized medicine of synthesized chemicals, which can only treat patients in one way and do not in and of themselves heal at a soul level.

The processing of essential oils—delicate liquids distilled from plants—retains the life force of the plant. Consequently, these oils radiate an electrical frequency in the form of megahertz (MHz). This energy is measurable and typically ranges from approximately 50 MHz to 320 MHz. For comparison, fresh fruits and vegetables have a biofrequency of up to 15 MHz; fresh herbs, 20 to 27 MHz; the human body during waking hours, 62 to 68 MHz; our brain, 72 to 90 MHz. Essential oils compress and encapsulate the life force of the plant. Studies have proven that use of these oils can increase our biofrequencies or restore our biofrequencies to a normal range.

The New Testament makes many references to essential oils. Perhaps the most prominent account is the gift of frankincense and myrrh by the three wise men to the Christ child. This gift was considered more precious than gold. The value of essential oils lies in the fact that, for example, the manufacture of one ounce of rose oil requires sixty thousand rose blossoms.

Molecularly, essential oils are so minuscule they can be absorbed into our systems even when cell walls are hardened due to oxygen deficiency. They act upon every cell in the body within twenty minutes. In fact, essential oils reoxygenate and nourish depleted cells. Cells require oxygen for the processing of nutrients. Without proper cell oxygenation, disease begins. Essential oils are also strong antioxidants and have antibacterial and antiviral properties. During the Great Plague of the Middle Ages, perfumers were reported as being essentially immune to the disease. What truly makes essential oils precious, though, is that they also restore balance to the human body. For all of these reasons, aromatherapy deserves a more elevated status in our homes and lives.

The Egyptians pioneered the use of essential oils for medicinal healing approximately five thousand years ago. A preserved medical scroll titled "The Ebers Papyrus" lists more than eight hundred prescriptions and documents the successful treatment of eighty-one diseases. The Egyptians also used essential oils for embalming. The Greeks were first to ascribe to essential oils their more subtle, spiritual properties. Romans, true to their hedonistic image, indulged their senses completely by using essential oils to scent themselves, their clothing, and—perhaps most significant within this context—the walls of their homes. And so there exists a strong collective consciousness surrounding the healing attributes of aromatherapy.

In creating home environments that align with your goals and objectives, aromatherapy plays an important role. It is the kind of touch that carries much love because it is bound to be considered a fine detail by most. Specific suggestions for the appropriate essential oils to use are found in each chapter of Section Three. Scent is powerful in aiding memory recall, so choose your essential oils wisely and enjoy the many happy memories of Home you are bound to accumulate.

There are many ways to use essential oils. For our purposes, the most effective and quietly nurturing for the occupants of Home is to use a diffuser. Diffusers come in several different forms and are generally available where essential oils are sold. They are inexpensive and very unobtrusive. Some diffusers use a candle to heat a small, usually ceramic jar containing an essential oil, or blend of oils, causing their fragrance to be released into the air. There are also simple rings that can hold a small amount of essential oil that rest on top of lightbulbs, the heat of which diffuses scent into the air. One that I like is a small plug-in device. You sprinkle a few drops of your oil or oils of choice onto a pad, insert it into the electric diffuser, and plug it in. A similar product is also available for vehicles.

Although aromatherapy has many healing properties, it also offers the simple pleasure of fragrance. Refrain from using sickly smelling synthetic fragrances, such as those found in most commercially produced air fresheners; many other choices are available for making your home smell wonderful.

The double benefit of flowers is difficult to surpass: they are visually engaging and add the element of scent. Consider some of the following flowers: carnations, lily of the valley, freesias, mimosa, gardenias, narcissi, hyacinths, primroses, roses, jasmine, lilacs, geraniums, sweet peas, violets, and tuberose. Flowers are notably romantic. It is very important to remove dead blooms immediately because viewing dead plant life becomes a sort of visual affirmation for death.

Linens or a pillow scented with lavender are deeply relaxing and sleep inducing. To scent a linen closet with dried herbs, simply place them in a small cotton or cheesecloth pouch or envelope and then into your closet or under your pillow. On a cotton pad place a few drops of your favorite essential oil or perfume oil then toss it into the clothes dryer along with your clothes. Or try adding your favorite oil to the water in your steam iron—just a couple of drops will do—and then press the fragrance right into your shirts. Citrus scents work well for this since they generally produce a feeling of ample energy and optimism.

Cleanse the air in your kitchen after cooking by boiling dried herbs in a pot of water on the stove. Cinnamon works well because most of us have fond childhood memories of cinnamon-scented holidays. It is also said to attract prosperity. Real estate agents sometimes recommend it to help a home sell. Plant fragrant herbs and shrubs outside near windows and doors. In the spring and summer, keep the windows open wide and enjoy the freshness these plants bring. Lavender is associated with the goddesses Circe and Hecate, and it is said to bring luck. Plant it near your entryway; it is a living blessing.

Scent your mop water with essential oils. Place a cotton pad soaked with them in your vacuum cleaner bag—it makes a great diffuser—for instant cheer as you work. Again, lavender works well because of its antibacterial action, and remember that violets were revered by the Christian church in early New England as being sanctifying.

Use the essential oils listed with each home environment theme in Section Three singularly, or be creative and try blending some or all of them to create a signature scent for your home. I am quite sure that once you make a habit of using aromatherapy in your home it will become a tradition that you will find very therapeutic.

CHAPTER SEVEN

Color

*W*e think of color as visual, and truly color is inescapably woven into the components of our visual home. However, the importance of color becomes more salient when we introduce the fact that color is energy—vibration. This means we sense it with more than just our vision. Color can be felt, as shown by studies in which individuals have been able to identify color through touch while blindfolded.

Color is present in the aura of the human body—our energy field. These colors are not only seen by some individuals, but research is beginning to show that the colors seen in people's auras have measurable frequencies consistent within color groupings. For example, wherever yellow is seen in the auric field, the frequency reading is consistently in the range of 500 to 700 hertz (Hz).

This information is important to Home for several reasons. If we feel ourselves more strongly attracted to a certain color than in the past, it may be that we have actually developed a physical or emotional need for it. We could even speculate that putting on an article of clothing and having to remove it at once could indicate that its particular color is creating some kind of uncomfortable imbalance based on how it interacts with us. Some colors just seem to feel better, more inviting. And as with everything else in life, our needs change. Because we sense color on more than one level, imagine how important it is to pay attention to what your body tells you when investing in a new sofa, for instance. Simply knowing the more esoteric side of the topic of color raises your awareness and helps you to be more responsive to your intuition when selecting color to enliven your home.

There are many ways to approach selecting colors that are sensually appealing yet can be used to decorate harmoniously, but no matter what, color is personal. Never allow the tastes or professional training of another individual to supersede what you know intuitively about color. A Feng Shui practitioner could tell you that your entryway needed black accents. If your body or intuition says no to black, listen. Know there is a reason you are rejecting a certain color—a reason that perhaps is worth exploring.

At this time you may wish to reflect on the notes you took during your mental tour of Home. If strong color themes did not arise during the exercise, clear your mind and focus for a minute. What color or colors are you currently drawn to? Still need more information? Open your closet. The information you find there can be interpreted literally, or it can be loosely translated. For example, my clothing is primarily navy, black, and white, with a little brown and aubergine. My clothes tend to be plain or simply tailored and with simple patterns, if any. But in my home I love greens and reds, and I like the way the starkness of my solid-colored couch makes my intricately patterned chair stand out. Perhaps it is the play of color, the contrast I am most drawn to. Maybe it is just that I wear so much navy that it's the last thing I want in my house. Perhaps it is the more intimate connection between wardrobe color and body that rules out specific colors for use in the home.

While these are all points to consider, the only way your home is going to feel loving is if that feeling is being emulated. It has to come from you first. And that means you must love the colors you live with. When visitors come they will feel it. For this reason, never decorate with colors you feel indifferent about—you might as well not like them. Unless you really love the colors of your home, there will always be a line of demarcation between you and it that will be felt by everyone.

If you're still stumped about color choices, think about the color of any recently purchased items, or the color of anything you've admired lately. Does that color, or some variation of it, resonate with you in some emotional way? Does it excite you, inspire you, make you feel kind and loving, romantic, or clear? If so, and you would like this to become a theme on some scale, make a note of it. It could be that this color would make a wonderful signature color for you. A signature color is one that carries a theme throughout most of your home. If it is red, then perhaps it is an accent color in the living room, a contrasting and poignant color in the dining room, the color your kitchen cabinets are stained, and the color of the luminous glass accents in the hallway. Color expressed in this manner can be subtle, yet unifying. Additionally, a particular color can serve as a base from which to begin developing a home environment, providing an organizing element.

When selecting color, be practical as well. If you make an impractical choice, you will feel uncomfortable and anxious—and so then will your family and friends. Always consider the activities conducted within each room. Is it a room your children will play in often? Don't use white, off-white, or a pastel color on anything they will sit or stand on. I recently purchased a small couch for our newly remodeled basement. This couch was primarily for my kids to sit on while watching television or playing around with friends. It had to be a small couch so as not to overwhelm the space, and yet I wanted it to be one that could fold out into a bed for guests. I found the perfect couch and it was available in two colors: a sage green and beige. The beige would have looked better—at first. But the darker color was the better choice for this particular purpose.

In any space where creative work is done, color must be carefully considered as well. For many people creative energy is drawn as much from our surroundings as from our imaginations. Color is important to most creative people. Color these areas beautifully and to the tastes of the individuals using them most. Even colors normally considered neutral, such as shades of white, when placed side by side will likely elicit strong and immediate responses from you.

Always contemplate and examine the many different shades of your color. Because color is also an expression of light, it changes throughout the day. Wall colors, because they are painted on large, flat surfaces, are particularly susceptible to the effects of light. If you are feeling uncertain about a wall color, paint a small area or two on opposing walls with the color. Just observe it and how it makes you feel over the next few days.

Cool colors—colors with shorter wavelengths—tend to visually recede. These colors are blues, greens, violets, and grays. Warm colors—those with longer wavelengths—advance. Warm colors include reds, oranges, and yellows. Whether a color is classified as being cool or warm has nothing to do with intensity. Contemplate violet walls in your living room, for example. Most of us would probably be overwhelmed. But it could work with just the right lighting, the perfect shade of violet, and certain furnishings in just the right size room.

Monochromatic color schemes are uncomfortable for most of us. Just conjure up into your mind a picture of you sitting on a light green sofa in a room with soft green walls and a deep green rug with lots of green plants in it. Don't you feel out of place? On display? This color scheme draws attention to anything not green. Though we normally would not consider green to be a stark color, it becomes one when applied in this manner.

There are many ways to bring color into your home. In addition to paint and fabric, place crystal prisms in your window to create rainbow light (first read Chapter 4 for information on proper placement), or strategically place colored glass vases where they become luminous when the light passes through them at certain times of the day. You can replace standard lightbulbs with colored bulbs, or string playful colored lights across doorways or amongst plants.

Feng Shui also has a lot to say about color, and some of that is discussed in Chapter 4. Don't translate Feng Shui suggestions about color too literally.

Blue can mean the entire range of blue, including turquoise, for example. Pink can mean mauve or magenta. Purple can include all of the subtle shades roughly classified as purple, such as violet, lavender, or plum. Red and blue, the primary colors blended to make purple, can also be effectively used in tandem.

Through the ages humans have applied spiritual characteristics to color, though meanings can vary in different cultures. Off-white, for example, signifies death and mourning in some cultures but is an appropriate color for marriage and new beginnings in others. Still, you may find some of this information helpful in excavating your own thoughts and feelings about color. Make a note of any strong reaction that may come up during your review of the following list of colors and their qualities.

White White represents sanctity, innocence, purity, cleanliness. It can also feel cold and isolating in some situations. White is very projecting and is therefore considered masculine. Most white paint is overly stimulating; it is just too crisp. Before the advent of latex paint, it used to be that white paint was actually a wash, possessing a dusty quality and texture. It yellowed over time and hence was much warmer and easier to live with.

Black Black has an impressive, powerful nature. When misused it can signify hiding. It magnifies our emotions. It is considered mysterious, and therefore feminine.

Brown Brown is earthy, grounding, and therefore stabilizing. It is especially successful in a decorating scheme when represented in wood furniture and flooring.

Purple Purple is a very spiritual and sensitive color that can be inspiring and conducive to reflection. It also supports creative energy. It often is associated with truth-seeking. When misused it carries the feeling of abuse of power.

Violet Soft violet is generally soothing to the body and mind. It is peaceful and tranquil. It is a very spiritual color. Violet has been used to help balance skin conditions, induce sleep, and balance emotions. It is said to control hunger.

Blue Blue is peaceful, calm, restful, and somewhat introverted. It is the color depicting loyalty. At its worst it can seem too cold and therefore withdrawn. It lowers the heart rate and blood pressure, and can also reduce inflammation.

Indigo Indigo is midnight blue. It is said to advance psychic power and increase daydreaming. It has been used to restore balance and stability, and is a good choice for a meditation room or healing space.

Green Green falls exactly in the center of the color spectrum, and therefore is associated with harmony, peace, reassurance, contentment, and balance. It often symbolizes freshness, birth, and potentiality. When misused its primary attribute is jealousy, but it can also manifest as indecisiveness. Green has been used to treat headaches, stress, and related conditions such as ulcers.

Yellow Yellow raises energy levels. It is alert, joyous, happy, and clear. It also symbolizes intellect. Sometimes it has the negative attribute of cowardice. Yellow has been used as an aid to sharpen memory.

Orange Orange is optimistic, confident, and social. It is sometimes referred to as a creative color as well. When misapplied it can fuel hyperactivity and can be overpowering. Orange is said to stimulate the appetite, and it has been used to help stimulate the human immune system and to heal depression and alcoholism. It is an excellent choice for a sickroom.

Red Red is vivacious, outgoing, and assertive. It can be characterized as active, and therefore it is a good color to use if you procrastinate. It is also warm and can feel intimate. It is the color of passion. Red can also evoke anger and irritability. It has been used to increase the pulse and improve circulation, and to regulate respiration and brain activity.

In the color descriptions you probably noticed that many colors have been used to treat physical conditions and disease. This science, now called color therapy, was used—just like aromatherapy—by the ancient Egyptians, Greeks, and Romans. The Greek goddess Iris governed color. When you see a rainbow, or when you witness rainbow color streaming through a dangling crystal prism, think of Iris, for her path between divinity and humanity is said to be a rainbow. Hang a prism in her honor.

Most of us approach color intuitively, and that is probably best. But it helps to understand relationships between colors. For the purposes of this book, just know that colors falling next to each other on the color wheel are considered harmonious. On the other hand, complementary colors—those which oppose each other on the color wheel—feel stronger, more lively. A harmonious home environment or family life is supported by the use of harmonious colors in a color scheme that augments this feeling. Complementary or contrasting colors are used to accentuate or strengthen a theme.

If you are seeking to increase a feeling of peace and tranquillity in your life, consider a soothing shade of green as your primary color. Adding blue accents further evokes tranquillity. Green and blue together constitute a harmonious color scheme. If that feels too cold you could add a bit of warm yellow or gold. If you had felt lethargic, sedentary, or reclusive for months, you might choose red or orange as a primary color in your overall scheme. To increase the energetic feeling red possesses without completely overwhelming yourself, you could accent it with green, which would make the red stand out without making it feel too hot or intense. If family unity is something you want to promote, a family room decorated in several related colors could really emphasize that feeling. One possibility is navy, turquoise, purple, and magenta combined. The magenta would provide a subtle contrast, but not enough to feel disruptive.

In this way you will be able to choose stronger, clearer color schemes with confidence. The end result will be exactly as you intended and in line with what your home and life are all about.

CHAPTER EIGHT

Flower Essences

*T*he powerful yet subtle medicine of flower essences may not leave a physical imprint on Home, yet it can play a significant and magical role in helping our souls move into a more comfortable space. In that flower essences encourage our evolvement on a soul level, we can align this medicine with our dreams and aspirations, as we do our home environments, to contribute toward a major shift in consciousness to our good.

Flower essences are tinctures prepared from the blossoms of wildflowers and cultivated flowers. These tinctures are alive, just as essential oils are alive. They carry the resonance of the souls of the plants from which they were produced. Vibration, whether it be in the form of sound such as music, or color, or light, is a soul-healing element. We know this to be true because our most profound moments tend to be the result of something vibratory in nature: a glorious sunset, the sound of ocean waves, a masterful work of art, or an enchanted garden spilling over with life. These things move us; they transform our lives.

Resonance is fascinating. A guitar string will vibrate when its matching note is sung by a human voice. If you strike a tuning fork and hold it near another tuning fork, the second one will begin to sound as well. We are no less magnificent in our ability to resonate. And so these delicate extracts, each with its particular attributes born of its flower heritage, subtly pull forward the qualities in our souls with which they resonate, working in tandem with our own energy fields.

In the 1930s Dr. Edward Bach pioneered a mind-body approach to health care. Although trained as a traditional physician, he found himself diagnosing patients' conditions based more on their attitudes and emotions than merely on their physical symptoms. His practice grew into a homeopathic-based one because of his appreciation of this whole-person perspective. Dr. Bach began investigating the healing properties of wildflowers at a time when the world was extremely conflicted and filled with hatred and fear, during the Nazi regime. By 1936, the year of his death, Dr. Bach had documented a fairly extensive list of flowers and their healing properties.

Flower essence therapy is homeopathic. Health is seen as the acceptance, the embracing, of all of life, even when it seems imperfect. When we are sick or in pain, we are receiving messages. Our bodies are calling us to go deeper within, to know ourselves better, to grow. It is perhaps better to accept and embrace and truly heal than to deny by seeking only to eradicate the attacker. Traditional medicine seeks to repair. It revolves around illness as opposed to good health. Homeopathy seeks to achieve a more expansive experience of wholeness and balance.

Flower essence drops are taken orally, but they are not drugs. Their vibratory nature renders them alive, and they have no biochemical effect as do pharmaceuticals. Flower essences encourage our souls to change, leaving us completely free to learn the lessons our ailments present to us.

By far the most intriguing aspect of flower essence treatment is that a particular essence will affect the full range of one particular ailment, from its decline at one end of the continuum to its full expression at the other. I am speaking of polarities, the yin and yang of all matter. Fear and courage are really one and the same, even though they seem to be opposites. To treat fear with a flower essence is to bring forward an enhanced state of courageousness. Flower essence therapy truly revolves around the concept of oneness and balance.

Flower essences that will conspire with your soul to manifest your dreams will be presented in each chapter of Section Three, "Home Templates." If you are primarily seeking a greater experience of peace in your life, you will most likely be drawn to the peace template. Woven into the messages of that chapter will be some suggestions for flower essences that will promote a feeling of inner peace and calm. This will further align your feelings and inner intentions with your physical reality, creating authentic harmony.

CHAPTER NINE

Guardian Spirits

*T*hroughout time human beings have recognized and honored their own divine nature through acknowledgment of spirit beings. To polish your home environment with love, it helps to invoke the presence of the celestial realm. Not only will your home glisten with warmth and comfort, it will transform itself into something grand enough to house all the precious souls inhabiting it.

Spirit beings may be angels and guides, animal spirits, or the souls of trees. They protect and direct us in our daily lives. They bring comfort and wisdom. Perhaps more important, though, they enlarge our view of the Beyond and bring perspective. We become aware that we are part of something wonderful and mysterious, something bottomless and vast. Our acknowledgment that life exists beyond this plane helps define our sense of place in the universe and creates authentic trust in life. Some of us have been fortunate enough to have felt, from a very early age, the presence of spirit beings in our lives. We may have been called eccentric. The wisdom of years makes us more comfortable with our sensitivities, and it delivers tolerance for those who are not yet as open.

To get closer to your spirit allies, find a quiet place to sit with your eyes closed and your heart and mind open. What kind of spirit magic are you most drawn to? Call into your mind a picture of an entity you feel you resonate with. Is it a radiant angel with glowing wings of gold and a frosty halo? Is it a frolicking butterfly? Is it a strong and stately elm, its protective branches extending over the roof of your home? Who comforts you when you are certain another human could not possibly understand? To whom do you pray in times of scorching pain? When you are brought to your knees in one fell swoop by a universe set on showing you an unpleasant piece of yourself, whom do you ask for deliverance? As this spirit being makes itself known to you, be mindful. Allow it into your daily life; let it bathe your home in its kindness and brilliance every day.

There is no need to recount stories of angel encounters. Just as Spirit is always there, poised to respond to the faintest recognition, so is a legion of angels. Some angels have wings, some have human bodies. Some enter through our senses and feelings as a warm wash of love. Some are with us from the time we are very young, some come to us as our souls advance toward them. If it is an angel you feel you are being guided by, draw yourself to it and it to you by placing—with thoughtful attention—symbolic representations of angels throughout your home. Each time you see these representations a part of you will become quiet and peaceful, loving and compassionate. Just as it is difficult for a couple who prays together to turn away from one another, your angels will encourage you to live to your highest ideals.

You can call forth your guardian spirit—however you picture it—by simply speaking to it, silently in meditation or aloud. When you invoke the presence of your guardian spirit, identify how you would like its presence to affect your home. Call forth angelic energy for joy and festivity in your dining room, for solitude and restful sleep in your bedroom, for clarity and industriousness in your office, for example. Contemplate your words; make them beautiful in your own way. "Angel, come forth into this sacred space; infuse it with your limitless love and unwavering peace. Stand guard and see that we are blessed. I give thanks that you are here with us." It is a nice touch to leave a love offering, something found in nature perhaps, as a gift for your guardian spirit. Undoubtedly you will recall your encounter each time you enter the room, and this will respirate your home with soulfulness and meaning.

Trees are considered great transmitters of protective and healing energy. Their energy varies according to tree type. The energy of the alder is strengthening and balancing, that of the ash is tranquil, while aspens have a stimulating, almost scattered energy. The energy of the chestnut tree brings determination, the linden is intellectually stimulating, and maple trees have a harmonious energy about them. Oaks convey strength and stability. The energy of pines is cheerful and purifying, as is their scent. Poplars and willows facilitate emotional healing. If you have a tree on your property, tune in to its energy and enlist it in maintaining a happy home. If you have a strong resonance with a tree on your property, dedicate it as your protective house tree. Allow yourself to imagine what that tree's soul is like.

Do you often dream of animals? Do animals migrate into and out of your consciousness? Perhaps you have recently received an elephant figurine as a gift, and now they appear to you everywhere. Linear thinking would dismiss this as coincidence, but it might just be your initiation into higher awareness. I believe there is a message and a touch of magic in every encounter. If we pay attention, we may be able to decipher it.

If you truly bond with animals and feel you encounter their souls when communicating with them, yet there is not one particular animal of significance in your life, you can seek one out. Animal totems will be suggested throughout the template chapters. If you decide to invite joy and festivity into your life, Butterfly or Hummingbird enchantment might be especially meaningful to you at this time. Or perhaps before retiring at night you can center yourself and ask Spirit to reveal to you a meaningful totem. The image of a particular animal may come to you during your sleep in a dream, or it may casually introduce itself to you in real life somehow. Simply tune in.

Another way to discover your animal totem is to make a list of all of the personality traits or habits you wish to change. Find the animal with the opposite traits; its energy will balance out yours. If you do not instinctively know which animal carries the traits you desire, you can refer to my list of some common animals later in this chapter or to a book of animal totems.

You can also scan through the lists at the end of this chapter for an animal associated with your birthdate. These three lists can also be found in Brad Steiger's wonderful book *Totems: The Transformative Power of Your Personal Animal Totem*, an excellent resource for further information.

Once you have discovered your animal totem, find a physical representation of it to display in your home. Then, invite it into your life and home as an energetic protector and guide. This can be done quietly while focusing your conscious intention upon the totem. Remembering that all of life resides within us, seek to learn all you can about your totem's characteristics. You will intuitively know a lot about your totem's energy and how it corresponds with your current experience of life. Anything else can be learned by studying the actual animal, or reading about its habits.

Because so many people appreciate Native American wisdom or feel a strong connection to animals, a list of the primary spiritual attributes of some totems follows.

Antelope Antelope signifies proper and swift action. Antelope medicine is graceful and agile. It strengthens the heart and mind. There is also communication with higher realms of consciousness.

Badger Badger is very self-assured and persistent. It is assertive in accomplishing objectives and uses anger as a motivator to action.

Bat Hanging upside down is a symbol for rebirth—just as a child enters the world through a mother's womb. Bats indicate that change is necessary. There must be a letting go of old ways that no longer serve.

Bear Bear signifies introspection and truth-seeking through going inward. It conveys extreme receptivity. Bear is a very right-brain symbol.

Beaver Beaver always keeps all options open, never backing itself into corners. It is especially adept at teamwork, and is industrious, especially at home.

Buffalo Buffalo represents prayerfulness and the recognition of abundance in all areas of life.

Butterfly Butterfly represents self-transformation. It can bring mental clarity and depth to soul searching. Note that the Greek word for *butterfly* and *soul* is the same: psyche.

Cat Cat energy implies mental and physical agility and grace. Cats represent intuition and the search for mystical truths. They are also highly independent.

Cow Cow is nurturing and peaceful. It represents caring for families, communities, global issues. Cow medicine is that of cooperation.

Crow Crow is a spirit helper that is able to get you in touch with the knowledge of higher order; one that is beyond humanness. Crow is very perceptive and intelligent.

Deer Deer symbolizes a gentleness powerful enough to heal all wounds.

Dog The primary attributes of Dog are loyalty and dependability; also allegiance to one's personal truth and goals.

Dolphin Dolphin energy is that of laughter, joy, and playfulness on the surface. This totem is also deeply attuned to the cyclic rhythm of nature.

Dove Dove brings peacefulness, love, and harmony into life. Some Native American tribes believe that beings take the form of doves after death to facilitate their heavenly transcendence.

Eagle Eagle represents personal power achieved through the passage of spiritual tests, opportunities to rise above the everyday, astute mental power.

Elephant Elephant is strong and assumes great responsibility. It symbolizes wisdom.

Elk Elk represents stamina. During most of the year elk prefer the company of their own gender and therefore signify camaraderie.

Fish Because it swims in water, fish signifies emotions and deep or ancient mysteries.

Fox The essence of Fox is quick physical and mental response; cleverness. Rather than paying attention to the words of others, Fox tends to observe their actions.

Frog Frog energy is that of cleansing and purification. It may also symbolize the riddance of distraction to clear energy and the replenishment of spirit.

Hawk Hawk is extremely aware and sees things other people don't see. Hawks are messengers.

Horse Horse is a symbol of true power, the kind of power that comes from being compassionate and caring, from sharing your gifts and love with the world. Horse also evokes a sense of being free-spirited and lively.

Hummingbird Hummingbird symbolizes joy and an intense love of life.

Lion/Mountain Lion The essence of Lion medicine is primarily leadership; it also connotes majestic power.

Lizard Lizard is symbolic of dreamtime.

Otter The playful energy of Otter encourages sociability.

Owl Owl medicine is clairvoyant and magic—perhaps because of its keen night vision. Owl is comfortable in and curious about the dark unknown.

Rabbit Rabbit is quick-witted and articulate. Rabbit also symbolizes abundance and fertility.

Snake Snake embodies wholeness because of its willingness to accept and embrace anything that happens in life. Two snakes intertwined represent healing.

Swan Swan medicine is that of confidence and poise. It is an aid to developing social skills and personal style. Black swans may symbolize highly attuned intuition.

Turtle The nature of Turtle is grounding; it is very connected to Earth. It can bring stability to relationships and is an excellent booster for a good family life.

Whale Whale medicine is that of clairvoyance, having access to universal mind. Whale people know things and don't know why they know them. It is a good totem for spiritual development.

Wolf Wolf is a great teacher and friend; a sharer of gifts. It is characteristically a very communal animal and therefore a good totem for families.

Whatever our belief about what is beyond our three-dimensional existence, our lives are enriched exponentially when we recognize that there is more. We are enriched when we make room for the Grace that allows us to be here in this moment.

ANIMAL TOTEMS

Native American Zodiac

January 20–February 18	Otter
February 19–March 20	Cougar
March 19–April 20	Red-tailed hawk
April 20–May 20	Beaver
May 21–June 21	Deer
June 22–July 21	Brown flicker
July 22–August 21	Sturgeon
August 22–September 22	Bear
September 23–October 22	Raven
October 23–November 21	Snake
November 22–December 21	Elk
December 22–January 20	Snow goose

Astrological Birth Sign

January 21–February 19, Aquarius	Eagle
February 20–March 20, Pisces	Fish
March 21–April 20, Aries	Ram
April 21–May 21, Taurus	Bull
May 22–June 21, Gemini	Dolphin
June 22–July 22, Cancer	Crab
July 23–August 23, Leo	Lion
August 24–September 22, Virgo	Lamb
September 23–October 23, Libra	Owl
October 24–November 22, Scorpio	Scorpion
November 23–December 21, Sagittarius	Horse
December 22–January 20, Capricorn	Goat

Chinese Zodiac

The Rat: 1936, 1948, 1960, 1972, 1984, 1996

The Ox: 1937, 1949, 1961, 1973, 1985, 1997

The Tiger: 1938, 1950, 1962, 1974, 1986, 1998

The Rabbit: 1939, 1951, 1963, 1975, 1987, 1999

The Dragon: 1940, 1952, 1964, 1976, 1988, 2000

The Snake: 1941, 1953, 1965, 1977, 1989, 2001

The Horse: 1942, 1954, 1966, 1978, 1990, 2002

The Sheep: 1943, 1955, 1967, 1979, 1991, 2003

The Monkey: 1944, 1956, 1968, 1980, 1992, 2004

The Cock: 1945, 1957, 1969, 1981, 1993, 2005

The Dog: 1946, 1958, 1970, 1982, 1994, 2006

The Boar: 1947, 1959, 1971, 1983, 1995, 2007

CHAPTER TEN

Numerology

$\mathcal{N}$umerology is the descendant of number symbolism. The magical or symbolic value of numbers is ancient, with roots that trace back ten thousand years or more. Number symbolism enjoyed its first real blossoming during the time of the Pythagoreans and their successors. Pythagorus—often referred to as the father of modern math—believed everything could be represented by number relationships.

Every number carries with it sacred meaning and characteristics associated with that number's vibration. Some of us instinctively know our personal association with certain numbers, such as those we consider lucky.

There may be some reason for your attraction to particular numbers. Unleashing the enchantment of numbers on an environment can augment a sense of harmony, when correctly applied. It is helpful to know that even numbers are more yin—passive, receptive, feminine—and odd numbers more yang—assertive, active, masculine.

A process called mystical (or diagonal) addition is used to calculate the overall vibration of complex numbers. This method reduces a number to a single digit in order to reveal the number's essence. This will reveal to you another energetic nuance of Home. You add each digit of your home's street number together. If the sum of the digits results in a two- or three-digit number, then add those together. Continue until the address is reduced to a single number. Using the example 6249 Cherry Street, the method works like this: $6 + 2 + 4 + 9 = 21; 2 + 1 = 3$. This house would have the energetic influence of a 3 vibration. Below I've charted the mystical relevance of numbers one through nine.

One One is the symbol of totality; it represents the center from which all things emerge. The essence of one is completeness. It is the number of new beginnings and individual growth and development. A house possessing one energy is great for individual creative exploration. If you live alone in a one house it could be a little isolating. If you do feel isolated or lonely, balance your environment with color: sunny yellows and oranges; fragrance: citrus scents; and the flamboyance and sociability of three energy: group things in threes, employ triangular shapes, and so on.

Two Two is the number assigned to the element Earth. It represents balance between opposites: the dance of yin and yang. A two house necessitates tact and diplomacy, cooperation and patience. To minimize polar energies, choose a color scheme centering on green. You may wish to refer to Chapter 21, "Peace," for advice on countering conflict.

Three Three represents the element of Water and the triune nature of all life. Three is the symbol of fulfillment, as in three wishes, or achievement, as in three tests to pass. Three characterizes fun, sociability, and entertainment. It encourages friends and gatherings. Be careful not to tire yourself out by being constantly on the go in a three house.

Four Four is a manifestation of Earth; that is, four seasons and the four directions. It is a symbol of harmony and stability. Four connotes organization, practicality, wholeness, and strength. Four is a good house for a busy family. If stubbornness is a problem in a four home, try introducing contrasts in the home environment using contrasting colors, such as green and red, and textures, such as silk and linen or wool.

Five Five is the unification of two (feminine) and three (masculine). It has been considered the symbol of marriage. It represents our five senses, five fingers, the five wounds of Christ, and much more. Five is the number of freedom, change, spontaneity, and physical energy. All these things make a five home a dynamic one.

Six Six is a good number for home and family life. It is characterized by a keen sense of familial and social responsibility, compassion, and love. The energy of a six home places a great deal of importance on the beautification of the home and garden.

Seven The energetic influences of seven include a deep inner life and introspection, the welcome hush of solitude, the flowering of spirituality. This home is not conducive to a busy social life, and if that is something you desire, you can bring in a more extroverted energy with the inclusion of sunnier colors and fragrances.

Eight Eight symbolizes abundance and prosperity—worldly success. Eight energy allows for much accomplishment. You can be confident in all business dealings. You command respect. It is the number of greatness and infinity.

Nine Nine is the number of completion. It is good for finishing projects. Completed projects and old relationships that no longer serve will pass out of your life in a nine environment. A sense of selflessness, generosity, and giving away love is also the essence of nine. A new relationship is not easily obtained under this energy; however, old relationships are rekindled.

If, after calculating the numerology of your home, you decide that number's meaning does not correlate well with that which you desire to attract into your life, there are a couple of things you can do. The first is that you can name your home. Naming your home is a lovely thing to do anyway, because it establishes your home as an entity. According to ancient traditions, letters have corresponding numbers. You can effectively alter the numerological energy of your home by giving it a meaningful and appropriate name.

The following chart shows how to determine the numerology of any name.

A	B	C	D	E	F	G	H	I	J	K
1	2	3	4	5	6	7	8	9	10	11

L	M	N	O	P	Q	R	S	T	U	V
12	13	14	15	16	17	18	19	20	21	22

W	X	Y	Z
23	24	25	26

In the Cherry Street example described earlier, the home carried the energy of three. Perhaps the occupant of the home is a newly widowed or newly divorced woman with a tremendous need to dig deep into her soul for answers. Seven is perhaps a better number for her during this time. She could give her home a name with a seven vibration, such as Francesca.

Using mystical addition, the numerology of Francesca can be easily calculated:

```
F    R    A    N    C    E    S    C    A
6 + 18 + 1 + 14 + 3 + 5 + 19 + 3 + 1 = 70;  7 + 0 = 7
```

The power of the number seven is evoked each time the name is used. The energy becomes more and more imprinted on the environment over time, and with all energetic impulses correctly aligned, this woman's home can become a haven of peace and reflection. She could further enhance the magic power of the number seven by placing seven candles on her mantle, seven plants in her garden window, and seven polished stones upon her dressing table, and by inviting seven angels to watch over her in sleep.

Several other adjustments would enhance her comfort during this difficult time. She could provide herself with a quiet corner in which to meditate and pray. She could decorate and dedicate an altar to inner growth and renewal. She could accent her home with the colors of a midnight sky. She could adopt Bear as her totem ally to remind her of her process and guide her through it.

Now that you understand the power of numerology, use this ancient wisdom to help make your home more comfortable for you wherever you are at in life.

CHAPTER ELEVEN

Stones and Minerals

The immense power of stones and minerals has long been acknowledged by human beings. All sacred texts refer to it. Although it seems
that stones and minerals are esteemed today primarily for materialistic rather
than spiritualistic reasons, it does also appear that increasing numbers of
people are beginning to understand the tremendous energy encased in these
brilliant particles of earth.

As with all matter, stones and minerals express on a microcosmic level
what is true on a grander scale. Subtle consciousness and energy reside in
them. For this reason we are attracted to certain stones. They possess a
quality that mates with a need we have. Of course, our energy levels, and

therefore our needs, change subtly from day to day, and over a period of time may change dramatically. Consequently, our attraction to stones will vary and change from time to time.

This chapter will give you a little information about the more common—and a few not-so-common—stones and minerals, especially as they may relate to the home environment themes in Section Three. There is much to know about stones and minerals from both spiritual and scientific perspectives. As you read through the following list of stones and their spiritual characteristics, pay particular attention to those stones that especially interest you. Your intuitive guidance may be sending you a signal about what will most benefit you.

Agate Agate has the ability to call forward and bond together the earthy qualities of human beings. Agate naturally draws out truth. The subtle gathering force of agate makes it an excellent facilitator of teamwork. It promotes peace and helps to spread joy. Agate can help you accept yourself and others.

Amethyst Amethyst has always represented royalty. Spiritually, it is quite a powerful stone, emanating love and healing. Amethyst can help you surrender your consciousness to the higher collective spiritual mind. It has the ability to draw out unnecessary or unwanted energies, diffusing them to the ethers. Amethyst also can receive, purify, and disperse all healing energies. It is calming. If you live in the city or have any kind of respiratory condition, amethyst is said to positively affect breathing.

Aquamarine This stone works well for meditation and reflection. It is intrinsically peaceful and serene. It is said to reduce fluid retention.

Bloodstone Bloodstone energy is grounding and detoxifying. It has the ability to align the physical body with the spiritual. It is said to improve clairvoyance, and hence, decision making.

Carnelian Carnelian can propel individuals who tend to be too passive, languid, or lazy into action. It helps remove lethargy and creates personal power. Its energy reminds us to seek to be highly energetic and positive, yet balanced, without compulsion.

Crystal (Quartz) Quartz is a generic name for a number of stones that are very pure and clear, mostly without color. These physical properties have much to do with the spiritual attributes assigned to them. Crystals are widely known as amplifiers: the energies present in the environment or being will be magnified. Rose quartz resonates love, beauty, and warmth. It is an aid to those who are lonely. It is an excellent choice for children, or for individuals who needed more parental love as children. Smoky quartz is very grounding and is said to bring abundance.

Diamond Diamond emphasizes the infinite search of the soul. It encourages us to be completely open and present. It purifies mental energy.

Emerald Emerald has an energetic presence of love and kindness. Emeralds strengthen the heart and character. Emerald energy is amplified by the moon, such that when the moon is at its fullest the stone is its most effective.

Fluorite Fluorite is a great balancer of mental energies and is an excellent choice for meditation. It helps expand mental power and clear out psychic clutter related to stressful living.

Garnet Garnet is an excellent choice to help bring about a deep sense of well-being. Red garnets inspire love and creativity. They heighten passion in general.

Iolite Iolite is the stone of discernment, saying true or false to matters of the heart.

Jade In China and Japan jade is considered to be the most precious stone. Jade is piercing in that its energy makes obvious the root of a problem. At the same time, it is a stone of tranquillity, its energy steadying the individual to look at an issue calmly and rationally so that the solution can be recognized. The various colors of jade also take on the spiritual attributes those colors typically represent.

Jasper Jasper is said to stimulate our sense of smell. It possesses a very subtle positive or uplifting energy.

Kunzite Kunzite is a good stone for individuals desiring to become more disciplined. It also seems to provide relief to those who have undergone trauma or extreme stress. Kunzite is also touted as being beneficial to the circulatory system.

Lapis Lazuli Lapis lazuli refines mental processing. It calms the mind, allowing a person's strength of will to come forward. It is renowned for deepening psychic ability. It also benefits all interpersonal relationships.

Malachite Malachite is a stone that acts somewhat like a mirror. It brings forward an individual's energy patterns, or personal truths. This allows the individual to see her or his own qualities—positive and negative.

Moonstone Moonstone can help balance out emotions and helps link the individual with moon-based cycles.

Onyx Onyx is a stone that is beneficial mostly in times of great need, such as in times of desperation or personal crisis. It soothes nerves and lends emotional stability. It is centering. Onyx is also said to help reduce fevers.

Opal Opal tends to accentuate the prevailing or dominant characteristics of a person, either positive or negative.

Peacock Ore Peacock ore is said to increase physical stamina and energy by stimulating the nervous system, muscles, heart, and lungs.

Pearl The luminescent pearl symbolizes beauty, purity, and compassion. A pearl is a soothing thing of beauty that is born of the irritation and rubbing of a grain of sand. Such is the soul.

Peridot Peridot is a subtle and soothing energy that protects against nervousness. Its energy is very light, however, and so is best suited to individuals who do not face overwhelming challenges. It is also said to benefit the parathyroid glands.

Ruby Ruby has forever signified love, including self-love; it strengthens the heart. Rubies inspire courageousness and valor.

Sapphire This stone is centering and accentuates intuition. When worn on the finger it sends out healing. When used in meditation it is calming.

Tiger's Eye Tiger's eye is a confidence builder, providing courage to help meet new challenges. It also allows clear thinking to flow and be projected through words and gestures. It actually strengthens the mind. Tiger's eye also draws Into being what is good and nourishing for its owner's soul.

Topaz Topaz radiates love in a way that the surrounding environment is able to easily absorb. Its energy is more delicate than that of the diamond. It is a joyful and light stone.

Turquoise Turquoise carries honor, glory, wisdom, and a strong sense of spirit. Its energy is steady, rhythmic. A deep bond tends to develop between the owner and the stone. This connection facilitates truth-seeking and clear communication. Man's reverence for this stone could fill volumes.

Zircon Zircon helps heal the spirit, bringing temperance and peacefulness. It symbolizes and emanates harmony. It is especially effective for individuals who are by nature quiet.

You may wonder how these stones could possibly assist with creating an aligned home environment. Aside from being the striking, luminous, objects of beauty they are, stones give us information about what our souls need. For example, over the past eighteen months I have been strongly drawn to smoky quartz. I am not a person who likes to shop, yet I have discovered or been drawn to large prisms of this stone, usually set in silver earrings or necklaces.

Small pieces of the stone are not nearly as attractive to me as big ones. I finally realized that what I needed was more grounding—a more pronounced connection with the earthly plane—during a time of expansive spiritual growth. I did finally purchase a brilliant pair of smoky quartz earrings, which I love wearing. More importantly, I gained a physical representation of a very real personal need. This stone showed me that I currently need more stability in my life, and that I crave more than ever to be able to rely on loved ones, rely on Spirit, and feel safe in my process. I need to turn my attention inward without fear that my outer or material world will fall away.

This experience led me to another realization—that there are other ways, many of them physical, to help myself feel grounded. In my home environment I have worked to clear out, organize, and beautify our basement. It now truly supports the physical and spiritual beauty abundant in my life. During the process of this remodeling, we resupported and leveled our home; it is now very strong and stable. I have also resuscitated some very important, close friendships, and I have established a stronger network of friends. I have learned important lessons about releasing my dreams into the universe—into Spirit's hands—while keeping my feet firmly planted on the ground and staying poised for action.

Awareness of this timely message life wanted to communicate to me began with my attraction to a beautiful rock. If it were possible to be truly awake in every moment, our every instinct would feel the prompts nature continuously provides.

Perhaps you have noticed that you have felt attracted to a particular stone in the past few months. Or maybe there is a stone you have loved since childhood. When you're out shopping, do you find yourself gravitating toward one stone in particular? Perusing the list earlier, did you catch yourself thinking you would love to have one of those stones? The stones you are attracted to will serve you well in the form of jewelry or as loose objects placed upon your altar, at the energetic center of your home, on your desk or computer, or on a bedside table. If you resonate with a larger crystal or stone found in nature, you could dedicate it as a house stone, imbuing it with inspiring messages for constant replay to everyone who enters or dwells there.

Pay particular attention to choosing a house stone. If it is a natural stone, such as a river rock, it will carry the energy of the place from where it came, and it will be imprinted with the occasion on which it was discovered and claimed by you. If this was a happy time and place, then all of that love will continue to radiate from it into your environment. If it is a crystal that was traumatically torn from its beloved earth, its energy may have been altered. Just pay attention. If the energy of the stone feels good to you, then it is good. Still, it is a good idea to clear the stone's energy patterns so that it will be more responsive to yours. This is achieved through cleaning. I highly recommend cleaning even if you have chosen a river rock or other opaque stone to center your home. Your intention strengthens the act of cleansing. I will suggest several methods here, but there are many ways to do this; the "right way" is whatever method most resonates with you and your rock.

- Hold your stone or crystal underwater in a clean, gently moving stream.
- Place it on a piece of natural fiber fabric and lay it in the sun for a few hours.
- Place it in a bowl of water and let it bathe in the light of the full moon.
- Rub it with a purifying oil, such as eucalyptus (crystals only).
- Allow it to soak for approximately twenty-four hours in a purifying bath of two parts water to one part salt. Sea salt is best.

Once it is cleansed, hold your stone to your third eye. Focus your energy and your intention for the stone upon it, dedicate it to what you desire to bring forth in your life, give thanks to its presence, and place it in its new home. If it is a crystal, you may wish to keep it out of the direct presence of visitors, because crystals tend to collect energy. Occasionally—whenever you feel the need—you may wish to cleanse and reprogram your stone.

Opening your life to the delicate messages of the natural world will help finely tune your sensitivities and intuition. Stones will grace your environment and being with a certain lightness and purity of spirit.

CHAPTER TWELVE

Sound

Consider the idea that the world was sung into existence; this is the belief held by the Aborigines. We know of the power sound has over our emotions, and we are becoming aware of its ability to caress us into good health and to lead our minds into patterns conducive to more complex reasoning.

Sound comes to the foreground when discussing components of Home, for it is perhaps more expressive and tangible than the sweet, faint gyrations of any other component. We are somehow more aware of its impact on our physical, emotional, and mental states. Because of its dominance in daily life, we often feel lost and lonely when sound is absent and silence takes over.

Sound, music in particular, can lift our spirits to levels that make us feel renewed, strong, and almost unstoppable in executing our mission in this life. When our emotions are fragile and raw, music can easily collapse our hearts, deflating our desire to press forward. Sound can hypnotically carry us to places only dreamed of, and can cause our souls to ascend to other planes. How is it that sound can affect us so multidimensionally? Perhaps its thick, rich, declaration demands that our response match its drama. As much as sound stirs the fabric of our being, it is equally forceful in rearranging the energy in our homes. This is generally good because it greatly lessens the likelihood that this energy will become dense and less pliable. As with all vibration, sound leaves its mark, and so it pays to be careful about what we invite in.

There are many sounds competing for a resonant match with our cellular makeup. These can take many forms: playful splashing water, laughing children, purring kittens, the solemn ticking of a clock, a mesmerizing voice reading a story, the random melody of wind chimes that sing us to sleep, bells that awaken us. If we are fortunate, we can hear nature beckon through its crashing ocean waves, a meandering stream, the clap of thunder, or the melodious screeching of a legion of angels.

Sound doesn't mind intruding. It does so with the telephone, the doorbell, our blessed coworkers, and even the voices of our loved ones. It descends on us in the form of traffic, street and air, and the sounds of thousands of people breathing together. It can intrude in the form of an excited crow, or the frivolity of a midweek party next door. Dogs bark without concern for our mental health. Motors whir without asking permission. Home can provide sanctuary from these intrusions.

As you move through life your body is keeping pace with the sounds it encounters. Your blood pressure, heartbeat, digestion, muscles, breathing, gait, brain waves, mental patterning, and mood all make an effort to harmonize with what is around you. That is why the discordance of heavy metal music can make you feel anxious and edgy. When a sound arrives at an inappropriate time, such as a police siren early on Sunday morning, the results can be nerve shattering. Even certain voices can overwhelm us, either by their tone or their cadence. Not only does the quality of the voice—the sound we hear—affect us, but it is a fascinating fact that certain patterns of speech are more pleasing to our ear. The exquisite patterning of Shakespearean language, iambic pentameter, is said to speak directly to our hearts. No wonder the precise meaning of the words may escape us and yet their lyrical essence is still deeply felt. As more research is completed regarding the effects of sound, some municipalities are finding a correlation between soothing sounds and the decrease of crime on their streets and so are piping music into their public squares.

While I cannot instruct you on how to mitigate your exposure to all unwelcome sounds, I hope to raise your awareness of their impact and encourage you to create literal harmony in your home. When sound aligns with soul, a sense of authentic well-being results. Just as essential oils carry oxygen to our cells, new research is finding that chanting and singing as well as listening to certain types of music can produce the same result. Proper cell oxygenation is said to deter immune deficiency and certain degenerative diseases. It has also been said that a half-hour of soothing music can produce the same relaxation as does ingesting ten milligrams of valium. While the behavior generated through loud, harsh, hard rock music may somehow facilitate independence of thought for teenagers, for most of us it is probably unhealthy physically and emotionally to be exposed to it for long periods. And complex music, such as the music of Mozart and other masters, helps establish complex neural patterns conducive to performing higher brain activities such as mathematics.

Sound can be used advantageously in our homes in several ways. The first is that it can become a physical attractor of whatever energy we need present to manifest our dreams. Think of sound as a powerful tool. If you become determined to shake off a state of lethargy you have carried around for some time, tuning in to some lively music at appropriate times will not only physically energize you, it will energize your spirit. Subsequently, you will be more likely to attract that which is active by nature. You might suddenly find yourself with new friends with whom to engage in activities and events, offers of club memberships, or invitations to sporting events.

Secondly, the right music and other types of sound can heighten our receptivity to the sacred symbols present in our home and underscore our home's overall theme. If you decide, for instance, that you want your home to support you during an inward journey, playing sacred music on your sound system will accentuate the spiritual icons on display. The music will cause you to pay more attention to these things, thereby empowering them, and they in turn will reinforce your process.

Music can simply produce a desired ambience. We all know about this. Music is an instant mood enhancer: instant romance, instant party, instant introspection, and so on, can be accomplished through appropriate music.

Sound can help us in any physical or emotional healing process we might be in the throes of. If you've lost your love, you may find yourself playing music that reminds you of cherished times together. You may, in fact, need to allow yourself to feel all that pain in order to acknowledge and then release it. We can use music to calm and soothe, to make us determined and strong, or to help us dream or reminisce. Other research indicates that certain sounds can provide relief of physical pain. It is just a matter of finding the sounds that work.

Sound can also very effectively clear and reset energy patterns in our home environment. This is discussed in depth in Chapter 3.

If you haven't invested in a sound system, especially if you live in a noisy city, make a plan to do so. If you have a sound system, acquire a wide variety of recorded music and nature sounds. Base your purchases on what you most desire to create in your domain. You will find musical suggestions aligned with specific goals in each chapter of Section Three. Some general guidelines follow.

To increase your energy level and aid in the release of deep emotions held in the body's tissue, listen to music of African descent: calypso, soul, reggae, the blues, and jazz. Latin American music can also provide an energy fill-up: samba, salsa, and rumba are good examples.

Impressionist music acts on us much the same as impressionist painting does. It is conducive to daydreaming and imaginative creative work. Debussy is probably best known for this type of music.

Music that is somewhat neutral, such as New Age, helps open our minds and sense of space and time. In this way it is peaceful, expansive.

The sounds of sacred or ritualistic music can map out pathways to introspection and meditation and help us to be present with our feelings. Drumming, chanting, and strains of church music, such as Tudor church music, are wonderful examples. Music carrying great inspiration and emotion, such as gospel songs and hymns, has an earthy quality that is grounding and uplifting at the same time. If you have not had the experience of drumming, you may wish to invest in a handmade drum and try it. It is a wonderful precursor to meditation. If your mind is tired of being busy and you wish to create a feeling of simplicity and wholeness, Gregorian chant is an excellent choice.

To create a feeling of consistency, predictability, and stability, try baroque music. It is great music by which to perform repetitive tasks.

Romantic music, evoking images of slowly sipped wine, significant and tender chitchat, and luminescent indigo skies is best represented by the masters Chopin, Schubert, Liszt, and others. This music lends an air of poetic refinement.

For traditional elegance, clarity, and an atmosphere of excellence, choose classical music. This, of course, is a large musical category—examples are Mozart, Brahms, Beethoven, Bach, and Tchaikovsky.

Popular music is very personal. Because of its prevalence we tend to have strong associations with it. Always go with your gut feeling. Big-band music can fall into this category, although it tends to simply create a sense of fun and nostalgia. Rock and roll can make you feel optimistic and energetic, and it can help you release tension. It can also increase tension if it is dissonant with your mood.

Remember that these are only guidelines. You should always go with whatever strikes a definite chord within you.

CHAPTER THIRTEEN

Sacred Symbols

The word *symbolism* is based on a Greek word meaning "to toss together" or "join together." The objects we refer to as symbols are actually icons providing a link between ourselves and their deep meanings. Our collective consciousness holds a veritable web of symbols linking everything. What better affirmation that everything is one! Perhaps this is the true function of symbols.

Delving into the meaning of symbols is an important endeavor. Most symbols have roots in antiquity; some are cross-cultural, some are culture-specific. Without question, unless we examine their meanings, symbols can become buried in a sea of optical stimuli in an age that too often uses them merely to grab attention. However, symbolism is far too broad a subject to do more than graze in the pages of a single chapter. I suggest that you allow your lineage and your personality to guide you in your search for symbols that convey meaning to you and that you in turn empower them with your attention.

What is your heritage? Like most of us, you may be of mixed descent. If so, does one side of your family seem more rooted in its culture and traditions? If the memories are fond and shaped your life in a positive way, why not adopt some of the icons of that tradition? Embracing your roots is one way to bring more strength, groundedness, and resilience into your life.

Below is a list of basic and common household symbols and their meanings. Understand that everything and anything can be symbolic, depending on the meaning we assign to what we see. All of the things you've saved from childhood and long lost loves are symbols. Colors, rocks and minerals, and numerology are also symbols, but they are explained in earlier chapters, and I've left them out of this list to avoid redundancy. You will also notice that saints, gods, goddesses, and all other such protective guides and governors are largely absent. Look to your culture, your lifestyle, your path, and see if there exists a guide carrying special meaning for you. As you read through the list, make note of anything that touches a nerve or brings a smile to your face.

Anchor Fidelity, consistency, stability
Ankh Everlasting life, authentic wisdom
Bamboo Good luck, spiritual development
Basket Fertility, abundance
Beans Fertility, good fortune
Bee Social organization, royalty, hope, intelligence, poetry
Bell Connection between heaven and earth, cosmic harmony
Birds Mediation between heaven and earth
Book Knowledge, wisdom, unity
Branches (green) Honor, immortality, fame
Candle Light, faith
Castle Fulfillment of all wishes
Chain Connection, relationship between heaven and earth

Cherries Self-discovery

Cherry blossom Good fortune, beauty, purity

Circle Wholeness, completion, the life cycle, eternity

Clouds Habitat of the gods

Clover A sacred and magical plant (Celts); good luck

Coal Hidden power

Copper The goddess Venus; warmth, femininity, a conductor of beauty

Corn Happiness, prosperity

Cornucopia Abundance

Crocus Love, majesty

Cross Victory over death, eternal life, divine protection, Christianity

Crown Power, the elevation of spirit over body

Cube Firmness, solidity

Cup Overflowing abundance

Cyclamen The flower of Mary

Doe Womanliness

Door Transition

Dove Peace, reconciliation

Drum Heavenly powers, the path of the sun

Egg Fertility, perfection

Elephant Power, peace, wisdom, happiness, chastity

Eye Light, spirit, the sun, perception, vision, clarity

Fan Sovereignty

Feather Power

Fire Holiness, purity, divinity

Fish Spiritual nourishment

Flower Feminine beauty

Forest Introspection, mystery

Fountain Youth, health, good fortune

Gazelle Speed, beauty, piercing spiritual knowledge

Gold Heavenly light, love, the soul, the energy of money

Goose Love, marital fidelity, vigilance

Grapevine Life, abundance

Hand Friendship, a sign of blessing, devotion

Heart Love, friendship

Hippopotamus Pregnancy, a protector of women

Honey Tenderness, sweetness

Horn Psychological balance

Horse Strength, youth, freedom

Hyacinth Yearning for heaven

Iris The rainbow reconciliation of God and man

Ivy Fidelity, friendship

Janus Guardian of transitions

Jewels Heavenly light

Labyrinth Discovery, enlightenment

Lamp Individual spirituality

Laurel Poetic inspiration, victory

Lily Purity, virginity

Lotus Cosmic harmony, light, meditation

Marigold Salvation

Mirror Self-knowledge, clarity, truth

Moon The feminine aspect, receptivity, the unconscious

Mountain Closeness to God, strength

Mushroom Long life, creativity

Myrtle Peace, joy, virginity

Net Gathering, interconnectedness

Ocean Infinity

Ostrich Truth, justice

Pansy Fidelity, coyness

Parasol Power, high status

Pegasus Poetic and intellectual creativity

Pentagram (five-pointed star) Knowledge, health, balance,
protection against evil

Peony Honor, wealth

Pyramid Ascension, alignment of earth and heaven, secret
knowledge

Quail Dance of yin and yang

Rain Heaven's influence on earth, cleansing

Rainbow Promise, reconciliation between God and man

Reindeer Guide to souls

Rice Spiritual and material wealth

Ring Eternity, fidelity

River Time, continual renewal

Robe Protection, high position

Rock Solidity, stability

Rosary Prayer, meditation

Rose Love, complex relationships

Salamander Inner peace while under attack

Salt Protection, purifying, intellect, wit, hospitality

Sand Limitless potential

Scale Balance, fairness

Scepter Higher power

Ship Journey

Silver Purification of the soul

Snow Innocence

Spiral Development, growth, quest, renewal

Square Earth, the four directions

Staircase Acquisition of a lofty position, spiritual and emotional development

Stars Acquisition of dreams and goals, fame

Strawberry Modesty, readiness for marriage

Sun Light, cosmic intelligence, clarity, joy, vision, the masculine principle

Sunflower The sun

Sword Courage, strength, decisiveness

Throne Sovereignty, rulership

Thread Connection

Torch Illumination, cleansing

Tower Rising above mediocrity

Triangle The triune nature of God or Goddess, harmony, divine qualities

Trumpet The voice of God or of angels

Turtle Diligence, immortality, universal wisdom, earth

Unicorn Strength, power, purity
Veil Mystery, secrets
Water Femininity, mystery, life; associated with the moon
Weaving Structure and movement of the universe

I submit this list to inspire you, to challenge you to ask yourself about the deeper meanings of all things. When intentionally selected, symbols are silent affirmations for our fondest dreams. When strategically placed in your environment, their power increases exponentially. A meaningful symbol placed in an area you don't frequent will not be as effective as one placed just above your computer monitor where your eyes drift while you are deep in thought.

Whether universal or deeply personal, overt or subtle in nature, symbols constitute the organizing and unifying principles of Home.

CHAPTER FOURTEEN

Intention

*T*hroughout this book I refer to the power of our own intention in creating our lives. What I mean is that, just as "we are what we eat," we are what we think. Our private and worldly lives are the fruit of our thoughts. Many of us have allowed ourselves to understand this in only a limited sense; we understand that positive thinking attracts positive results. We know that positive thinkers are more healthy and more successful than those who think negatively. And yet, perhaps we have not discovered how we deprive ourselves of life-enhancing energy by not fully recognizing the Divine in each of us.

An invisible universal unity supports all things. Materially, that presence could be described as energy or ether. Mentally, it could be described as divine consciousness. When we position ourselves in harmony with this energy, our thoughts become masterful transformers. By aligning ourselves with the energetic flow of the Divine mind, much can be accomplished. In fact, we can create every experience we can imagine and believe about ourselves. The actions I prescribe in this book will increase your awareness of the power of aligned thinking as it relates to creating harmonious spaces and beyond.

If your thinking is restricted and limited, what you attract into your home and life will likewise be restricted and limited. We often refer to this as the law of cause and effect. We seem to know and understand this law a little better in a scientific setting, but it applies to our daily lives. Everything is complete in itself while being part of something larger. Because life is layer upon layer upon layer of pattern, we as human beings are microcosms of the universe. Therefore, we are not exempt from the law of cause and effect. For every action there is a reaction. And because we are able to reason and choose, we can determine effect by defining cause.

It is important to understand that beyond the law of cause and effect there is a Universal Intelligence at work—the essence of life itself. Even science agrees that life comes from antecedent life. Universal Intelligence lovingly breathes meaning into all we are and all we do. All we accomplish is channeled through this intelligence, this Spirit. We release to it our desires, our knowing, and it reproduces them in form. Proof of this is literally everywhere. The universe continues to create as we constantly create through our thoughts, whether they be beautiful or less than beautiful. And so we experience effect. If our thoughts are aligned to that loving presence of Spirit, our experiences are harmonious, pleasant. Applying this principle to our environment enables us to create sanctuary. It is also true, then, that if we think thoughts that come not from love but from fear, they bring into our lives experiences that we would probably rather not have.

It pays off to capture our thoughts, to become aware of them, to monitor them, and to change them when necessary. We must align our thoughts in a way that brings us harmony and does no harm to anyone. Of course, learning what is in our best interest and in harmony with the universe is an unfolding process. Perhaps it is impossible to know what is for our greatest good in every single moment. But by learning to listen to the faint voice of our intuition—which is how Spirit speaks to us—we surely will come closer to living in harmony with life.

Studies have shown that positive thought and the expression of positive thought, such as in the form of prayer or meditation, raises the frequency of the human energy field. Raising our consciousness to the highest possible pitch will help secure the highest possible benefits for ourselves. The key is to find a place inside yourself where you know and can affirm for yourself the truth you seek. Through acceptance, which is the practice of simply claiming whatever it is you declare as your highest good, the best possible outcomes will become your real experience.

Rise up to the truth that is present in, around, and through you: you are a creative expression—an individuation—of Spirit. Created in the likeness of Spirit, you too have tremendous creative power. When understood and unleashed, this creativity can help you manifest supportive, sacred space.

You were born to be godlike: a radiant, glorious, courageous expression of the highest qualities imaginable. It serves neither you nor the world to think any less of yourself. No matter what conditions surrounded your entry into this life, no matter what circumstances surround you now, you are always who you are in this moment. Neither guilt, nor shame, nor desperation, nor any other tormenting emotion works in your best interest. If you truly want this world to be better, then love yourself. Cast off anything that is based in fear; savor all that comes from a place of love. Remember who you are, always.

Underlying the content and premise of this entire book is a message of love. Love yourself, love your family, love your things, love your home. Count everything as sacred. Coursing through this book are words of love. I make no excuses for them because I know these words are powerful. What I intend to do with my words is send love and comfort out into this world. I know that as I do others are inspired to become aware of their thoughts, and perhaps they, in turn, are inspired to grant themselves and the world more love.

I believe that our power to better our life conditions depends upon how much good we are able to draw into our own imaginations. However much good you can imagine, I believe it is yours to have. The path is not always as we envisioned, the package may not be exactly as conceived, and yet our utterances of belief and longing bring us a perfect result. The result being what we in essence asked for through a chain that began with our own thinking. Some of us have difficulty thinking we are worthy enough to have everything we ever dared to want. Wake up! You have received in exact measure what you believe. What you believe is exhibited in how you live, and that is driven by what you really think, not what you merely philosophize about.

Dare to dream big dreams and think big thoughts. In order to have peace in your life you must first conjure it up in your mind. Before having the family life you wanted since childhood you must be able to imagine it first, and in full-blown, exquisite detail. Before becoming president of the United States you must surely be able to feel in your gut the power it takes to be that. And because we all need a starting place, let us practice in the sacred space of Home. Every adjustment to Home ushers in personal change, for the precursor to the adjustment was an equivalent enlightened thought. All this fuss about Home is really fuss over you. You deserve to be fussed over. Here is an affirmation you might use:

> *Knowing that I am what I think, I declare that I now act in harmony with the universe. I recognize Spirit in my life, in myself, and I allow my heart to rest in that holy space. I release myself from fear, and live from love. The love inside me generates the gentlest, most loving thoughts. These magnificent thoughts are unleashed into the universe. I see the results in my beautiful home, in my family relationships and friendships, and in my every encounter. And yet I know my thoughts travel beyond what I can see and experience, and that my powerful love touches those in distant places. For simply knowing these things I am blessed and I am grateful. It is good to be aware.*
> *Amen.*

SECTION THREE

Home Templates

CHAPTER FIFTEEN

Balance

Balance is the still point within a steady being; it is the equipoise between the forces of yin and yang, introspection and worldly prowess, feeling and doing, honoring and disengaging. Balance means living within our own evolved idea of integrity, without being overly smitten with any one aspect of our life. Every component of our life receives the amount of attention needed to allow it to support us as we journey along our critical path.

Whether we seek it or not, balance seeks us out. Many people describe this phenomenon as life teaching its lessons. When we have invested too much in our own independence, a romantic interest suddenly presents itself in some irresistible form. When we speed along missing the important things of life, an unfortunate accident forces us to contemplate them. When we deny mounting pressure to make a decision, someone makes it for us. When we bury emotion deep within our bodies and don't attend to it, we become ill. All are messages; the nudging of life trying to call us back into the natural state where we belong.

Finding Balance

In this hectic, busy society, balance is an extraordinarily challenging state to achieve. I find it useful to do two things: peel back the layers of life to just a handful of important components; and prioritize.

How does one transform a scrambled clump of tasks, obligations, and habits into a streamlined life teeming with meaningful experiences? While I cannot reveal this to you, I know life will. Whenever your faith becomes big enough to cause you to act, the applause of your angels will lift you to a place where the next step is clear. Don't dwell on the details of your current life, or the differences between the life you have and the life you desire. Keep your eyes on where you intend to go, and you will.

EXERCISE • PARING DOWN AND PRIORITIZING

This exercise is intended to help reveal what your heart deems a balanced existence. You will need some paper and a pencil or pen and highlighter. You will also need a great deal of honesty and courage in order to articulate your heart's desires. Your heart instinctively knows balance. This exercise requires the use of logic and deductive reasoning; however, the heart must instruct the brain, not vice versa.

Begin by taking six or seven deep breaths, and then follow your normal breathing pattern for a few minutes. Being receptive with every sense you have, allow your awareness to rest on your heart. Pull as much energy as you can from that beautiful heart space. Ask Spirit for guidance in completing this exercise with honesty and to your highest good.

Draw a large circle to represent the pie chart of your life. Tuning in to the guidance of your heart and using appropriately sized slices, assign each component of your life a slice and label it with the approximate percentage of your time that you believe it uses up each month. My life pie encompassed the following slices: mothering/time with spouse: 26 percent; writing, researching: 11 percent; managing the family business and personal consulting business: 10 percent; household management: 15 percent; social/family activities: 6 percent; personal time: 5 percent; sleep/renewal: 27 percent. Time I spend on my own spiritual practice is embedded in a couple of different categories.

In examining your chart you will probably notice some glaring misappropriations. You might want to eliminate an entire slice. Go ahead, cross it out. This is like decluttering, so be ruthless. Anything you don't want, or that drains your energy or joy away, or is a constant source of irritation must go; do not allow your brain to overrule your heart's decision. If an entire slice is eliminated, redraw the pie chart with percentages reallocated to equal 100 percent again.

Now, unless you're completely happy and fulfilled with how you spend every moment of your time within each category, draw an individual pie chart for each segment of the master chart. When I did this exercise, I saw that, while all of the categories belonged in my pie chart, my time needed to be redistributed. I needed to eliminate some undesirable tasks within a couple of the categories. In particular, my heart desired to spend less time focused on the family business and more time on my writing and consulting. I listed the activities relating to the family business, creating a separate pie chart, and crossed out every task and habit that, on a personal level, was not uplifting. In one five-minute session I obliterated nearly the entire chart!

This surprised me because I have always held my responsibilities as being extremely important for the well-being of my family. I realized that these responsibilities had nothing to do with my own growth, evolution, or enjoyment, however practical they might be in helping support us. I also saw that the time I spent participating in family business activities took time away from what I love doing—and what I love doing undoubtedly makes me feel more prosperous than those things I feel a mere obligation to do.

I understand, of course, that some things must be done regardless of how little I enjoy them. I have a commitment to keep regarding a special business partnership. But by redrawing the pie chart representing that segment in my life, I affirmed that there are options yet to be discovered. With my heart intent on balancing my life by recognizing my desires and finding creative ways to honor myself, my endeavors, and my path without shirking my commitment to the family business or compromising my family's standard of living, I have created the possibility for change. Through this opening of consciousness, opportunities for my personal betterment will show up.

Don't just list activities in your pie chart. List habits. If, for instance, you drink several glasses of wine in front of the television each night, give that a place on a chart. Ask your heart if each item serves you or disserves you, if it is balancing or throws you off-center. Most likely the wine and television will go. On the other hand, if everyone cuddles on the sofa for family night each Friday while munching popcorn and viewing a movie and you cherish those cuddles, keep that on your chart. Go a step further and explore ways to enhance this time even more.

Draw and redraw, if need be, the master and component pie charts until you have an exact representation of the perfect balance your heart wants. It is unlikely your heart wants relationships that eat away at your self-esteem, self-destructive habits, or inertia. Continue redrawing until all items born strictly of logic or fear are wiped out. When your charts exude love in all of their components, when nothing about your charts hurts anyone, when they radiate brilliance, excellence, beauty, and integrity, you're finished. You've achieved a personal representation of a balanced life.

Display your charts in a protected place, but one that you see several times daily. Tape them to the pull-out writing surfaces of your desk, put them on the music stand of your piano, or tape them to the inside of your pantry door.

Don't forget to thank Spirit for guiding you through this process. When you truly listen to your heart your path becomes clear. Keep your eyes open and opportunities for balance will appear.

❧ SPACE CLEARING FOR BALANCE

The best examples of balance are found in nature, where large stones steady swift water; where a passive insect falls prey to a clever bird; where stately trees with open arms shelter countless small animals. Although each component delivers its role in perfect balance to its counterpart, each also embraces a delicate balance within itself. There can be no imbalance where everything carries out its role according to nature's plan. To see the oneness of all life is to be balanced. Achieving this oneness, a state of living your authentic nature, is the objective of this space clearing.

Choose an auspicious date to conduct your space clearing for balance, such as during the new moon or on an even-numbered date. Consider performing this clearing between the hours of 11 and 1, A.M. or P.M., when yin and yang energies are at their peak and transforming into their opposites—a good time to transform your space into one of greater balance.

For this space clearing you will need the following materials to make offerings for each of your main rooms: a large beeswax pillar candle and a large flat rock to set it on, and enough flowers (preferably wildflowers) to surround each candle. Balance the colors of the flowers. For each candle I suggest four large flowers such as white daisies, with one facing each of the four directions. Fill in between each of these with some small yellow flowers, representing earth, and an equal number of proportionately sized blue flowers to symbolize the vastness of heaven. In all of the other rooms a smaller beeswax candle will do. You will also need a drum, possibly a rattle, and a spray bottle filled with charged water with a few drops of essential oil—either spruce, to create a feeling of balance, or ylang-ylang, to balance the masculine and feminine energies. The rattle is necessary only if you feel the energy in the house is stuck or negative enough to require three passes, the first with the drum, the second with the rattle, and the third with the mister.

If necessary, review the space clearing guidelines in Chapter 3, "Space Clearing," for more detail; the following instructions are specific to this particular space clearing.

Step One

Beginning at your front entrance, and moving in whichever direction you plan to move during the space clearing, light and dedicate each candle you come to. Use thoughtful words to dedicate each candle to a balanced life. For instance, in your entry hall you could say, "I dedicate this candle to the presentation of a balanced lifestyle. May all who enter my home feel the balance my life now exudes." In your living room, "I dedicate this candle to the memories of a balanced life, joyous social gatherings and intimate moments, games and the quiet pursuits of the soul, and the sharing of both laughter and raw feelings." In your kitchen, "I dedicate this candle to perfect health born of the balanced blending of yin and yang in all food prepared here with love, as well as for the souls who partake of it and grace this room." In the bedroom, "I dedicate this candle to the presence of masculine and feminine energies present in each individual who rests here. Their perfect rest rebalances and renews these forces."

Step Two

Following the steps outlined in Chapter 3, begin your space clearing for balance at the entrance of your home. Because you are clearing your home and invoking an overall feeling of balance at the same time, be very measured in how you use your space clearing tools. For example, when beating your drum, do it consistently, resisting the urge to beat harder and more sporadically where the energy feels thicker. Instead, simply spend more time in these areas. Be the essence of balance: rhythmic and steady. Apply this same methodology to rattling, if you choose to make a second pass. Finally, infuse each room with a misting of spruce or ylang-ylang.

Step Three

Seal each room off by standing at the entrance of the room and facing into it. Place one hand on each doorjamb, if possible, and visualize activities and discussions being conducted in the room by centered, balanced family members. If you live alone, project a feeling of balance into the room. When you feel the clearing is complete, etch the sign of infinity in the air and go on to the next room. If you will be home during the period immediately following your space clearing, leave the candles burning as long as it is safely possible.

❧ AN ALTAR TO BALANCE

Create an altar to the poetic yet practical balance of nature. To accentuate balance, all altar items should be from nature and of earth-toned colors.

Place a golden beeswax candle upon a flat rock at the altar's center. Surround the candle with small pinecones—bearers of new life. Now position a small vase of any kind of white flowers in the back right-hand corner of the altar, for beauty and purity in all your relationships. In the front right hand corner place a representation of your animal totem, or of the animal whose qualities you most admire, to invoke the protective spirit of your animal guide. This will also serve to invite into your life the wisdom that particular animal offers. In the back left-hand corner of your altar place a small, tabletop fountain fashioned with river rock to activate wealth and keep it smoothly flowing and accumulating. In the front left-hand corner place a small bowl of sand, indicating awareness of your limitless potential for knowing yourself in finer and finer detail for all the years of your life.

Scatter beautiful leaves all over the altar, for they are possibly the finest and most abundant representations of a natural state of perfect balance. Dot your altar in a symmetrical pattern with small garnets or pieces of onyx; both stones are good balancers of mental and physical energy.

Visit your altar regularly, lighting the candle and checking in with Spirit about your path to balance. Refresh your altar with a misting of spruce-scented water.

❧ COLOR

Individuals working toward a more balanced psyche and lifestyle will appreciate the centered feeling an earth palette will bring. Contrasting and complementary colors should be injected into your color palette for balance.

In Feng Shui, yellows and earth tones bring forward the essence of the element Earth, which is grounding and balancing. Because many people find browns dreary when they dominate a color scheme, a golden, earthy saffron might be more appealing. If this is a color you find easy to live with, you might wish to adopt it as a signature color, allowing it to wind its way throughout your home in varying degrees of tonal depth. Other choices for the base of a balanced color scheme range from a hearty mustard yellow to a paler, more sophisticated sand.

To provide contrast in living areas and to strengthen the earthiness of your decorating scheme, try using, in moderation, very dark browns, such as the color of coffee beans. This look is instantly elegant, yet comforting. For more sophistication add a little pearl, and for a feeling of richness add a little garnet or a deep plum or aubergine.

In your bedroom couple a sunnier yellow with a very warm white and caress your psyche into sweet dreams with a dash of lavender or a warm blue such as cornflower or turquoise.

Imagine a honey-pine color enlivened with a warm green, such as olive, in the kitchen. A smattering of terra-cotta or brick will invite healthy appetites and great conversation, and may even inspire some exciting Mediterranean dishes.

A bathroom lapped in golden walls, gleaming ivory tiles, and a vanity of mahogany feels exotic and provides a strong connection with the earth.

Anchor the entire range of colors you use with a good number of dark green houseplants in every room. Plants have very responsive energy fields. To help your plants stay balanced, rotate them throughout the house regularly.

❧ SOUND

When feeling slightly off-center, nothing has a more instantaneous balancing effect than the appropriate music or sound. It is critical to eliminate unwanted sounds from your home environment to as great an extent as possible. Only you can say what these are. If you live in the city, the constant grind of life on the streets can cause stress of which you might not even be aware.

If you own your own home, consider insulated windows if you don't already have them. They are quite expensive, so if this is not an option, perhaps you could invest in window treatments fashioned of heavier fabrics—the more layers the better. Whenever you are in the market for a new appliance, it pays to spend a little extra for a quieter machine.

Some people find nature sounds soothing and at the same time balancing or even renewing. Some nature sounds, however, can be quite irritating. I have in my CD collection a rainforest recording with an insect buzzing in the background. It may be authentic, but it is excruciating for me to listen to. Rhythmic sounds, such as of a steady rainfall, are best.

New Age music, the type often used for guided meditations, is excellent for inducing a state of zenlike balance. Gregorian chant can also produce this effect. I tend to gravitate toward music incorporating flute and drumming sounds, for centering.

If you play a musical instrument, I don't have to tell you how useful it is to have one around to play when feeling off-kilter or upset. Use your gift to promote or restore your own sense of balance whenever the mood strikes. If you don't play an instrument, there are some that require little skill—such as a Native American drum, chimes (the kind you strike), or even a xylophone. It is nothing but luxurious to sound yourself back into a natural state of being.

✌ AROMATHERAPY

Spruce is an excellent choice to filter into the main rooms of your house for a solid sense of balance. It has the nice side effect of smelling clean and fresh—just the way most of us want our homes to smell anyway. Cypress has similar attributes. Ylang-ylang, the ultimate yin-yang balancer, is best used in the bedroom, where it also becomes romantic and passion-inducing. For an exotic flair, try amyris. This oil originates from Haiti and has a sweet overtone, as does sandalwood. The spicy-sweet scent of clary sage has a centering effect for some people, and at the same time helps with visualization—an excellent choice for those of us trying to calm our busy minds. Geranium is a popular scent. In addition to being normalizing, it's deliciously sweet. Other balancers to try are cedarwood, chamomile, and frankincense.

❧ FLOWER ESSENCES

A number of flower essences help restore a sense of balance from within. As always, the recommended dosage is two to four drops under the tongue or in a small amount of water, four times per day. It may take several weeks to begin to feel an internal shift.

Nasturtium is often used to bring mind and body—specifically metabolism—into a state of balance and integration. This is the best flower essence prescription for those who are overtaxed with worry, extreme mental activity, and stress. Nicotiana integrates the forces of the heart with the strength of the body. It helps you feel connected with earth and at the same time helps you foster your soul's inner life. Morning glory helps bring your lifestyle and habits into a state of balance by helping align them to the cycles of nature. Calla lily brings your own internal masculine and feminine aspects into balance.

❧ ENERGETIC DESIGN

The metaphorical scales of your home landscape have been calibrated to better your chances of achieving a balanced environment and life. Now it is time to add some weight by considering and introducing design elements geared toward balance. This is one of my favorite templates because I expend so much mental energy that I genuinely rely on my home to keep me grounded and balanced.

Symmetry is very helpful in creating an ambience of balance, for symmetry provides the eye with a deeply satisfying feeling of wholeness. The essence of symmetry is a definite correspondence between position, size, and shape of relative objects. It has a lot to do with balanced proportions. We rely so much on our vision that we are more dependent on visual equality than any other form of balance. Being off-balance does necessitate heavier use of visual symmetry, but if symmetry is not intuitively easy for you, it is best to use a light hand when decorating, opting for a more sparse look.

Take note of the scale of your home's interior. How high are the ceilings? Is there a lot of wall space? Or are there lots of windows breaking up the walls? How big are the windows in proportion to the room? What is your home's style? How does that style affect scale? Be sensitive to your home's size, scale, and style. Notice I didn't say conform to those things. Just be sensitive. If your home is a cottage with a lovely dappling of soft light pouring through each of the many small, leaded glass windows, which leave little wall space, a life-size velvet painting of Elvis in your tiny entryway would probably give most occupants and visitors a headache. Not only would it completely violate your home's scale, it would clash with its quaintness.

For symmetry's sake place appropriately sized works of art on your walls. Small walls generally call for fewer and smaller wall adornments. However, if you have smaller living spaces and prefer a very clean look, you could probably get away with a couple of larger-sized (not large) works if adequate blank space remains on the walls surrounding them. Larger walls are more accepting of a variety of sizes of art. Allow your embellishments to punctuate the walls at balanced intervals between doorways and window openings.

Opt for art that depicts symmetry. A still life that is painstakingly balanced and is itself centered in your dining room and flanked on either side by matching candle wall sconces could be very dramatic—even in its simple symmetry. Some artists, such as Maxfield Parrish, are masters of balance and symmetry in all components.

Unless you are a very skilled arranger, stay away from clusters of art and objects on small walls. Although the objective might be to accent a wall in an interesting manner, clusters can easily look messy. The most common mistake is groupings of family photos. The cherished faces and memories become obscured by frames haphazardly purchased on sale. Transform these groupings into symbolic webs of connectivity by purchasing frames of the same simple design. Choose one or two areas in your home to display them. Group them in a balanced manner, such as in groups of four identically sized frames, two on top, two on bottom, making a square. Make sure all immediate family members are represented equally and that everyone likes the photos displayed.

Be scrupulous. Adorn similar spaces similarly. If two adjacent walls in your living room frame windows of identical size and placement, echo that symmetry within the space embraced by the walls. Complementary artwork on each of the walls is in order, as is treating the space as a unit. In other words, design that space for one distinct purpose: make it an intimate sitting area, or place a gaming table there. Don't functionally divide the space. In the same vein, if the doorway between the entryway and the kitchen is perfectly centered in the wall, treat each side of the doorway equally. If you put a large potted plant on one side, put a matching or similar one on the other. In this way you highlight the symmetry that already exists.

A room will also feel out of balance if you disregard its architectural centerpiece. This could be a grand fireplace or commanding window seat. Find each room's strength and design around that. Any other scheme will typically fail, even with the very best planning.

Choose furnishings that reflect both your home's scale and personality. If you live in a craftsman bungalow, your home will naturally exude a lot of balance, characteristic of craftsman style. However, because the style is heavy and chunky, smaller rooms would be completely overwhelmed by large pieces of mission-style furniture. You would undoubtedly begin to feel boxed in. This doesn't mean you should go to the opposite extreme, cluttering the space with all manner of curvy, intricate Victorian things. You could soften your interior overall in more subtle ways. For example, you could install lace panels in art deco patterns on the windows or employ furnishings with the same simple lines on a less dramatic scale. You could also use nonperiod fabrics on period sofas and chairs to bring the decor into balance with the home's scale. Also, in a smaller home, try not to choose furniture that uses up too much vertical space. If you have an eight-foot ceiling, a towering wardrobe coming within a few inches of it will make your home feel less grand, and will make you feel as though your home is closing in on you. Also, leave ample space in between pieces for Chi to saunter through.

There is much more to balance than symmetry or visual evenness. Balance can be obtained through the play between animate and inanimate objects, for example. If you live alone and spend little time at home, have no pets of any kind, nothing that moves, and you love still-life paintings, your home will feel like a museum. Add movement: an aquarium or a water fountain, a cat, artwork depicting motion, indoor electric wind chimes, a cuckoo clock. Even plant life will make your home feel as though it has motion.

Always make sure that all the elements of Feng Shui are present and in balance (refer to p. 132).

Room by room, take inventory of everything inhabiting the space. Don't forget to notice the flooring, which is often wood. Once you've assembled your list, note any major imbalances. Refer to the lists on page 50 of Chapter 4, which indicate the nourishing and controlling cycles of the five elements. This list will tell you what element to bring in to counter the effect of a dominating element. What you ultimately strive for, however, is equal representation of all the elements.

❧ FINISHING TOUCHES

In numerology, the essence of balance is the number two. Two represents equal play between equal and opposing forces, which results in perfect balance. In life, two is normally symbolic of human relationships, their male and female aspects. If this kind of balance is your objective, then allow yourself to acquire pairs of things that are very similar, complementary, or even identical. Identical objects, such as candlesticks, are powerful enough without being placed right next to each other. However, if you allow them to frame something, such as a plant on your dining room table, it is imperative that the thing they are framing be perfectly healthy, pristine, or in excellent working order. If the framed object is dysfunctional in any way, the metaphor is that of two things fated to be together while separated by some dysfunction or problem. If you are married this image will be of particular concern.

If you are spiritually oriented and/or self-aware, you may find a stronger pull to balance with threes, which represent the triune nature of everything. Threes are inherently soothing to the eye and arrange easily. Three golden

Element	Represented by
Earth	Square and rectangle shapes and flat surfaces
	Earthenware, ceramics
	Brick, tile, and adobe finishes
	Yellows and earth tones
Metal	Circle and oval shapes
	All metals
	All rocks and stones, including gemstones
	Whites and pastels
Water	Free-flowing shapes
	Water features of all kinds
	Reflective surfaces such as mirrors and glass
	Black, charcoal, dark blues
Wood	Columnar shapes: pedestals, beams, columns, stripes
	Wood furniture and finishes
	Textiles
	Floral prints, indoor/outdoor gardens, flowers, plants
	Greens and blues
Fire	Triangular shapes
	All lighting: natural, kinetic, and artificial
	Sun symbols
	Animals
	Animal skins, feathers, bone, and wool fabrics
	Reds

candles—which represent wisdom, strength, and beauty—together on a shelf along the stairway could highlight your ascent to a higher level in your spiritual evolution. Three gorgeous plants in the wealth area of your home (refer to the bagua map on page 56) could symbolize and encourage growing prosperity in a balanced way—one that honors your perfect, triune nature.

As mentioned earlier, onyx and garnet are great examples of stones that balance. Their relative affordable cost might enable you to find an excellent specimen to dedicate as a house stone or even to wear. Balancing is also a matter of countering undesirable or irritating traits. For instance, if you classify yourself as an extremely linear thinker and you wish to embark on some spiritual exploration or self-discovery, employ a stone such as azurite to bring you to center. Azurite is highly stimulating to a person's intuition. If you believe you have held back love and kindness in your dealing with yourself or others, emeralds would be an excellent choice for you to wear because they are known to stimulate love and kindness. Finding a stone that possesses characteristics opposite of those in yourself you wish to balance may require a bit of self-exploration and then research, but it is interesting and worthwhile.

When feeling out of sync with life your tendency may be to call on a higher power. If this is your inclination, ask, as specifically as possible, for the blessing and presence of your angels to show up as balance at home. In your bedroom you could call forth your angels and say:

> *Angels, watch over me in my sleep that I am renewed at a*
> *cellular and spiritual level each night, rendering me more*
> *balanced in my perspectives and mental energies each day.*
> *Reveal to me in my dreams information to help me lead a more*
> *balanced life.*

Animal totems, being directly connected to the spirit of earth, can help balance our energies in much the same way rocks and gemstones can. Once you have identified personality quirks that you believe keep you from being balanced, locate the animal totem that possesses opposing characteristics that will bring you back to center. If you have been feeling naive, the perceptiveness of the crow could be just what you need. Totems are best placed in areas where your eye will be drawn to them easily and often.

Perfect balance is a state of comfort and authenticity. With your home balanced you will receive tremendous support in leading a balanced lifestyle. Home becomes a collage of daily affirmations for balance, and that is very powerful.

❧ AN AFFIRMATION FOR BALANCE

Once you have emotionally disengaged from activities that disrupt that perfect state of balance, the next step is to affirm to yourself your acceptance of that balance in your life now. It is the intent of this affirmation to help you draw in the universal energy necessary to express a balanced life. Once you have captured this power, you will be able to dispense its essence as you walk through life, causing opportunities to stay in that state of balance to come to you. The cycle becomes self-perpetuating. This is the law of attraction.

Just as the stars are suspended in heaven, I create balance in my life today.

I allow the universal dance of yin and yang to frame my place in life's activities. These activities are perfectly aligned to my life's purpose and path. I am poised to respond with grace and gratitude to the prompts of an evolved life. Because my life's activities are relevant to my purpose and are meaningful to me, I am balanced, centered, and lifted. And like a star, I shine.
Amen.

CHAPTER SIXTEEN

Creativity

*C*reativity is the expression of universal power. Creativity is what cause is channeled through to produce effect. The result is everywhere. Everything has energy, therefore everything creates something. It can be as subtle as an impression, as violent as a war, as masterful as a painting, as functional as a fence. To create is to give birth to part of oneself so as to see it, touch it, admire or loathe it, and contemplate it.

People with abundant creative energy often funnel it into art: dance, music, painting, theater, written words. Some funnel their creativity into process or product. Some haven't found an outlet for their gift and it goes bad.

This chapter is about allowing creativity greater expression through formal recognition of a desire to make room for it in your life.

Creating Creativity

Home is a place to incubate and give birth to ideas. It can be a breeding ground for creativity. Here is a fun exercise for discovering how to support your creativity.

EXERCISE ONE • CREATIVITY MANDALA

A mandala is essentially a patterned diagram inviting contemplation. Visual representations of our objectives are more powerful than a hundred words. By creating this mandala and hanging it in a place of distinction, we fuel and honor our objectives all at once.

For this exercise you will need a large piece of poster board, some string or thread, glue, scissors, lots and lots of magazines, catalogs, and brochures, and a photo of yourself that you like.

Begin by thumbing through all of the journals you've assembled looking for photographs of creative activities or work you want to expand into doing. It makes no difference whether you've had training in these activities, or whether you think you could master them. If you want to paint with oils but you have not yet even experienced holding a brush in your hand, it does not matter. The emphasis is on process and pleasing your soul, not on the end result.

Clip photos of anything and everything meaningful or inspiring to your creative self. If you play the piano, but rarely, you may wish to photocopy sheet music for use in your mandala. If you love nature photography and would like to try your hand at it, clip pictures that inspire you. If you want to sew hats, clip illustrations of fabric patterns you love. If you have a brochure advertising some coursework you would like to sign up for, clip meaningful photos from it or even some key words, if they are in large print.

After clipping for a few minutes you will shift. It's the same thing that happens a few pages into a good book. Something else envelops your consciousness and all cares and worries are gone. That is why there is no need to meditate or center yourself beforehand. This is your very own guided meditation, so play music that opens up your soul and enjoy.

You will know when to stop clipping. You will either have gone through every periodical you have, or a sense of completeness will settle over you. Prioritize your clippings into the following categories: 1) want very badly to do right away, or is something very close to your heart; 2) want to do in the near future; 3) want to experience whenever the opportunity arises.

Attach your string to the end of a pencil. Anchoring the other end of the string to the center of the poster board, draw the radius of a circle. Make it as large as you can. Cut out your circle.

Beginning with the items you have classified as number threes, glue the pictures to the circular board in collage style around the outside one-third of the mandala. Glue the number-two items in the center one-third of the circle, and the number ones in the inner part of the circle, leaving a spot in the very center for your photograph.

Dedicate your mandala to uncovering the yearnings of a soul to create. Bless it. Then hang it in your bedroom where you will see it upon rising and retiring day in and day out until every activity has been drawn into your physical experience. You will be amazed to discover how powerful and immediate the results of such a simple exercise are.

EXERCISE TWO • MAKING ROOM TO CREATE

If you have affirmed to yourself that you want to learn to play the piano and you don't have a piano, you have work to do. That work involves clearing out an honored space for your new piano. If you have decided that you will explore your feminine essence through belly dancing, you need a place to move and some room in your closet for the right attire. If you plan to paint daily you need to find the most inspiring place in your home to set up your easel and paints. If you're finally going to produce those beautiful quilts you have kept inside your head all these years, your craft needs a place to unfold.

Whatever it is you intend to create, it is the right time to make space in your life for it. The world will be touched that you love yourself enough to give your soul a gift.

❧ SPACE CLEARING FOR CREATIVITY

Creativity requires a conduit in order to transform raw energy into effect. You are the conduit. During this space clearing for creativity you will produce a magical atmosphere charged with energetic impulses to spark your imagination. Although I can make some suggestions, I highly recommend tailoring this clearing to your very own creative style.

For this clearing you will need about two dozen tea lights with their own metal casings for each room to be cleared. Some home and craft stores sell these in large bags. Make sure they are the ones with the metal casings. With all those candles to light you will probably want a torch-style lighter. You will need either a deep-sounding drum or a gong. Also, prepare a bowl of charged spring water with a few drops of either myrrh—to arouse mind and spirit and increase concentration—or an uplifting citrus scent such as bergamot, orange, lemon, or grapefruit.

Plan to wear clothing that hugs the body, at least from the hips down. Exercise leotards paired with a long top—belt it if you would like—is perfect. Unless you have very cooperative family members or friends, plan to do this clearing alone.

An excellent time for this space clearing is 1:00 A.M. during the new moon. The number one is the number of beginnings and also of creativity and instinct. The power of the new moon accentuates embarking on a journey of soul exploration through the creative process. If 1:00 A.M. is impossible, perform this clearing after nightfall during the new moon.

Clean your home thoroughly earlier in the day, and while doing so move all large pieces of furniture that occupy the main rooms to the periphery. The process of shifting furniture will in itself stir up stagnant energy. Try to make available for your use six feet of space in diameter, more if possible. In each of the main rooms, and especially any room in which you perform creative work, make a large spiral pattern with the tea lights on the floor in the center of the room. Space the candles several inches apart. Spirals are symbolic of the creative process. The center of the spiral should be large enough for you to sit in comfortably. It is quite sufficient if the spiral loops around its center twice.

If necessary, review the general information in Chapter 3. At 1:00 A.M. and beginning on the main floor, light every candle in the first room to be cleared. Clasping your gong or drum, carefully seat yourself at the center of the spiral. Close your eyes and summon your angels. Ask them for their blessing upon this room. Declare that as you gong or drum all negative energy will be instantly and completely transformed into energy inspiring and encouraging to you in your creative journey, and specifically name your work.

Strike your gong loudly once. Feel the sound waves traveling out to every part of the room. As these waves encounter pools of stuck energy, visualize the old energy fizzling out and being replaced by luminescent light. The color of the light should be whatever color inspires you to create. Allow each sound wave to fade to a level just below your hearing range before striking your instrument again. If using a drum you can strike it hard one time and then drum very rhythmically and quietly as you focus your intention on transforming the energy of the space. Repeat this process ten times.

Once this is done, dip the fingers of your dominant hand into the bowl of charged water. Flick the scented water into all the corners of the room, knowing that your intention that the room support you in every creative endeavor is now fixed upon it. Blow out all of the candles prior to moving on to the next room. Customize your blessing for each room based on how you think it can best support you as your creativity unfolds.

Save for last the room where you envision spending the most time creating. As you sit in your sacred spiral in this room, you must center yourself by envisioning your happy self spending countless hours doing whatever it is you love. Visualize every detail, including your favorite time of day for working and the exact quality of the light the room receives. See yourself creating and feel the blissful feelings your work is generating. Notice there are no interruptions and no worries to steal your creative or mental energy. See the convenient arrangement of all the tools you need for your work.

When you feel you have explored all your dreams relating to your creative work, bless your space. I cannot tell you what these words should be, and neither should you rehearse them. Allow your words to pour out of your inspired vision, releasing them with vivacity and thorough conviction to penetrate the space. When you feel your work is complete, begin the drumming or gonging and proceed as you did in every other room.

Thank Spirit for the opportunity to live creatively.

❧❧ AN ALTAR TO CREATIVITY

According to some Feng Shui experts, the most exalted position to place this altar is in the creativity/children area (the middle-right section) of your home. If this is not practical, erect your altar in a protected area in your studio, wherever that may be. Remember, an altar can be a small shelf; the space requirement is minimal.

Here is the stuff of creativity:

- The color orange, which helps release feelings of limitation and produces feelings of enthusiasm.
- The color red, which moves to action and emphasizes attachment and passion.
- The color violet, for inspiration in all creative endeavors.
- Symbols or examples of the type of creative work you like to do. If that's writing, an inscription of your finest or whatever is most inspirational to you in your work will do nicely. You could place these words inside a prayer wheel or a small handcrafted box. If it's painting, a well-loved brush is an excellent tribute to your craft. If it's music, you could decoupage your altar with sheet music. Add whimsy: a string of tiny white blinking Christmas lights will do nicely. Be creative and even eccentric here!
- Anything with a spiral patterning to it, such as some seashells.
- Three blue or violet candles. These are to help you remember that your potential for creative work is limitless.
- A fluorite stone to help actualize mental energy. Or try covellite, which adds force to creative thinking. It's a beautiful iridescent mineral with a primarily indigo sheen.

Assemble your altar in a way that inspires you in your creative quest. You may wish to place the candles in the creativity/children position on your altar. Again, this is the middle-right position as you stand facing it.

❧ COLOR

Color is always a significant consideration. For someone who desires that their creativity flow freely, it is paramount. Creative thinking is an expression of life force. The mental energy released during creative visualization and planning or a creative act can drain you or cause you to lose your sense of reality. For these reasons I recommend that you use orange, or reddish earth tones, as the base of a creative color scheme. Because they are warm colors they are spiritually grounding, definitely cheery and uplifting, and they inspire confidence, spontaneity, and action.

The choices are tremendous. Just allow your mind to sense these colors: persimmon, coral, flame, terra-cotta, tomato, brick, garnet, cinnabar, copper, redwood, tangerine, and melon. To strengthen the color scheme add a little bit of a contrasting color, such as deep purple. To make it more soothing, add lots of natural or neutral color. Imagine the inspiration a color scheme of willow, terra-cotta, and sage could bring. If you do your best work when you're cheerful, use the same idea, but make it clearer using eggshell, geranium, and grass. One of my favorite colors is garnet, and it is wonderful paired with pine and very light honey. To breathe inspiration into your color scheme, complement the oranges with violet and a creamy neutral. The optimism and confidence of the orange blended with the inspirational accent of the violet is a winning combination for creativity.

Imagine your living room glowing with golden oak, dusty white, and tangerine: people will love to stay and socialize. Punctuate the space with green leafy plants or violet accents. Persimmon walls cooled with the staccato of silver-framed artwork in the dining room will invite conversations that linger long past the food. A kitchen dotted with vivacious redwood and subdued with spruce and muslin or eggplant is fun to work in. A primarily crisp, antique white bathroom is made warm with terra-cotta floors.

To create a restful space of renewal, however, you must be careful with reds and oranges. In your bedroom you may opt for a comforting cream, apricot, and touch of azure or lavender to encourage rejuvenation and sweet dreams.

Many people find shades of blue, such as periwinkle, indigo, or midnight blue, inspiring. However, they are also cool and very calming, and so they may not move you to actually do something with your creative energy. You may wish to have your studio in a place where it receives the cool, clear light of morning. This is especially good for painters.

❧ SOUND

Music that is conducive to unbridled imagining can be a great primer for a creativity session. Freely flowing impressionist music, such as that of Debussy, is the audio counterpart to daydreaming. Prior to beginning your work try listening to some impressionist music for approximately fifteen minutes. This will help your brain shift and open to creativity. Then spend five to fifteen minutes stretching your body, and you will then be ready to begin working.

As you move into your work you may wish to tune into some jazz. The chaos of its musical phrases and its characteristic unpredictability are exceptional for bringing into physical form the creative messages you receive. Within the many strains of jazz you are likely to find something inspiring to you. If not, any music that has about sixty beats per minute will get you moving.

There is a wide range of other music to choose from to support creative work, including New Age, baroque, and ambient music.

❧ AROMATHERAPY

Just as the color orange inspires spontaneity and confidence, so does the scent. In general, citrus scents all provide the same motivating and uplifting result. If you want to move into experiencing the creative process, to take what has been buzzing around in your head and express it physically, these scents are truly helpful.

In addition, to strengthen and clarify your thinking, try rosemary. To improve your power of concentration choose peppermint, myrrh, lavender, juniper, eucalyptus, cypress, cedarwood, or basil.

For an aromatherapy session during your creative workouts, use a diffuser of some sort. I use the type that plugs into an electrical outlet. Simply sprinkle onto a small pad a few drops of your essential oil of choice, insert it into the diffuser, and plug it in. You can enjoy the effects of a very few drops of oil for an hour or so, and it will probably correspond nicely to whatever it is you love doing.

✿ FLOWER ESSENCES

During your first few weeks of manifesting your creative energy, iris will protect you from feeling intimidated. Blackberry will help motivate you to harvest your ideas. For those whose passion is dance or any type of movement, dogwood will allow you to feel inner harmony and grace, helping you to feel less awkward. To bring an earthly vitality to your work try indian paintbrush. Performing artists will benefit from trumpet vine, which will enliven verbal expression. Zinnia brings greater spontaneity—a quality that will enhance other aspects of your life as well.

✿ ENERGETIC DESIGN

To inspire creativity it is necessary to have done a thorough decluttering, as described in Chapter 2. (Of course, my assumption is that you have already embarked upon your decluttering adventure prior to your space clearing to make it as effective as possible.) Creativity requires space: mental, emotional, and physical. When your physical space is encroached upon by things, so is your emotional space, and the effect is crushing to creativity. If there is clearing left to do in your home that you just haven't felt like tackling yet, please consider doing so now.

From a Feng Shui perspective your work areas—all the places where you create or generate prosperity—must be pristine. Your mental energy combined with the energy generated by your tools and equipment should produce harmony and peace. This minimizes distraction and maximizes clarity of thought. Keep your studio organized and orderly, with easy access to the things you use most often. Devise ways to stave off disarray. Allow yourself ample time to clean up and put away after each session.

Your studio should be as spacious as possible, but even if your home is small and all you can allot for your art studio is one corner of a room, make it a lovely shrine to your craft. Be sure that whatever it is you station yourself at, be it a desk, a computer, a piano, or an easel, is placed in the most powerful and commanding position possible. This is normally such that your back is not to the door, allowing you dominion over your environment and diminishing nervousness.

Make sure the lighting is appropriate to your task. The purpose of overhead lighting is to provide general lighting. It is not usually soothing to the nervous system. Natural light is excellent, as is task lighting, which will purposely highlight whatever you're working on. Even if your creative expression is dance, you may feel more inspired by soft ambient wall lighting, such as provided by wall sconces, than by overhead light. At the very least you should install dimmers on all light switches so you can change the level of lighting to suit your mood.

The element of Fire comes into direct play in producing creative ambience. It is interesting to note that Fire is associated with reds—including oranges and pinks—which, as already discussed, are decidedly motivational for artists of all kinds. This element also controls the heart, the eyes, and the hands. Literally and symbolically, these are the three most prominent tools necessary for creative work in general. The values associated with this element are fun and variety.

Bringing in the element of Fire is not limited to decorating with reds. Also associated with Fire are light, triangular shapes, pets and wildlife, and animal-derived textiles such as wool. Be creative about how Fire is expressed in your decorating theme. For example, use plenty of light of varying types, employ triangular shapes, such as pyramids, and let your pets roam freely. Remember that the Fire element should be part of a fairly balanced environment, though. If you need to refresh your memory about balancing elements, you will find this information in Chapters 4 and 15.

A creative home might also have a thread of the offbeat winding through it. This is easily accomplished by employing ordinary objects for purposes other than what's intended. A small red glass vase becomes a pencil cup. An ornate picture frame may showcase a bulletin board. Tiny blinking Christmas lights could highlight works of art in your living room. Trinkets and charms might peer out from under the leaves of potted plants. Scraps of fabric too striking to throw out can become wall covering. A miscellany of cabinet knobs might become hooks when screwed into the back of the bathroom door. Creativity expressed via the platform Home is limitless.

If you are inspired by free-flowing thought, reflect that in the fabric patterns you choose. Random patterns provide a much better backdrop for creative thinking than do repeated ones. Allow this idea to influence your furniture arrangements. Rather than conforming strictly to the dictates of a square room, soften it by arranging furniture in a way that's more meandering. Keep things uncluttered so there is plenty of room for Chi to circulate without obstruction. Another way to interpret the randomness of creative processing is through animal life, such as fish darting to and fro in an imaginative aquarium environment, or a playful cat—consider the machinations of a cat contemplating a bird. All enunciate spontaneity—creative fuel—and, again, emphasize the qualities of Fire.

If there is a window in your creativity/children area, you can amplify creative energy by hanging a round crystal prism, approximately thirty millimeters in size, from a nine-inch piece of red ribbon. It is very important that the ribbon be nine inches in length, since nine is considered the luckiest number, symbolizing the abundant nature of heaven and earth. Red activates the energy of the crystal.

❧ FINISHING TOUCHES

Tempt yourself to create by making it easy to fall into your projects. If your best time to work is early in the morning before anyone else has gotten out of bed, but you have to have a cup of tea first, outsmart yourself. A lure in the form of an electric teapot, a small basket full of a variety of teas, and your favorite cup conveniently positioned next to your drafting table might work wonders.

The most significant number for creativity is the number one, for the essence of one is that of an individual's unfolding and progress. If you like to group objects, the number three is the number of expression, of flamboyant and open communication, making it a great decorating tool. Tibetan object arrangement is based on groups of threes, each object representing either heaven, man, or earth; the arrangement describes relationship, giving form to life. If you are a photographer, group three of your favorite photos together on a table or wall where you will visually visit them often. You could also position three golden candles in the fame area of your home (the back center section) to symbolically illuminate your reputation for your work, if this matters to you. Three flowers in a vase will remind you of your blossoming creativity, and so on. Remember the life-altering influence of your intention and the power of your thoughts. If when you place those three flowers in that vase you consciously say to yourself "These flowers are my creative self in full bloom," they become enlisted to support your mental attitude.

The perfect totem for creative work is Butterfly. Butterflies enlighten mental processes with clarity. They bring joy and are the epitome of successful metamorphosis, another way of envisioning the creative process.

❧ AN AFFIRMATION FOR CREATIVITY

To keep your intention focused on a creative life, highlight your creativity using daily affirmations. You can revise the following affirmation to name specifically the creative work you are engaged in or aspiring to do. Or, allow this affirmation to inspire you in crafting your own.

I delight in seeing the manifestation of myself through my creative work.

My creative work is a profound reflection of my soul. And yet it allows me to explore my humanity. As I explore, I become more able in and anchored by my craft.
When I create, miracles happen.
And so it is.

CHAPTER SEVENTEEN

Physical Well-Being

An energetic sense of well-being is essentially the tactile engagement of our self with our environment. While some of us quietly glide through life in a way we feel won't disrupt anything or anyone, active individuals seem to actually touch life. Some of us engage with life on a spiritual or metaphysical level; some with lots of mental energy. Physical people engage with life primarily in a physical way—but the benefits bring joy to their souls and relief to their minds.

There may be many reasons why a sense of physical well-being is attractive to you now. It could be that you wish to finally do something about that quiet inner pleading to honor your body by being more active. Maybe you've been despondent for some time. Maybe you've healed yourself of an extended or serious illness and you want to celebrate your body's usefulness. If you've ended a long-term relationship you may just want to channel some of that energy into yourself to see what happens. Whatever the reason, this chapter can help you find ways to create a home environment that supports your sense of well-being. Do not mistake physical well-being and an abundance of energy with being overly busy. It's really about physically engaging with your world and feeling it in your body.

EXERCISE • VISUALIZATION FOR PHYSICAL WELL-BEING

Read through this visualization exercise and prepare to either take yourself through it silently or to customize it somewhat, tape-recording your instructions to yourself with some ambient or New Age music in the background for a lovely guided meditation of your own.

Sitting on the floor, on a cushion if you would like, center yourself. Try taking a few very deep, slow breaths, followed by normal breathing and a quiet mind for about five minutes. In your quiet mind allow a sense of vitality to come over you. Feel what that's like from the tips of your toes to the top of your head. Find that place inside of you where all is well. Envision the results of excellent self-care. Allow yourself to feel comfortable in your body. Allow whatever feelings that come out of this, be they feelings of relief, incredible joy, or confidence, to wash over you now.

See yourself suspended over your front yard looking down at it. What are you doing there that makes your heart well up with joy? (Do not be disturbed if you cannot see yourself in your front yard or anywhere else during this journey; just move on.) Measure the light and time of day. Engage all of your senses. Does the delicate scent from your lilac bush waft around you on a warm, gentle breeze? Send yourself messages about all that you're enjoying.

Glide around to the backyard. What are you doing there? Are other people involved? Identify the activities and individuals that bring you happiness in your backyard. Do you see yourself with a friend or romantic interest sitting on lounge chairs in the dark, covered with wool blankets and stargazing? Are you jumping into the cool waters of a swimming pool under the mantle of a hot July sun? Playing croquet? Lying on the grass, journaling in the protective shade of an oak tree? Are you making a repair to your home? Note everything. See yourself at various times of the year if you'd like.

Now move around the house, returning to the front, and when you feel ready, enter through the front door. As you enter, what sounds do you hear, what scents do you smell? Know that you are ecstatically happy. What are you doing in the living room? Are you playing board games with friends or family? Are you playing a musical instrument? Are you dancing to music that creates a sense of aliveness you haven't felt in years? Notice the arrangement of your furniture, the fabric patterns of the upholstery and drapes, the art work on the walls, any symbols present. Notice differences between your current life and the life of your heart. Notice what is absent.

Move around your floor plan, asking these questions concerning each room you enter. When you get to the kitchen, pay particular attention to every detail, for the kitchen is the hub and nurturer of an active life. Notice the foods you are preparing. What are they? Do they differ from the foods of your current diet? How do you feel as you prepare them? How do you feel as you are eating? How does it feel to be in your body? Are you alone? Are you entertaining? What are you wearing? Is there anything substantially different about this kitchen than your current one?

Continue until you have examined yourself engaged in the environment each room of your house offers. When you are finished, gently return to the present moment. With a journal or notebook, allow yourself a page per room to describe the experience. Begin not with the first room, but with the room in which you had the most significant insights or that excited you the most. Detail what you saw in any way that pleases you. Again, note the differences between your current home and the home supporting you in physical well-being. Note the obvious absences of things, such as photographs of individuals, or actual people, pieces of equipment such as the television or telephone, and so on. Use your notes as a working model of a healthier lifestyle tailored to your soul.

❧ SPACE CLEARING FOR PHYSICAL WELL-BEING

To engage your environment in supporting your well-being, this space clearing focuses on blasting thick, stuck, despondent energy right out of the house and replacing it with energy that vibrates subtly and happily. This space clearing will take some time; if you have a three-bedroom home allow three to four hours.

Follow the general preparation guidelines presented in Chapter 3. This space clearing should take place early in the morning, at dawn if possible, when energy is clear and strong.

You will need one candle for each room. I recommend white for burning up all the negative energy you'll stir. You will also need a leather rattle or some other kind of noisemaker that you can shake. One more tool is necessary to finish the clearing. Choose something you delight in using that requires a lot of movement, such as a tambourine, castanets, or maracas. Follow these steps.

Step One

After lighting candles, mentally connecting with your home, and invoking the presence of your angels or guides, begin clearing the space using a rattle in the manner discussed in Chapter 3. Truly tune in to the energy by using all of your senses. Shake the rattle vigorously wherever your intuition tells you to do so, and spend a little extra time in corners and hidden or out-of-the-way areas. As you shake the rattle with one hand, use your other hand to spread the energy out and around. Begin lower to the floor and move up as you move around the room. Engage your entire body in the process.

Work the energy hard and ceaselessly all the way through the house. Do not stop in between rooms to seal them off, but as you leave a room envision it encased in white light. When you're done with the last room, leaving all candles safely burning, return to your home's main entrance, where you first began.

Step Two

Place both hands on the doorjambs. Feel a gathering of power into both hands. When your hands become so full of power that they begin to ache, remove them from the doorway and stretch them out in front of you. As you do, imagine streaks of white light shooting out across your home and yard. Turn and perform this procedure in each direction, including down and up. Visualize this lighted area as being enveloped by a large, open parachute or blanket.

Contained within the blanket and neutralized by the white light is all of the negative energy your rattling disrupted. Focus on clearing all the old energy patterns. Mentally using the blanket or parachute, lift the energy up high in the air, where the ends are then tied together. Your guides and angels then carry it off to be transformed.

Step Three

This is a time when some music would be appropriate. Select music that is joyful, uplifting, and fun to you. Then, taking your noisemaker, whatever that is, dance and make noise all over the house, intentionally filling it with your renewed sense of well-being and deep joy, setting the intention for a happy, healthy Home.

❧ AN ALTAR TO ENERGY AND PHYSICAL WELL-BEING

If your health and well-being is of particular interest to you because of illness, loss, or despondency of any kind, it is paramount that you feel loved now. In any case, it is very important when on a path to a greater sense of well-being that you learn to love yourself enough to invest in your health. This altar is about feeling loved by others and feeling love for yourself.

Your altar is an excellent place to go to when you need support—actually, when you need to *remember* that you *are* supported. Placing this altar in the family/health area of your home is especially meaningful. Identify the people or entities whom you know love you. They can be real people in your life, past and present, or helpers, such as saints, angels, or guides. Excavate representations of them—photos, personal items that belonged to them, gifts they gave you, or statuettes—and give them a place of honor on your altar. If you have bundles of these things and they all mean a lot, consider placing spill-over items in the helpful people/travel area of your home—the front right corner, according to Feng Shui principles. This will strengthen your emotional ties to them and they will feed you in your venture to love yourself more expansively.

Blend these icons of love with things that represent the renewed sense of love you have for yourself. Refer to your notes from the visualization exercise. Did you see yourself doing yoga in the sunny spot in your living room? Find something symbolizing this. It could be a clipping from a magazine, a drawing, or a symbol. In fact, you could even make a mini collage on letter-sized paper of things you love doing, if you wish. Assign this collage a distinguished place, such as the center of your altar.

From where else do you draw strength? Do you find it on long walks in nature? Exalt found objects on your altar, such as shells, leaves, or stones from a favorite walking place or memorable excursion. If you feel empowered when you're working out at the gym, find a mental link to it to grace your altar. Even a pair of shoelaces will work if you intend them to. Do you feel strong through self-discovery? Perhaps your journal has found a new home.

Anything from the sun gives an instant sense of well-being. I've seen candles in the shape of the sun. You could accent your altar with yellow or gold. Citrus fruits are from sunny climes. Try peeling a lemon or orange and placing the peels in a wooden or metal bowl atop your altar. This type of offering will energize your space, as long as you remove them before they begin to turn bad.

Carnelian is said to increase energy, power, and motivation. Of course, there is always the revered turquoise. Its long list of attributes includes the addition of vibrancy and overall physical toning. Up the vibration by framing something important on your altar with five small stones—five being the number of physical energy and aliveness.

The idea of feeling whole is closely linked to feeling strong. So give your altar a strong, deliberate theme and make it obvious that much energy has gone into placement. Avoid a free-flowing style here. Make an overt statement to yourself that you are definitely loved. Your sense of well-being will soar.

❦ COLOR

Because the emphasis is really on well-being *and* increasing energy levels, balance is critical. Some people would say that red would be the obvious base for an energetic color scheme, but for someone making a lifestyle change from a delicate spot, red would be too intense, too dramatic.

Yellow is the color of the sun's powerful rays, the thing that sustains life. It is the color that evokes joy and heightens a sense of well-being, making it the perfect basis for this environment. Notice how the varying yellows make you feel. Lemon is decidedly cool. Warmer yellows, such as ochre or saffron, contain a tinge of red or orange—infusing them with confidence and an easily digestible amount of energy. In Japan, orange is the color of happiness.

Team yellow with green and the result is uplifting and healing all at once, and easy to live with. Green is healing and promotes willfulness and persistence. This color scheme definitely can create sunny comfort in any room.

Refer to your notes from the visualization exercise again and choose specific color palettes for your rooms based on activity level. If you want your space to support you in more intense activities, such as any kind of movement, allow yellow to dominate the scheme. Choose a warmer yellow, pair it with creamy white, and downplay the green tones. Your space will invite you into it and support you without overwhelming intensity during your workouts. Activities that are in themselves intense and finely detailed, such as any kind of handiwork—needlepoint, for example—can at times build frustration. Too much yellow, or yellows that are too warm, would contribute to frustration when it flares. Allow soothing shades of green to preside over the room, such as a pale lime green. Add a second green if you wish, such as spring green, some soft white, and light, airy yellow. The layering of the greens will bring depth to your healing process.

Where food is concerned, such as in the kitchen and eating areas, know that green tends to suppress the appetite. In the kitchen, where it feels good to socialize and you want to impart joy to your concoctions, yellow reigns. A warm buttery yellow or yellow-gold as a backdrop for light maple cabinets actually brings a lustrous glow to the wood.

Be aware of how dramatically light affects coloration. Incandescent bulbs will brighten warm colors and mute cool colors. This is good information to have ahead of time. If you are thinking of painting, first try to get a sample of the color under consideration and try it out in a couple of different areas. Inspect the color during different times of the day and under varying light conditions.

Your increased levels of activity will hopefully tire you into a good night's sleep. Here is a departure from the greens and yellows I've been recommending. Rose and pink are said to promote a general sense of well-being. These delicate shades warm hearts. I visualize myself being wrapped in a rose-colored blanket when I need to comfort or physically warm myself. These colors are the quintessence of self-love.

❧ SOUND

What sounds instill a sense of well-being deep within you? Think of the lilting sounds of birds chirping, water flowing, chimes chiming. All of these sounds either contain life or are the result of energy moving. They uplift and cheer. You can bring them into your home by throwing open the windows if you're lucky. Or you can bring them in with recordings of birds chirping (and maybe adopt bird-watching as a hobby), or a water fountain, or electronic chimes.

On days when you need a little coaxing into the rhythms of life, find music that gets you going. This is highly personal, but popular music, big band, or Top 40 will usually move you right along and generate a sense of well-being too. Be sensitive to other individuals living with you—people tend to develop strong associations with popular music.

Most important to establishing a feeling of well-being and strength is beat. Music without an organized beat could eventually even annoy you. Music that you feel comfortable with that also has a strong beat will subtly invigorate you. Another lethargy-lifting technique is to hum and move while listening to music you love. Most often you will not even remember what was bothering you in the first place.

Studies suggest that women move in a more controlled, coordinated manner when they have the outside influence of a steady, rhythmic beat than when they regulate their moves based on their own internal body rhythms. To pump up your inner strength listen to music that has about ninety beats per minute.

❧ AROMATHERAPY

Essential oils extracted from plants grown in sunny climes encourage sunny moods. (Eating these types of foods is also uplifting to your soul.) The following oils will energize you: basil, cinnamon, clary sage, eucalyptus, ginger, grapefruit, juniper, orange, peppermint, pine, and rosemary. Most of these are also good thought clarifiers. If you are feeling low or depressed, try bergamot, chamomile, hyssop, lavender, orange, or yarrow. Your spirits are bound to perk up immediately.

❧ FLOWER ESSENCES

There is much to learn from the subtle energy fields of flowers about well-being and maintaining the appropriate energy levels. In fact, the choice of flower essences can be overwhelming. This therapy is a wonderful demonstration of the incredible wisdom of our natural world.

If you have been suffering through what is termed "the dark night of the soul," sweet chestnut is your friend. Try hornbeam if daily life frequently overwhelms you. If you are not sure why you are blue, or if you often have mood swings, mustard can help. Cayenne, true to its essential nature, helps break up stuck energy patterns and motivates. Tansy will help you energetically engage with life and will move you out of lethargy. California wild rose will encourage enthusiasm for life.

ENERGETIC DESIGN

When we feel emotionally strong, we feel physically strong—I've noticed that time and time again in my own life. Feeling good is an honorable endeavor, and one which Home can effectively accommodate you.

In your space clearing, you broke up and bundled up the old tired energy of your environment, and you can now feel excited about life again. Now, to sustain that feeling of well-being, there is much to look at. Again, it is very important to follow the prompts your soul gave earlier during the visualization exercise. Throughout this section, look to see what else can be incorporated into your plan for Home.

Prior to making any physical changes in your home, thoroughly examine Chi flow. Pay particular attention to areas where you spend a lot of time, such as your office or your bed. Are there any corners or obstructions, such as beams or pillars pointing toward you? These things can cause fatigue. An adjustment would be in order.

There has been much debate about the possibility that electromagnetic fields generated by electrical equipment may be harmful to your health. A common source is an electronic alarm clock. We spend eight hours a day with our heads just feet away from these. An easy precaution to take is to move the clock across the room, or to the floor, or to obtain a battery-operated alarm clock. Never have a television set or computer in your bedroom.

To avoid or correct other health imbalances, make sure your home gets plenty of natural light. Also, make certain your home is not overwhelmed by a taller building next door. If so, position a mirror to symbolically turn away the negative Chi.

Decorate with lots of indoor plants. Many of them purify the air you breathe. Some flowering plants that do this are moth orchids, gerberas, tulips, cyclamen, Christmas cacti, chrysanthemums, and peace lilies.

Flowing water counters adrenal exhaustion due to allergies, stress, and burnout. So punctuate your interior landscape with tabletop water features wherever possible.

To infuse your home with an energy that motivates, keep things moving gently. One way to do this is to avoid furniture that looks like it is intended to lure you into lying down and never getting up again. Anything that looks too comfortable, or anything that when you sit down on it swallows you so you can't stand up, will curb energy. If you find them too enticing, stay away from things that contour to your body perfectly, or that have huge round arms, for example. Do have cozy furniture, such as sofas you can curl up on with a good book (and remain awake), chairs you can swing your legs over, tables inviting enough to use them more than just at Thanksgiving. Clean, rounded lines for tables and other pieces of furniture will also keep energy moving, and will be less likely to encourage you to hang out for too long. Feng Shui says that curvy lines are more healthful and auspicious than straight ones.

To create a subtle sense of motion, choose patterned fabrics instead of solids. If the patterns slant they inspire even more movement. If you just purchased an expensive couch and it is solid green, try adding some interesting pillows and perhaps a patterned throw. Choose a balanced mix of textures, but stay away from anything knobby or furry, for example, because this can cause energy (and lots of other things) to stick, and can feel almost claustrophobic. Soft, smooth fabrics, such as brushed cotton, allow energy to glide over them more easily. Shiny textures, such as satin, can be overly stimulating. If you choose fabrics that shine, make sure they are part of an integrated, balanced group of textures. The frailty of lace could become a metaphor for physical health, so avoid using it altogether.

Movement can be easily and brilliantly depicted through artwork: ocean waves, wild horses, birds, butterflies, and sailboats are good examples. They can also enrich your environment when they possess deeper symbolic meaning to you. If, for example, you love horses and the strength and freedom they represent, a horse print will serve a dual purpose. Seeing the horses will make you feel strong *and* lift your spirits because you hold so much love for them. If you are drawn to decorate with statuary, always consider bronze, known for its capability to balance energy. If the work of art also shows movement, an excellent metaphor for solid health and abundant energy is created.

South-facing rooms receive more sunlight and therefore more energy—this will help you feel more alive. Whenever possible, then, it is an excellent idea to use south-facing rooms as places of activity, such as work, working out, or crafting. If your house faces south, the sun kisses and blesses every room with more vitality.

To ground your well-being, you may wish to symbolically highlight your home's center. You can emphasize your home's center, and your health, by placing some source of illumination there, a green candle or a little table lamp, perhaps. Lamps with beaded shades are perfect because during the day, if the sunlight hits the beads, they glisten and shine just as your health does

❧ FINISHING TOUCHES

I mentioned earlier that the number five was an excellent choice for this home environment because the essence of five is aliveness and vibrancy. Luckily, objects clustered in fives are visually pleasing and arrange easily. Focus on collections of things that make you feel more alive. If you have five river rocks from a recent rafting trip, artfully arrange them on top of the coffee table for a kind of Zen feeling. They will tempt all who enter to play with them too.

For stamina, you may wish to adopt Elk as your totem if you don't already have one. The message of Elk is about pacing yourself so as not to burn out. Often, when we embark on something new, our own enthusiasm sabotages us. It's interesting that elk seek out the company of their own gender except at mating time. I've often heard that coaches tell their athletes not to have sexual intercourse prior to an event. There is something about saving that raw energy up for the sake of endurance. However, I like the idea of seeking out the camaraderie of my women friends during times of transition. Elk would reinforce that tendency.

Another good totem is Horse, who naturally represents power. It reminds us that genuine power is foresight—the ability to see the entire process or journey laid out before us. Antelope symbolizes action, and yet its true strength lies in its ability to find solutions, or the appropriate critical path.

🌺 AN AFFIRMATION FOR PHYSICAL WELL-BEING

Dramatic, beneficial life changes come to those who are willing to get out of their own way and allow them to happen. The universe is infinite, and there is plenty of good to go around. You have to believe you are priceless. Anything less than priceless assumes the Creator is flawed, and of course that's not true. Allow this affirmation to become part of your daily quest for wholeness and invigoration. Recite it to yourself, to Spirit, to your angels, to your loved ones.

The power to live a full life resides within me.

Because I am a perfect and complete expression of Spirit, my power to live is an indwelling presence that cannot leave me desolate. This infinite life within makes me strong and it provides me with ample energy. I am propelled by this power to fully engage life within me to fully express all that I am in everything I undertake.
Amen.

CHAPTER EIGHTEEN

Excellence

$\mathcal{W}$e all possess mental atmospheres, and these are primarily the results of our thinking and its aftereffects, our words and actions. The present is always the perfect place to be, for we can plant ourselves in the moment knowing that who we are is who we are right now. Yet our strength of mind and feeling allows us to revisit our thinking of the past to see how it has led us to the present.

A person versed in authentic excellence knows that thoughts are things and treats them as such. Thoughts are made up of fluid energy. They create, bringing concept to matter. They are not things that should be wasted on pondering the faults of oneself or others, or channeled into counterproductive processes, or used to express fear or doom. Instead, excellence cuts out time spent on such things and channels energy wisely and lovingly. Your thoughts should be used to make you vibrantly alive and healthy, to bring to you all the good the universe has to give, to hug you to a meaningful life full of love and joy. When you're focused on excellence, filtering out counterproductive thoughts, the negative will fall away. There won't be anything for it to stick to.

Excellence is a climate of knowing the power of thought and of using it wisely in orchestrating life; it is pure thought, springing from a pure heart. Excellence is not hard-driving, denunciating, perfectionist, judgmental, or unaccepting. It cannot alienate you from those you love. Excellence is a condition capable of cradling a family in warmth, bringing nourishment to exacting professionals, and smoothing the frays of a busy life. Excellence does not necessarily mean having a busy life. It actually pares down a busy life by removing from it time squandered in creating problematic situations to be dealt with later on.

If you can become aware of your thinking, you can arrest negative thoughts and change them to positive, life-affirming thoughts. Once you become aware of your thoughts you will always be aware. You cannot unlearn something. Our thoughts of yesterday may bring to life some unpleasantness to deal with today, but if today we channel our energy into clear, pure, purposeful thinking, each day will be happier and brighter.

Developing Awareness of Thought

There is one very powerful way to become conscious of our thoughts that works every time: with a sincere heart, call forth Spirit to guide you.

Some form of meditation is definitely helpful in accomplishing awareness. If you do not now meditate in any way, I recommend setting a few minutes aside each morning for reflection. Find a quiet corner in your house where you won't be disturbed for a few minutes. Put aside all thoughts of the impending day. If fear or worry start to intrude, gently put them out of your mind. Read something inspirational, a thought-provoking short story, something from a sacred text, poetry, or whatever speaks directly to your soul. Close your eyes and, after taking a few deep breaths, allow the words you read to sink deep inside. That's all you need to do. Just sit quietly with the words. When you feel ready to face the day, do so.

Words are powerful. Beginning the day with life-affirming words makes it hard to let negativity creep in. When it does, you will notice it because you invested some precious time in beautifying your mindscape. You won't want anything to ruin the good work you've done. In time, you will master your thoughts through your own built-in awareness—which just needed some sharpening.

🌺 SPACE CLEARING FOR EXCELLENCE

Excellence in life requires uncluttered thought. The obvious parallel between Home and mind is that an uncluttered environment serves excellence well. Before proceeding with a metaphysical space clearing, do a thorough literal space clearing. As discussed in Chapter 2, you contemplate each item in your possession and ask yourself how it serves you in the logistics of life and achieving your objectives. Part with anything that doesn't serve your vision in some way. Make everything meaningful and relative to the clear thoughts you hold for your life. If you believe excellence will be a long-term theme in your life, it will benefit you to develop a zero tolerance attitude for clutter.

For this space clearing you will need yellow candles for each room being cleared, one or two aromatherapy diffusers, and one of the following essential oils: grapefruit for cutting through old energy to give way to new, clear energy; or lemongrass, which has a cleansing effect on the atmosphere. Place a diffuser on each floor of your house and begin the aromatherapy session approximately thirty minutes before you begin your space clearing. You will also need a crystal bell—a symbol of extreme clarity. If it appeals to you, place offerings in each of your main rooms by floating four daffodils—which inspire optimism and mental clarity—and four candles in crystal bowls.

Step One

After placing and lighting candles and making offerings, begin your clearing at your front entrance. Invoke the help of four spirit energies, each standing watch at the four cardinal directions: north, south, east, and west. Set your intention by dedicating your space clearing to the clear thinking that will produce good things in your life. Once you have spoken your dedication in your own prophetic and wise words, visualize a golden glistening light descending on your home, settling into every room, every nook and cranny. Know that your house now supports your dreams.

Step Two

Begin by clapping out the entire space. Clap vigorously and persistently in areas where the energy is stuck or wherever you have a remembrance of a negative occasion. Clap until the clapping is crisp and clear. Pay special attention to those areas that directly correlate with your goal. If your dream is to have a consulting business of your own, be scrupulously thorough in your office area. If you are clearly focused on finding a life partner, be particular about clearing energy in the bedroom.

Step Three

Once you have completed clapping, make another pass using the crystal bell. As you work the space with your bell, use your unoccupied hand to further disperse the crystalline energy using smooth movements. As you gloss each room with clarity, feel excellence emerge. As you complete each room, seal it off by making the infinity sign in the air, or by imagining it sealed and protected.

AN EXCELLENCE ALTAR

An excellence altar pays tribute to and helps keep you focused on the good things. Allow yours to trace the path you've taken to get wherever you are today. Feed it, allow it to evolve as you do, and make it a testimony to the power of your own thinking.

Begin by assembling things that symbolize milestones in your life. In doing this, sometimes a theme will emerge. By focusing on this theme with your altar bearing witness, you will reaffirm that thoughts are things. Everything placed upon your altar will represent the good thoughts behind it that brought it into being.

For example, if you are now the director of a local chapter of a nonprofit organization, you may be able to see the roots of that by reviewing the milestones or synchronicities of your life. In college you developed the model for a major service project; in high school you served on student council; in grade school you spent time at an elderly neighbor's house cleaning and running errands. You can pick out that thread of service running through your life. By somehow honoring your life upon your altar you develop a visual affirmation for living your purpose and giving voice and therefore emphasis to your higher thoughts. This will encourage you to continue thinking clearly, focusing on being your true self, and knowing that this is the way you create your life.

Sift through your mementos of achievement, remembering that these things need only to empower you in keeping what is important in mind. Your altar to excellence need not make sense to anyone else. Be sure to include a symbol of your next step or steps in life, to help you keep a clear focus on your objective.

Energize your altar with the color yellow for clarity and joy in all you've done and all you do and will do. The number eight is significant for you because its essence contains the seeds of leadership: original thinking, self-power, public recognition of your work, and the ability to command respect. Perhaps placing a total of eight items upon your altar is meaningful to you: two from childhood, two from young adulthood, two from your current life, and two representing your blessed goal or goals.

❧ COLOR

Yellow is the color most often associated with clarity, fruitfulness, joy, and a powerful intellect. Yellow inspires. It is no coincidence that yellow is also the color of the human body's third chakra, or energy center. The third chakra, also termed the will center, is located in the solar plexus area. It controls our ability to focus clearly and purposefully on our direction in life.

This center is connected with mental processing, including analyzing and creating new thoughts and ideas. Gold—closely related to yellow—connotes royalty, luxury, and power. From the pale yellow of creamy butter to the glistening yellow of the midday sun to the polished glow of gold, there probably isn't a more happily diverse color to decorate with than yellow.

Violet is associated with the seventh or crown chakra, located at the top of the head. This energy center concerns itself with our life's purpose and the path to that purpose's unfolding. It allows us to connect and disperse our own talents and gifts. Purple, related to violet, is associated with wealth, majesty, and royalty, and it also symbolizes intuition and psychic awareness. The choices are nearly as diverse as that for yellow, ranging from deep plum to sophisticated eggplant to healing lavender.

Capturing the essence of an excellence environment, yellow and purple together are powerful, symbolizing clarity and strength of will in fruitfully accomplishing our life's purpose. The heaviness of the purple will accentuate the lightness of the yellow. This rich combination creates a sense of luxury and physical comfort. In fact, you may wish to employ purple to activate the wealth area of your home. The wealth corner, as you face the front of your house from the street, is the back left section of your home. This combination can even be used successfully in the kitchen. I saw a striking example in which the lower cabinets were a clear natural maple and the uppers were maple dyed a very pale lavender. A gorgeous backsplash of imported tiles in white, gold, lavender, and burnt orange gave this kitchen an updated yet homespun look.

In the bedroom, for relaxation, allow lavender to dominate. It will sing you into slumber and increase your chances for sweet dreams. In the office or study areas, use a clear yellow for exceptional clarity. Yellow combats all the confusion and despondency the teenage years can evoke. Work with your teenager to see if there is a way to incorporate yellow into his or her bedroom landscape. For harmony and healing, to smooth out that edginess, you may wish to add green.

Although white is associated with purity and cleanliness and some could argue that white is a great backdrop for excellence, white is often overly stimulating. It can also make you feel alienated from your surroundings and therefore uncomfortable. White can be considered neutral, which is not the best mental space to be in for excellence. People living amidst a neutral color scheme could find it difficult to make decisions or feel motivated by anything. A white flag indicates surrender.

❧ SOUND

It is believed that classical music, specifically that of Mozart and Haydn, helps develop advanced reasoning ability. The personality of classical music, its clarity and elegance, seems to permeate our thinking in a way that improves our concentration. In work situations, classical music has been shown to increase accuracy by 20 percent. Evidence also supports a correlation between music and clearer, more advanced thinking. Studies have shown that students participating in music programs have higher SAT scores than those who do not. They score 51 points higher on the verbal portion of the SAT and 39 points higher on the math portion.

❧ AROMATHERAPY

The scents most commonly used to increase mental clarity and concentration and to stimulate the memory are basil, camphor, cypress, cedarwood, eucalyptus, grapefruit, juniper, lavender, lemon, lemongrass, pine, peppermint, rosemary, sandalwood, and tea tree. You may also wish to try a less commonly used essential oil—cardamom seed, which has an exotic spicy aroma with floral undertones. Fir, frankincense, geranium, ginger, jasmine, marjoram, rose, rosewood, spruce, thyme, and ylang-ylang are said to help clear up mental confusion. Lemongrass is also good for cleansing the environment of emotions after there has been a release. I keep a spray bottle of spring water mixed with a few drops of this oil handy. I even use it to cleanse my own energy field by spraying it all around me. On warm days, it's refreshing.

There are so many essential oils to choose from that you may wish to try several and decide on one or two that are most effective or appealing to you.

Or let your intuition guide you in making a selection. Group some of the oils together, then close your eyes and run your fingers over the bottles until you feel drawn to one particular oil. You can make your own special blend from several of your favorites. To craft a blend, carefully add oils drop by drop, testing the scent as you go until you reach your objective. Again, allow your intuition and your sense of smell to direct the process.

When studying, working, or mentally fashioning your life, use these oils in a diffuser. Go lightly though if the space is small. You might opt to place the diffuser just outside the door, in the hallway.

🌺 FLOWER ESSENCES

Flowers add beauty to life in so many ways. To connect with a strong sense of self-worth—vital in an excellence environment—try buttercup. Scleranthus is helpful in bringing about confident decision making. To help clarify your life direction, try using wild oat. Peppermint enhances mental attention. Madia helps overcome distraction. Two to four drops of any of these, four times a day, should yield a discernable difference within a few weeks.

🌺 ENERGETIC DESIGN

Designing to an excellence theme is a great initiation into practicing mental excellence, for this process will require you to bring thought into form with clarity and precision.

As discussed earlier in this chapter, a cluttered environment cannot support clear thinking. An environment that promotes excellence works best when there is a feeling of spaciousness. Aside from getting rid of unnecessary items, there are other ways to create a sense of spaciousness.

To create a feeling of openness, paint your ceilings white. Use simple, sheer window treatments to allow as much natural light to stream in as is practical. This too will produce a feeling of spaciousness. You may even wish to consider placing small skylights in areas where clarity is most beneficial, for instance in your office and in the self-knowledge/education area of your home (the front left corner of your house as you face it from the street). In any case, make sure these areas are well illuminated with natural and task lighting to practically and symbolically accentuate clarity of thought where it really counts.

Make adjustments throughout your house to ensure there is sufficient Chi. First of all, make sure everything in your home is in good working order. Negative Chi oozes through broken windows, from behind blocked doors, and from under creaking floorboards. Make sure every lightbulb works. Make sure your front entrance is exquisite and that it is used every day; this is the main portal for Chi. Chi loves color, light, sound, movement, living things, beauty. Without cluttering, make sure the entrance to your home environment is visually pleasing. Make sure Chi isn't pressurized in long hallways and stairways by placing Chi attractors in these areas. A crystal prism is excellent: not only is crystal associated with clarity, but the facets of a prism symbolically disperse Chi out in all directions. Hang a crystal prism from the ceiling approximately one third to one-half of the way through a long hallway. The same approach can be taken with a stairway that faces the entry door.

Sounds invoking a sense of order without being monotonous energize excellence. Other than the music listed earlier in this chapter, the splashing sound of an indoor water fountain invites Chi and has a rhythm that is neither chaotic nor monotonous. Indoor electronic chimes are somewhat random but exacting in stirring up the Chi they've already invited in. A clock ticking and chiming adds a sense of order, not to mention coziness.

Enlist artwork that is meaningful to you into your excellence environment. Make sure the composition and message of any work of art or decorative object is clear. Meaningful yet simple abstract art using geometric shapes will be very conducive to clarity. Simple statuary, when well placed, will symbolically anchor and strengthen your thinking.

Dot your interior environment with lots of plants. Plants with round leaves will encourage Chi to flow around them and continue on. Plants with spiked leaves will cut up stagnant Chi. Lots of people seem to interpret the latter as being undesirable, but there may be an appropriate place for a spiked-leaf plant, such as in an inactive corner. As long as you are not exposed to the cutting Chi for long periods, such as while reclining in your favorite chair and reading, or while dining, it can be a great thing. Certain plants actually clean the air, and that is obviously good for clear thinking:

- Peace lily: Removes formaldehyde, alcohol, ethylene, trichloro-ethylene, and benzene.
- Ficus alii, golden pathos, red emerald philodendron: Promote general air purification.
- Dracaena: Removes trichloroethylene.
- Rubber plant, corn plant, weeping fig, spider plant: Remove formaldehyde.
- Kimberly queen: Removes formaldehyde and alcohols.
- King of hearts: Removes ammonia.

If you like fresh flowers, daffodils have long been said to stimulate the mind and inspire optimism. The number eight contains the energy of organization and efficiency, so position a crystal vase of eight flowers in your entryway. They will also invite in Chi and affirm your penchant for organization and leadership.

In your office or study, place your desk or workstation in its most powerful position, if possible. Your back should not face the door; neither should you be in direct line with the door. A commanding position has visual domain of the comings and goings of the room. If this is not possible, you can use a Feng Shui cure, such as a mirror that enables you to clearly see the doorway. Your office or study is an excellent area to display your credentials or symbols of achievement. These things represent success and are reminders of all of the qualities that enable you to rise to any challenge.

Furniture should be simple and clean-lined. Imagine the fluid simplicity of elongated curves. Furniture that is purchased as a set can work well. If you prefer antique furniture and have acquired several pieces that work well together, find or create a unifying trait. This could be the tone or finish of the wood, or you could have all pieces reupholstered in coordinating fabrics. Don't clutter up your sofa and chairs with lots of pillows and throws.

If you like to have these things close by, store them neatly in a wicker trunk or closet.

Stay away from busy patterns and overly lush textures. Opt for solids or simple geometric patterns, which enhance your life with the organization they impose. To increase mental stimulation, introduce subtle contrasts in fabrics used. For example, if your couch is covered in gold velvet, choose gossamer curtains. Or use contrasting colors in softer shades, such as discussed earlier in this chapter.

❧ FINISHING TOUCHES

Adopt the personal power of Eagle, who can assist you with rising above the mundane in life by extending your vision and perspective about what you can accomplish. The energy of Mountain Lion can help you make decisions quickly and cleanly. Elk's energy is that of stamina and strength in accomplishing objectives, but without burning out.

The stone carnelian helps to actualize personal power, and it is warm and beautiful. Use it to grace your altar, or in jewelry.

Use the number eight to bring order to your environment, but also to bring prosperity, the reward for keeping a clear heart and mind in accomplishing lofty and honorable goals. Two groups of four photographs of whatever excellence means to you could be very affirming. If you love to sail, images of sailing will conjure ideas of mastery.

❧ AN AFFIRMATION FOR EXCELLENCE

To aid you in focusing your consciousness in shifting to a mental attitude of excellence, practice countering self-defeating thoughts with affirmative statements. At first, you may begin to notice many negative thoughts over the course of the day. A brief statement acknowledging your new, more positive way of thinking, such as the bolded statement following, will help combat these unwanted thoughts.

Today I choose to see and think clearly.

My clear, pure thoughts acknowledge my full and limitless potential. My words and actions are grounded in these pure thought-forms and reflect the infinite being I am. I recognize that in this way I can control the direction my life takes. For this I am so grateful. Amen.

CHAPTER NINETEEN

Intuition

*I*ntuition is heeded sensitivity. It is unwavering trust in one's own perceptions. Our intuition whispers to us through the vastness of our unconscious mind, protruding as that small clear voice, or as a poignant or disturbing dream. At times our intuition is placed on alert through the words of a stranger or a loved one. It courses through our veins, pulses in our stomachs, converges on our hearts, braces our muscles, emerges in our breath.

Sometimes our intuition arrives in a manner that is more grandiose, as when a brilliant idea streams full-blown into our mind, or when it speaks to us openly through the voice of another being. These instances are perhaps rare for most of us. Therefore it is helpful to cultivate a certain openness and stillness within ourselves so that we can recognize our intuition when it speaks to us, however it is that it speaks.

Intuition is not only in some of us, it is in all of us. Everyone has access to all the information they need to live an inspired life—a life that pulses in time with nature. We can, at any time, pull information down from heaven into ourselves. But we have to accept the process, trust it, and yield to it. The more we practice, the better rapport we'll have with our intuition.

Symbolically, intuition is associated with dark, watery depth and a smooth state of receptivity. It is linked with the mystery and inwardness of the moon and the deep violet sky she reigns. There is a very real connection between the moon and our inner states of being. The moon controls internal flow and shape of mass: it powerfully moves large bodies of water and even changes the shape of the earth. In Native American cultures, women physically withdrew from their families to seek solace in their own inner worlds during their menstrual cycles, which typically corresponded to the presence of the full moon.

Learning to Trust Your Intuition

There are many books written on understanding and learning to accept intuition. Many of their authors have honed their natural gift into a fine art. However, know that intuition is not the same as psychic ability. Intuition is not that specialized or flamboyant. Your intuition has undoubtedly served you well on many occasions. And most of us have experienced the regret of not having listened to it, learning that life gets its message across in one way or another. If subtle and gentle doesn't work, overt and messy often does.

With pen and paper in hand, review your life. Begin with the present and work backward in time. Note instances when you heard the small voice of your intuition and ignored it. What made you disregard your intuition? Was it that your mind or ego wished things would play out differently than what your gut was telling you was right? Did you decide to chance it anyway? How would you have been better off if you had only paid attention to your gut feelings? Now do the same thing remembering the times you did listen to your intuition. What form did your intuition take? Was it easy or hard to allow it precedence over your chattering mind or the opinions of others? What benefits came to you as the result of listening to your intuition?

When you feel you've exhausted your repertoire of classic examples of not listening and listening to your intuition, spend some time contemplating what you have learned. You may wish to conclude in silent meditation. Tonight, before you go to sleep, command your soul to give clear audience to your intuition from now on. Employ your angels and guardian spirits in helping you consult your authentic self when making decisions great and small. Learn to listen to the highest law: the one that channels itself in some unique way from Spirit through you.

♊ SPACE CLEARING FOR INTUITION

This space clearing is intended to help set the energetic patterns of your home to create more openness to intuitive guidance. As with all space clearings, the effect is dependent upon the power of your intention. For best results, perform the clearing during a full moon after nightfall. There is a bit more ritual embedded in this space clearing than most, which is appropriate to the link between the moon and intuition.

For this space clearing you will need a glass bowl and spring water, a few smooth stones, and anything that you may associate with your intuition, inner wisdom, or the moon. Some examples could be a moonstone ring or earrings, tarot cards—especially the High Priestess, which represents inner wisdom and intuition—crystals, rune stones, dream catchers, and so on. Whatever it is you treasure and associate with true wisdom is appropriate for this ritual. You will also need one large white candle and six smaller purple candles for each room you are clearing—white to burn up negative energy, purple to illuminate inner wisdom. The total number of candles used in each grouping, seven, represents intuition and is excellent for emphasizing a prolific inner life. If you have a singing bowl or access to one, use it for the clearing: the bowl represents the feminine state of receptivity. Or, if you prefer, use a drum—which can carry you into altered states of consciousness, sharpening your perspective. If you have some kind of wand, you may wish to use it to seal off each room once the clearing is complete. Wands symbolize intuition.

You may wish to crack the windows of your home to allow egress of the negative energy released during the clearing.

Step One

Once the moon is in view, bring your stones and other treasured symbols outside. Create a small circle with your stones and place the treasures you gathered inside the circle, all the while holding the intention that each will become charged by the powerful light of the moon to become your personal helper in accessing intuition. Spend as much time as you would like moon-bathing. If you are moved to celebrate the moon's magnetism by dancing in its light, do so. Leave your things in the protective safety of the stone circle for the duration of the clearing.

Place the glass bowl in the moonlight and pour the spring water into it. Allow it also to remain there until you have finished the space clearing.

Return to the house and light all candles. Dedicate each group of candles in a meaningful way. In the kitchen you may wish to dedicate your candles to opening up a greater intuitive awareness of how to honor your body with proper nourishment. In the office you might call forth intuition in dealing with all financial and career matters to your highest good. When all candles are lit, return to your front entrance.

Step Two

After connecting with the spirit of your home by placing one or both hands upon the doorjamb, call down the power of your angels and guardian spirits in assisting to clear all stagnant energy and setting the energy patterns in your home to facilitate access to your inner wisdom.

This is a time to let your intuition take over. Begin the clearing in whatever location you feel drawn to begin in, in any part of the room, and move in any direction or manner that seems appropriate. If you are using a singing bowl, you may choose to begin in the center of the room, moving in circles to the outward edges of the room, thereby pushing the negative energy out the open windows. If you are drumming, you may choose to beat the drum in a very steady, hypnotic manner, fusing yourself with the energy and sensing exactly how to manage it.

As you leave each room, blow out the white candle only, knowing any energy blocking easy access to your intuition has permanently evaporated. If you have a wand, use it to seal off the room by drawing the infinity sign in the air, or use it to cast a spell on the room to help you honor and be guided by your astute inner wisdom. Allow the purple candles to burn for as long as it is safe. If possible, let them burn until you go to bed for the night.

Step Three

Gather up your stones and precious objects from outside. You may wish to bundle them in a cloth of midnight blue velvet. Place them in an exalted, meaningful place, such as your altar, as a remembrance and affirmation of the power of your intuition. You may feel inclined to take them outside during the next full moon to celebrate your intuitive awakening.

Bring the bowl of water indoors, it has now been charged with the moon's mystical power. Before going to sleep, drink the water to increase your ability to summon your inner wisdom and to encourage meaningful, prolific dreaming.

AN ALTAR TO INTUITION

There may be no more meaningful or enjoyable altar to construct than one to summon intuitive awareness. There are many ways to symbolize intuition, but whatever you choose to place upon your sacred altar must be completely meaningful to you.

Start by assessing your spiritual life. What mystic symbols do you align yourself with? If you consult an oracle, your altar is a high place for your tarot cards or *I Ching* coins to call home when not in use. A crystal or colored-glass bowl filled with crystal prisms or natural crystals will amplify your intention to be guided by your intuition, and will be visually striking as well.

Float a lotus flower in a bowl of spring water upon your altar. The lotus depicts the seven circles of consciousness, as well as the seven chakras, or energy centers, of the human body that respond to spiritual experience. If you have a moonstone or selenite, you may wish to use these on your altar. Moonstone is said to open the subconscious and heighten intuition. Selenite was the magical stone of the moon goddess Selene and can be used to facilitate dream recall. By all means place a purple or indigo candle upon your altar for continual illumination of your inner wisdom. Personal items of great meaning will empower your intuition. For example, a feather or other token you found during a walk when you became enlightened about something might be especially meaningful.

The number seven is significant, so why not keep your altar uncluttered by limiting the total number of items upon it to seven? The more empty space there is, the more room there is to receive the blessings of the divine mystery. You can even place upon your altar an empty bowl that acts as a receptacle for inner knowing.

To energize your altar, place it in the self-knowledge area of your home, which is the front left area of your home as you stand facing it. Alternatively, place it along an interior wall that faces north—the natural amplifier of introspection.

While you should always make the occasion of creating an altar as meaningful as possible, it is perhaps even more important in this instance. Not only are you endowing your altar items to act as guideposts and confidants in your process, but you are launching a mystical journey. Design an appropriate ritual to dedicate and bless your altar and yourself in your quest. Set aside plenty of time and solitude for this ceremony; good beginnings are important.

❧ COLOR

To unify all components of true spiritual wisdom, with emphasis on intuition, allow three colors to wind their way through your home landscape: purple to punctuate intuitive awareness; blue to feed spiritual understanding and inspiration; and gold for clarity and grounding. Purple and blue stand next to each other on the color wheel and are therefore termed harmonious when used together. Gold stands across from them and is contrasting, providing interest, strength, and warmth. Use a very light touch with the purple and blue: they are intense colors. If the color is to be applied to the wall, use softer shades in most cases. If you prefer warm white or a shade of gold on the walls, you could use more intense shades of purple and blue in fabrics or in accent pieces.

There are many sumptuous variations of this color palette. If you have warm honey-colored pine floors or something similar, try combining a pastel blue-green and a medium-toned blue-violet. In a small or awkwardly shaped room—perhaps one with a sloping ceiling such as in an attic—try painting two walls in one color and two in the other for a very expansive and surprisingly soothing effect. If you have high ceilings and lots of natural light in your bedroom, ceilings of midnight blue, or slightly lighter, and walls of the palest smoky lavender with an earthy golden rug for grounding are inspirational yet feel whole and complete. There are companies that will paint a starscape upon your ceiling that is visible only at night. This would add to the celestial fantasy the ceiling would evoke.

Parts of the country, such as the sunny southwest, tolerate intense color better. If you love color, you could develop a sort of mineralesque color scheme with a sunny saffron or even a wash of tangerine paired with an earthy plum and accents of turquoise. The result is actually quite warm and needn't be flamboyant. If you want to cool it down a bit, frame any artwork in silver-toned frames, as opposed to gold-toned or wooden frames. These colors are found in nature more often than you might recall. Envision the sun melting into the slate blue sea, shadowy purple mountain silhouettes jutting into the horizon, or the desert sky at dusk, golden sand in the foreground, purple mountains in the background. They are actually very peaceful colors, creating a sense of quiet and wonder.

✌ SOUND

New Age music often brings up images of something emerging from nothing. It is a metaphor and backdrop for cultivating intuitive awareness. Music that flows without a prevailing rhythm is often an excellent choice for developing intuition. Gregorian chant creates a state of mental spaciousness, a sort of openness that reflects the expanse of the heavens. Shamanic drumming will deliver you to a place where humans are naturally closer to their intuition. Music highlighting the harp or flute—representing the voices of angels—evokes a soft, surreal feeling.

✿ AROMATHERAPY

To guide you into a relaxed meditative state, use frankincense, sandalwood, or cedarwood. Myrrh will help awaken your spirit. Sandalwood is also known for helping to balance several of the chakras. For enlightenment, try using helichrysum. Use any of these oils in a diffuser.

✿ FLOWER ESSENCES

To become increasingly receptive to more subtle states of awareness, use star tulip. Cosmos can usher in a state of higher mental consciousness. California poppy will help remind you that true wisdom comes from within, and hound's-tongue will enable you to see deeper meaning behind physical reality.

✿ ENERGETIC DESIGN

The direction north symbolizes introspection; therefore a north-facing house or apartment is ideally suited to someone developing intuition. If you are settled in a home with no plans to move and it does not face north, perhaps you can locate a meditation space in a room that does face north. If you do not already practice meditation, it is highly recommended for training the mind to become still and quiet enough to hear the faint voice of intuition.

A meditation room need only be the size of a small walk-in closet. Many older homes have large closets that have a window in them. If you can do without the storage space, you might consider converting it to a meditation room. If a dedicated room is impossible, perhaps a quiet corner can be found. A cushion on the floor is really the only prop necessary—anything else is just for personal enjoyment or to facilitate your transfer to that deep, relaxed state.

Fountains are significant features of a home dedicated to intuition because of their spiritual link to water. Set the fountain's pump to a lower setting so the water doesn't splash. The more still the water, the better the metaphor for a quiet mind. Allow the theme of deep, still water to thread through your home. You can achieve this through color selection, as already discussed, through the artwork chosen to grace your walls, or through very gentle wave or rippled patterns.

To accentuate stillness, stay away from harsh geometric patterns or anything possessing a theme of rigid organization, including stripes. In fact, try to opt for more solid fabrics in quiet textures such as velvet, wool, or heavy brushed cotton. Heavier fabrics, by adding heft, will help anchor and ground you during your journey. If you want to add a little shimmer, do so with your window treatment. To give play to the deep water or depth metaphor again, layer your window treatments.

Stillness can be translated in many other thoughtful ways throughout your home. There is the still simplicity of a miniature Zen rock garden—complete with sand and rake. Ancient forests connote stillness. Artwork depicting such forests can add depth to a small space that would otherwise cause you to feel cramped or forced upon in some way. Forests are, metaphorically, places of intense introspection. By simply conjuring up the image of a deep forest, a mystical and mysterious feeling will waft through your body. You can translate stillness in a more traditional sense through still life artwork. Stay away from artwork or objects of art that represent motion: horses (or anything) running, travel via automobile or airplane, lines that slant dramatically, and so on.

Mirrors symbolize self-knowledge and have a reflective surface, such as that of water. Tastefully positioned mirrors throughout your home will serve to remind you that you need only look inside yourself for answers—even to life's most challenging questions. Use mirrors in dark spaces to reflect and amplify natural light, which is especially attractive to Chi.

Display throughout your home anything that heightens your awareness of your intuition or is an affirmation for your introspective journey. Hang your drum on your wall to create sacred space. Place a crystal upon your journal to symbolize the magnification of your inner knowing. Hang crystals and sun catchers in blues and purples in your windows. Grace an area near your bed with a striking dream catcher to filter your dreams through.

Stand a natural crystal on your kitchen windowsill to focus on during meal preparation. A cauldron is a symbol of mystic transformation and renewal; in China it symbolizes prosperity and good luck. Put your cauldron to stylistic use by allowing it to hold a houseplant, magazines, or cherished objects or hobby supplies. These things will serve you well as you embark on your inner journey. When having to face a difficult decision, they can remind you to give primary consideration to that quiet little voice inside of you.

You may wish to create a more closed environment for introspection. This is especially true if your need to go inward is fueled by great loss. If this is the case, you may choose to go against traditional Feng Shui principles and screen the entrance to your home somewhat. This simply says to people that you prefer your solitude at this time, and this can be done in an inoffensive, loving way. Iron fencing along the front of your property will still enable your house to be seen but will clearly separate your home from the rest of the world. If the permanence of this change doesn't set well with your intuition, the same effect could be achieved through planting a symbolic fence of shrubs. Setting yourself apart from the rest of the world or your community is only harmful if you want to generate an active social life, or if you are in denial of or running from some issue or circumstance.

Arrange your furniture in a way that makes intuitive sense. Good design, including placement, allows intuition to guide it. This does not mean that you should select furniture and place it in your home on a whim. You should give tremendous consideration to how you live your life and allow the placement of your belongings to accommodate you in it. If your intuition directs furniture placement, you will most likely arrange it in a manner that also promotes the smooth flow of Chi throughout your home. After arranging your furniture, walk into the room and around your furnishings. If you can move around it without encountering obstructions or dramatic protrusions, Chi can easily flow around it too.

You may find it more comfortable and stabilizing to employ heavier styles of furniture for a design scheme supporting intuition. Doing so will add to a feeling of having a solid base from which to explore the outer realms of your reality and purpose. Always keep in mind your room's proportions and general layout. Instead of chairs with delicate legs, you may prefer stronger, heavier legs. I am not implying that you should stay away from curves, just that furniture should make you feel amply supported.

Make your life activities intuitively easy to perform. If the first thing you do in the morning is roll out of bed, stretch, and do a little yoga, then place your mat next to your bed. If you don't live alone and prefer that your mat not get trampled, store it in a trunk at the foot of your bed, but get everything ready the evening before. If you like to read something inspiring each morning over tea, install an attractive bookshelf in your kitchen full of your favorite inspirational works. It will also bring in a sense of coziness.

✌ FINISHING TOUCHES

Allow blue and violet translucent objects to accent your home. Seven small blue or violet vases of varying shapes placed upon a windowsill greatly enhance an intuitive design scheme during the day when the sun penetrates them. A forest of seven pillar candles upon a silvery tray metaphorically illuminates the water's surface, asking "What's underneath?"

Intuition is exploration, for what is spoken to you through your intuition not only provides timely instruction, it unveils the essential truths of your being. You begin to know your real self, and because you are listening, you honor yourself all at once. The journey can be a mystical experience, and you may become fascinated with things you have never had much interest in. Follow your intuition, and revere it as a high holy path. If fairies begin to entice you or if they begin to represent some newly discovered part of you, bring their magic into your home.

Cats are renowned for walking in darkness with great confidence. The power of cats is made obvious by the numbers of people who actually fear them. Great cat fearers of history include Napoleon, who would scream for help whenever he met up with a cat in his palace, Adolf Hitler, and Henry III of England. If you like cats, you can represent cat magic through cat statuettes. Black cats striking Egyptian poses are probably the most powerful. If you can secure a pair of larger ones, you may wish to flank your doors with them. If you own real cats, accentuate their mystical presence and enlist them in breaking up energy by allowing them to play with a harmony or chime ball. Cats are quite fascinated by them.

The totem animal of introspection is Bear, who epitomizes feminine receptive energy. It is said that Bear annually enters a cave—a safe haven—to digest all that it encountered during the year. Once your intuitive awareness is well-seeded and established, you may wish to follow nature's pattern by initiating a yearly return to deep process work during the winter months. Owl can see things others cannot see, and has attributes similar to those of Cat. Owls are extremely perceptive and, in this respect, wise. If you resonate with Owl energy, find ways to represent Owl in your home.

Obsidian is symbolically considered a door opener, allowing you to see into yourself more clearly, often in an intuitive or psychic sense. This is a very benevolent stone and is a superb choice for those seeking a house stone to expand their intuitive awareness. Generally, blue stones also augment intuition.

❧ AN AFFIRMATION FOR INTUITION

Your interest in this information indicates a certain readiness to accept your instinctive wisdom. The purpose of this affirmation is to help you realize and open to your intuition, for it is standing at attention waiting for your command to access it.

I surrender to the small clear voice that seeks to guide me.

I accept the gentle guidance of my intuition. I disengage the rattling of arrogant intellect and embrace creative intelligence instead. My mind and heart work in unison, bringing to me subtle prompts from Spirit. I heed the words of Spirit through the acknowledgment of my inner wisdom. It serves me well.
Amen.

CHAPTER TWENTY

Joy

*J*oy is an effervescent feeling. It sings out about trust, about faith, about hope in the promise that the universe is a gentle, kind, abundant, comfortable, loving, friendly, compassionate place; that everything we need to live healthful lives of wonder is provided to us, no strings attached. It has to do with the ability to recognize grace.

Many people mistake happiness for joy. Happiness is the silhouette of joy. It is what joy often looks like when one is looking at it from the outside. Happiness is a disposition. Joy, however, is a condition of the heart. Joy doesn't mean constant bubbliness or silliness. It isn't merely fun and games.

It can be these things, but joy is never inappropriate. A joyful person still mourns the passing of a loved one, still feels the cosmic ebb and flow, still feels low from time to time.

The distinctive mark of a joyful person is that his or her trust in Spirit never waivers. All life unfolds exactly as it should in every moment. From this plateau it is easy to find reasons to celebrate, and joyous people do so. Life is a creative wonder to those who cultivate joy. A joyful person's salutatory perspective fuels him or her through both good and difficult periods. Through unity with universal or divine energy flow, joy-filled people understand that all life is one, and that giving and receiving are the same thing. Much giving and much receiving goes on in a joyful individual's life.

EXERCISE • WHAT JOY LOOKS LIKE

This exercise will help you rate and analyze various aspects of joy as it is expressed through you. The goal, as always, is to achieve balance and wholeness. All that is required is some quiet time, a pen, and a notebook or journal.

Joy is identified through the following pairs of terms. Each pair represents the polarities, the yin and yang, of some of the aspects of joyful behavior. For each individual item, give yourself a rating of one through ten, one representing suppression of that quality through your personality or behavior, and ten representing extroversion in that particular area.

Giving	Receiving
Playful	Serious
Spontaneous	Organized
Social	Introspective
Busyness	Downtime
Carefree	Responsible

Now examine each pair. If you gave yourself the same rating, or close to the same rating, for both, that aspect is in balance, regardless of where the number falls in the range of one to ten. For example, if you gave yourself a seven for social and a seven for introspective, they balance. Even if you gave yourself an eight for introspective, relatively speaking, you have learned to balance those two aspects. If, however, you awarded yourself a nine for giving and a two for receiving—which is common for women—you could work toward balancing those aspects out. Do some brainstorming on paper about how that balance might be achieved or how it might show up in your life.

The closer we move toward balancing these opposites, the closer we will come to creating true joy in our lives. It is difficult to fully appreciate giving, in any authentic sense, if we find it hard to receive. Without ever being serious, being playful loses some of its luster. After a period of behaving spontaneously, it is refreshing to sink our teeth into serious matters—and we are refreshed and clear enough to do so. After the party is over, it always feels great to surrender to our own quiet bed for a few hours of sleep. Being truly carefree can only come after we've taken care of our responsibilities; otherwise, we're simply being irresponsible.

SPACE CLEARING FOR JOY

Home can most definitely support you in your joyousness. To create an environment that cradles your heart and provides quietness during periods of introspection and sizzle for festive occasions, follow these easy steps.

For this clearing you will need three gold candles and three orange chrysanthemums floating in a bowl of spring water for each of the main rooms being cleared. You will also need a single gold candle for each of the other rooms being cleared. The space clearing tools required are your hands and any tool that makes a clacking or clicking sound, such as castanets or click sticks.

Step One

Place a bowl of chrysanthemums in the center of each main room, making a triangle of gold candles around it. Make sure that one of the candles points south. Chrysanthemums symbolize happiness, as does the color orange. Triangles are powerful energy attractors, and the direction south is sunny. The sun is a symbol for joy.

Physically connect with your home by placing your hands on the door-jamb, as is prerequisite for any space clearing. As you do this, imagine golden light pouring in through the top of your head and through your fingertips into the walls of your home. Continue envisioning this until you see every wall in your home radiating a golden glow, causing every inch of air space within to shimmer. Ask your angels to guide and direct your space clearing for joy.

Step Two

Begin working the space, as directed in Chapter 3, by clapping. Clap vigorously in any area where negative emotions have been expelled. As you clap through each room, feel the negative energy diffuse and imagine the golden glow becoming thicker, more alive, pulsating.

Step Three

Make another pass through the house using your tool. Hum a happy song as you do your clearing. Move your body and your hands in any way that brings you joy. Imagine your entire being as a conduit of universal joy and happiness. See your angels hovering over you, sprinkling joy throughout the room. When the room feels unusually clear, bright, and happy, seal it off by drawing an infinity sign in the air at the doorway.

In each of the main rooms you can use a dampened flower head to flick the spring water throughout the room, seeding it with joy. Allow the candles to burn for as long as you are home and it is safe to do so.

🌹 A JOYFUL ALTAR

An altar to joy will sustain you during your process of moving into a greater experience of it. As with any healing or growth, you will sometimes feel incredibly joyful and other times you won't know where your joy went. It is a rocking back and forth, a pendulum, until your heart finds a balanced resting place in joy.

Start by assembling three things that represent joy to you, past, present, and future: a gift given to you on a happy occasion by a special person in your life, a souvenir from a recent memorable social event, an icon representing something you perceive as bringing you great joy, and so on. Locate one or two universal symbols of joy: a hummingbird, flowers, a clown, a butterfly, an otter, the sun, a laughing Buddha. Find a photo of you on a particularly joyous occasion, or one that was taken during a time in your life when you felt joyful.

Place the photo of yourself in the center of the altar and create a triangle of the three treasured reminders of joy around it. Situate the remaining items in any way that pleases you. If you energize your altar with fresh flowers—a very sunny touch—be sure to replace them before they begin to wilt and die. Alternatively, you could place a healthy flowering plant on your altar. It will grow as your joy grows.

Dedicate each individual item to the flowering of joy within your heart. Bless your heart, asking that its message of joy reverberate throughout the world, unlocking the joy in the hearts of people everywhere.

✿ COLOR

The color of joy is gold. Because joy emanates from the heart, pink is its companion. It is a subtle yet rich and sophisticated color scheme that will nourish and uplift the hearts of all who dwell within and enter your home.

Imagine your home infused with the royal colors of a joyous heart. Layer shades of gold with the slightest tonal differences, use cream for balance, and add the faintest swipe of pink and green to balance the heart chakra. Wherever there is a lot of light, you can use a heavier hand with the gold tones you choose. Where natural light is not very good, gold can look dull and lifeless for much of the day, especially on walls or other large flat surfaces, such as tablecloths. Use gentler shades of gold in these rooms.

Nothing is more elegant and timeless than the golden veins of marble. Reflective surfaces such as the gold finishes found on lacquered boxes or large Asian fans will create focal points of golden light in more public areas such as living and dining rooms.

In private spaces, such as bedrooms, allow flannel sheets of the softest petal pink to warm and rejuvenate your body during the night. You may wish to subdue the colors in this room to create a restful effect. Imagine the charm of pink roses in a sea of silken cream laced with green vines.

Bathrooms lend themselves to the warmth of gold and pink or gold and green. A tiled sea-green floor with a honeyed maple vanity makes for a delicate and natural effect. If you are bold with color and have lots of good lighting, you can obtain a retro effect by using sea green, petal pink, and gold fixtures together in a bathroom.

In intimate living areas, such as a small dining room, use warm color dramatically if you would like. A deep sienna on the walls of a dining room, brightened with artwork in gilded frames, will induce fascinating conversations.

If pink does not resonate with you, pair a vibrant, earthy orange—such as persimmon—with gold and add a deep sea-green for contrast and strength. Use the orange primarily as an accent color: pillows upon a sofa, a vase, a framed family of poppies on the wall, orange pillar candles, and so on. While pink supports the heart, orange is social and happy.

Whatever color scheme you choose, apply color more lavishly in areas where you envision gatherings to take place. Warm color is inviting and reassuring: it tells people that it's okay to express varying aspects of their personalities in this space. Stark environments tend to intimidate, causing people to stand at attention, showing only their most refined behaviors. The lack of warmth can dampen any social gathering.

✌ SOUND

Sound is imperative in a home you want to ring with joy. Joyful sounds include children laughing and playing, birds chirping, water splashing, and glorious music.

Voices singing in unison, especially in gospel and inspirational music, are particularly uplifting on a weekend or when you're alone at home. People singing together also metaphorically represent the presence of others in the home. It has a social effect, which may be why this type of music is so comforting when no one else is around.

The music of your adolescence may bring you much happiness. As you reminisce about the dances, spirit rallies, parties, and celebrations of your youth, your heart will be restored to those expectant times. If this is the case for you, use this music to your advantage. Consider recording a tape of your favorite pick-me-up songs, or look for a compilation CD of songs that create optimism and joy in your heart. Whenever you feel low or are doing chores around the house, this music is bound to create happiness.

The music of Latin cultures is invigorating and can be lifting and conducive to fun gatherings. Rumba and salsa make for lively parties. Soul, calypso, and reggae—anything with African roots—can achieve the same thing. If your gathering is more refined, consider classical or Spanish guitar. Other strains of world culture as expressed through music, such as Jewish or Greek or Irish folk music, can also create memorable gatherings. Save them until the crowd gets warmed up.

A prerequisite to any kind of holiday gathering is holiday music. Make it a point to acquire a new holiday CD or two each year. Before you know it, you'll have something for any holiday gathering you can imagine. For larger parties with mixed crowds, instrumental music may be best. For more intimate gatherings of close family and friends, you may wish to have the classics sung to you—so everyone can join in. Nothing beats gathering around the piano to sing Christmas songs together. The effect is instantaneous unity and an abundance of holiday cheer. If you have a piano in your home and you can play, you owe it to your own heart to brush up on some holiday favorites in the months just prior to the season. This is a precious gift to share. Your children may not remember every gift they receive, but they will initiate similar traditions in their own family lives as adults because of their fond memories.

Music and sound can awaken joy and warm the heart like nothing else. Your budget doesn't matter. The effect of upbeat music while you set up your dorm room or first apartment can be dazzling. Allow music to connect you with beautiful people and create a string of fond memories.

&c AROMATHERAPY

Entrances are extremely important in a home dedicated to joy. Allow the sociable scent of tangerine or orange to greet your visitors. Make good use of these two scents throughout your main living areas. Use them in a diffuser during gatherings, or reenergize your environment through a light misting. Place a few drops of either in a mister along with some spring water.

These smells work wonderfully in the kitchen. Next time you eat an orange, partially grind the peel in your disposal but don't completely rinse it down the drain. Never throw lemons away in the garbage if you have a disposal. They disinfect and freshen your kitchen drain.

For other rooms, such as your bedroom, bergamot is very uplifting. This scent is also effective for raising your spirits when you are feeling especially blue or even grief-stricken.

Other scents considered festive are jasmine, which is welcoming, geranium, which is friendly, and coriander, cypress, juniper, pine, tuberose, and ylang-ylang.

&c FLOWER ESSENCES

It's natural to allow flowers to propel the blossoming of joy within your heart. If you have been suffering from a lack of joy, baby blue-eyes will bring you back to center. If you find all of life to be mundane and uninteresting, hornbeam can help make life seem lustrous again. To help you feel joy for others, use holly. If leadership is a path you're on, spike it with charisma by using larkspur. But if you want to play more, zinnia will gift you with a childlike attitude.

&c ENERGETIC DESIGN

Joy springs from the heart, where it is held, cradled, nourished, disbursed. The heart is ruled by the sun. Allowing the symbolism of the powerful sun to dominate your home will undoubtedly create a sunny disposition. This symbolism can be applied through color; through direct representations of the sun in artwork, fabrics, and so on; and through things that thrive in the sun, such as flowers.

A south-facing home, associated with warmth, will amplify feelings of joy in your home. If your entrance doesn't face south, symbolically increase the sun's energy by placing a crystal prism in every south-facing window. As you hang each crystal dedicate it to a joyous home environment in fitting words of your own. The rainbow light these prisms bring in will affirm your intention for joy.

Create an especially joyful atmosphere in your home by honoring anything you own that has ever brought you joy. Don't hide those things away in a trunk. Find a place in your home. If it is a Viewmaster from 1964, display it where you and others can not only see it but play with it. If it is your stuffed pink kitty given to you by your favorite aunt, put it on your bed. Sleep with it sometimes. Allow it to fill your heart with comfort and joy.

In a joyful house, toys may be important. It is an interesting phenomenon that people lose interest in toys, or transfer that interest to slick, expensive ones that can only be used with great effort on days off. I personally keep jacks on hand and sometimes play with them after the kids are tucked in. They are not stashed away in a drawer somewhere—they actually adorn a shelf near my entryway, which is where I love to play. I secretly kept a color book and crayons around all through college, and on rainy days I would sometimes color, just as I happily did on many rainy days as a child. If you have to encounter something with your eyes, you'll be more tempted to play with it. However, you may become oblivious to things on display if you don't move them around once in a while. If this is true of you, put your toys on view and move them around from time to time.

Collections of toys are catalysts for interesting conversation no matter your age. Give them a place of honor. A display cabinet full of your grandmother's, mother's, and your dolls is a shrine to your lineage. Arrange the dolls in different ways as often as you like. Use it (or something similar) to empower and strengthen your family by placing it in the family area of your home—which is the middle left section as you stand facing your home from the street. A collection such as this will imply a chain of joy running through your family. Intend it and it is so.

In your artwork, symbolically represent sociability and fun if you would like your home to take on these joyous accents. For instance, avoid artwork depicting singularity: a single rose, a single duck, and so on. Instead, opt for pictures of groups of objects: a beautiful and diverse bouquet of flowers can represent the diversity of the souls you plan to entertain at home. Things that dance together are incredibly uplifting. Dancing bears are a popular example. Ballerinas dancing, a couple dancing together, or butterflies flying together all contribute to a feeling of joy. I was fortunate to find an indoor water fountain with three happy frogs holding hands and dancing together; the water splashes up through their center. The sound of the trickling water brings joy to my heart whenever I hear it. It lives on our front porch, which is glassed in and has tile on the floor, which causes the sound to echo to the farthest parts of the house, spreading joy.

In fabrics, you may wish to stay away from solids, unless they are a social color such as orange. Patterned fabrics that are not linear are metaphorically more conducive to sociability and therefore to joy. If you like to entertain, these fabrics will show the aftereffects of spills and such to a lesser degree. Fabrics sporting flowers or perhaps even vines are excellent. Tribal patterns are great choices, and the colors are often very warm.

Arrange your furniture in ways conducive to play and entertaining. We recently added an entire closet between our kitchen and dining room expressly for housing a sound system and all the props necessary for gatherings: the music collection, games, and puzzles. If playing games is something you enjoy doing or that you would like to do more often, position your games nearest the place you envision gaming. For us, that's either the kitchen or dining room, hence the closet storage system. You may prefer a gaming table tucked in an intimate corner of the living room, with a game of chess or backgammon continually in progress. Keeping your coffee table clear or purchasing a larger coffee table will facilitate putting together jigsaw puzzles. Friends and visitors will find your puzzle irresistible if they stay for very long.

Games themselves are, of course, steeped in metaphor—and it's palpable. There is this mysterious and valiant energy about chess that is always very striking to me. Stop to consider a deck of cards: The fifty-two cards represent the weeks in a calendar year. The thirteen cards per suit, the lunar months in a year. The four suits represent the four directions, the four seasons. And the king, queen, and jack represent the holy trinity, the triple goddess or triune nature of Spirit.

Make it a point to keep a basket full of inexpensive musical instruments on hand. Tambourines, castanets, triangles, drums, rattles, recorders, and kazoos all make for fun when silliness breaks out. Whenever the musical instruments come out to play you can be doubly happy, because what follows is one of the best space clearings ever.

If you are a family, enrich your closeness through storytelling, conversation, play, music, and singing. Kids like it best, and it will be easier to adhere to if you make family night a ritual. Instead of engaging in splashy or expensive fun, make your own fun at your home. The energy patterns will make your house hum with joy. On family night, from the time everyone has arrived home, do whatever you can together. Assemble pizzas together, choose an activity, be it a craft or game, and play.

Remove the television from the center of your home. Give it a space in a den or basement family room. Television viewing is not conducive to knowing another person and is, except on rare occasions, not a social encounter. Having the television centrally located in your home could express an unbalanced sense of priorities and symbolically says that your own life is dull or not as important by comparison.

Celebration is more important than our culture recognizes. Celebrations mark milestones big and small. All are significant. They can bring families, friends, communities, even entire nations together. It is an understatement to say our lives meet up at these times. Celebrations help define us. They help us remember who we are. Look for reasons to celebrate your life.

Many of us feel funny about celebrating our own lives. On our birthdays we shy away from any attention people want to shower on us. Deep down inside though, we still need and desire that recognition. Nobody wants a birthday to go unnoticed. So, don't let it. Life is a precious gift. It is okay to live that way.

In addition to birthdays and secular and religious holidays, celebrate your children's coming of age. Don't allow them to pass silently and invisibly into adulthood. By celebrating their journey you say to them something words or a material gift can never express: I celebrate you. Show that you cherish your loved ones by noticing their firsts and accomplishments, both grandiose and modest. Your children's first words, their first tooth to fall out, each grade they pass through in school are all wonderful reasons to celebrate.

If you don't have a family of your own, celebrate your friends, your pets, the wildlife in your backyard, your coworkers. Give your time and money to organizations that do good in the world. When holding a gathering in your home, bless your environment by inviting mixed groups of people. The energy of young and old, varying ethnicity, and differing cultures enriches your home's environment. Celebrate with gratitude in your heart, spread your love out, and feel joy blossom inside.

Nature gives us plenty of reasons to celebrate. Celebrate the sun by basking in it. Relish the pale light and mysterious energy of the moon by taking a walk in it whenever it is full. Wish upon a star. You can honor nature by bringing her indoors at the change of every season. In the fall bring in bunches of beautifully colored leaves to grace your dinner table. Cultivate a flower garden that will provide cuttings for most of the year, if possible. Bring back a natural object from each of your travels. A family friend brought my son a lovely stone from the grounds of an ancient palace she toured in Europe. What made it such a thoughtful, precious gift is that she knows my son loves rocks and gemstones.

Plan meaningful holiday activities. Don't limit yourself to being a good consumer. Make it a point to understand the lore and symbolism of the secular holidays we celebrate. There are some terrific books available that are also very interesting for children to read. Make and keep family holiday traditions. In our family we read a Christmas story or sing Christmas carols together every night beginning on December twelfth. We make acquiring a Christmas tree a joyous excursion each year by taking a lovely drive out into the country to a tree farm and cutting one ourselves. We do this just a few days prior to Christmas so that the tree is still fresh when the holiday arrives. The entire day centers around the tree. Family rituals govern even the decorating process.

Gifts, for any occasion, are infused with your energy when you make them. Giving homemade gifts is an act of love that truly spreads joy. They don't have to be difficult or time consuming to make. If you're baking holiday cookies, increase the number of batches you make and deliver a few to your neighbors. If you're making holiday wreaths, why not let each family member make one and choose a neighbor to give it to.

If you celebrate this rare and beautiful life often and with meaning, your home cannot help but reverberate with love and joy. If you're making room in your life to receive more joy and to celebrate it more often, also plan a day of rest and reflection on a regular basis, so that you can wallow in all the joy you've created, allowing it to seep completely into your heart.

❧ FINISHING TOUCHES

Three is the magic number representing expression, entertaining, and expanding your social circle. Find ways to incorporate the power of three into your interior landscape. Three flowering plants on a sideboard in your entryway makes a sunny welcoming party for guests. Three guest soaps in a lovely dish tells visitors they're special. An eclectic ensemble of three birdhouses heralds joy, as does a grouping of three trumpeting angels.

Bring into your home the social prowess of Otter, Dolphin, or Hummingbird. Their playfulness and happy dispositions will add dimension and character to the theme of joy you've set in motion. Flank your home's entrance with friendly rosemary, which symbolizes remembrance and friendship.

Accentuate family playfulness by placing a toy in the family area of your home. For fun excursions, put one in your helpful people/travel area. For increased enjoyment in your marriage or relationships in general, place a favorite toy or game in the relationship area of your home. (Refer to the bagua map at the end of Chapter 4.)

❧ AN AFFIRMATION FOR JOY

If you are ready to enjoy the adventure of life fully by accepting more joy into your heart, affirmations can help attract it to you. Use this one, or craft one of your own using words that are more meaningful to you. Pay tribute to your joyous heart each day, until you begin to feel a shift.

My heart rejoices in all of life's adventures.

As I balance the aspects of joy in my life, my experience of life expands. This expansive feeling makes life adventurous and meaningful. I arise each day with joy in my heart anticipating the goodness Spirit has in store for me. I am never disappointed, for I am open and accepting of all that is mine. I trust, therefore I rejoice. And I am grateful.
Amen.

CHAPTER TWENTY-ONE

Peace

*P*eace is a deep inner sanctum that lives inside everyone. Peace is not something gifted to us on a silver platter, but it has always been our right to possess it. We need only turn inward toward our own intrinsic peace and accept it into our lives. Once we connect with peace, we contribute to a universal tipping of the scales away from fear in favor of love. Without doubt the angels sing with delight each time one of us chooses to embrace peace.

Peace is the product of self-responsibility. Peaceful people know that a truly tranquil world can exist only when every individual accepts responsibility not only for her or his actions, but for the words and thoughts that created them. Peaceful people also trust divine process, knowing that all life unfolds as it should according to Spirit's plan.

To foster peace, love yourself. There's no use in trying to give the world something you have not yet mastered. If the well is dry, you'll come up empty-handed every time anyway. To support yourself in love and peace, create a home environment that is peaceful to its core. Each time you retreat from delivering your gifts of peace to the world, your home sanctuary will replenish your peaceful spirit.

EXERCISE FOR PEACE THROUGH HOME

One of the premises of this book is that everything is alive, whether or not it is animated by the breath of life. This includes Home. If your home feels stressful, dissonant, or prone to argument, talk to it. Most of us talk to our automobiles, and nearly everyone I know talks to any piece of machinery when it doesn't perform as expected! If your home is out of kilter, maybe it will reveal the true source of the problem.

When you are home alone sometime, find the spot where the trouble seems to be most prevalent. Is there a particular room where arguing seems to frequently fester and erupt? Be very specific. You are likely to find that the spot of underlying discord is a certain area within a room. If your energy patterns are being influenced to fight in these places, the imprint of *sha*, or negative energy, has become more concentrated. Once you become aware of these trouble spots, you can begin to dislodge the *sha* patterns.

When you have located a place where the energies of the house seem to conflict or intersect in a disharmonious way, seat yourself there on the floor with four white candles positioned in a large square around you for protection. After lighting the candles, close your eyes and center yourself by mentally following your breath. Set the intention of unlocking the mystery of the energetic patterns converging in this area. Call forth your angels to assist you in completing your mission with ease.

When your mind is still and objective, ask your house, out loud and in a commanding rather than a passive tone, what it wants you to know about it. Listen quietly and with an open heart. Tune in to the energy. Pay very close attention to any pictures that come into your mind and to any bodily sensations. If something tells you this place was the scene of an emotionally dismantling argument, take it for truth. If your resulting feelings and sensations prompt another question, ask it. Continue until you feel complete.

Trust your instinct. When we moved into our house three years ago, we noticed right away that certain parts of the house felt really conflicted and grumpy. It was a challenge staying at first. We felt a very dark presence lurking. One day while I was meditating about it, a picture of an older man came into my mind. We had already done quite a bit of remodeling to the house, and I got a distinct feeling during my meditation that this man was very jealous about the changes we were making. This meshed with information about a previous owner who was quite a curmudgeon and extraordinarily antisocial. It confirmed a lot of what I had already felt and made so much sense to me. With it I was able to formulate a plan for breaking up the energy and getting this entity to move on. Space clearings have been very effective. My neighbors have commented on how different the house feels now.

Note in a journal or notebook anything you discover during your conversation with your house. If nothing springs to mind right away do not be disappointed. It may take some time for it to come to you—that might be part of the energy pattern. Or it may take you some time to pinpoint your feelings or find words for them. Be assured, however, that your probe will touch off a series of discoveries allowing you to determine the specific source of disharmony in your home.

🎔 SPACE CLEARING FOR PEACE

The purpose of this clearing is to completely and powerfully diffuse any negative energy and to blanket the house in peace. The clearing draws strongly upon Native American wisdom because of their tradition of living in peace with the forces of nature and their recognition of the oneness of all things.

Peace

🏵

203

For this clearing you will need a drum—preferably handmade by a Native American—a sage smudge stick, and a large feather (optional).

Step One

Connect with the spirit of your house and set your intention for breaking up the old energy patterns and smoothing them down until a feeling of peace is achieved. Ask that Spirit be present in your home now, bringing blessings of peace.

Then, invite in the spirits of the four elements: Air, associated with the east; Water, associated with the south; Fire, associated with the west; and Earth, associated with the north. Say something meaningful in connection with your peaceful objective as you invoke the presence of each element. For example: "May the spirit of the east be present in this home now, carrying peace on its gentle breezes. May the spirit of the south enter this home, its tranquil waters reflecting the inner peace of all who dwell here. May the spirit of the west bring love into our souls and purity to our thoughts through its flickering flames. May the spirit of the north bring nourishment to our bodies and minds through our Mother Earth." You may wish to face each direction as you address it.

Step Two

When you are ready, vigorously drum the entire house room by room. As always, pay attention to energetically sticky areas. Any specific place within your home that holds negative energy requires more time and perhaps more concentration. See the negativity break down each time you strike the drum. In addition to places where conflict seems to spontaneously erupt, pay attention to areas where you do not linger or feel like you need to pass by quickly, or places where you often trip or spill things.

When you've completed the drumming, move back through the home with a smudge stick. If you have purchased your smudge stick in a shop, follow its attached instructions. Normally, you simply light the loose end of the stick, blow out the flame, and allow it to smolder in a heat-proof dish or, traditionally, an abalone shell. The smoke is used to purify spaces and objects. Purification by smudging with sage is powerful. Walk through the space and around furnishings using the feather to push the smoke into areas you wish to purify. You may also use your hand.

Step Three

Sit on the floor at the energetic center of your house, facing east. Close your eyes and allow your mind to be still. Simply call forth the spirit of the east, feeling its gentle winds flowing all around you and through you, empowering your intellect with the true wisdom of peace. Thank the spirit of the east.

Now, turn to the south. When your mind is clear and calm call forth its spirit. Allow its rivers and streams to gently lace your emotions with peace. Its rains deliver peace to your feelings. Its fog brings sweet dreams to all occupants each and every night. Thank the spirit of the south.

Turn to the west and center yourself once again. Feel the heat of the sun's rays permeate your being with the energy of a peaceful and passionate warrior. Thank the spirit of the west.

Turn to the north and sit quietly and calmly. Establish a connection to the spirit of the north. Standing on its safe and sacred ground, feel its rich peacefulness rise up through the bottoms of your feet and spread throughout your being. Thank the spirit of the north.

✍ AN ALTAR TO PEACE

Peace allows our minds to rest quietly in our hearts. It comes in sweet little packages, but peace is a powerful thing. Recall the way your mother softly kissed your forehead as she tucked your blankets around you each night. Think of the saffron sunlight that hugs the mountain peaks moments before dusk, or droplets of rain pressed to the window by winter winds. Imagine the deep breathing of a child's sleep.

Allow the sweet power of peace to manifest itself upon your altar using a personal memento, such as a photo of the best friend who effortlessly calms your soul as soon as her voice is heard at the other end of the line; the wedding ring that belonged to your grandmother, whose hands reached out for you the moment your car pulled into the driveway; the rosary beads strung by your seven-year-old son in religion class and spontaneously given to you; a brilliant maple leaf gathered on a particularly peaceful walk during your favorite time of the year; words from a poem that speaks directly to your heart. These are the kinds of things that will bring an instant sense of inner calm on the wildest of days. Add to your treasures a green candle for harmony and healing and a statuette of a cooing dove or a deer. Dedicate your altar to a deepening awareness of inner peace and mindful practice of it in your life. Bless your altar and visit it often, especially when your nerves are frayed by the dizzying pace of modern life.

❧ COLOR

Peace is typified by green, which rests exactly in the center of the color spectrum. Green is the most common color on the planet. It is probable that Spirit planned this, for green is a healing color, restoring balance and calm. It nourishes the heart chakra, where the footings of peace lie. For this reason green is frequently used in healing centers such as hospitals and health retreats. Undemanding and kind, green is extraordinarily easy to live with.

Peace connotes harmony. Therefore, add to your palette harmonious colors, which are those residing on either side of green in the color spectrum—yellow and blue. Imagine this triad as replicating the holy trinity or triune nature of life. When mind, body, and spirit are unified, a feeling of completeness follows. Shades between green and yellow, such as chartreuse, and between green and blue, such as turquoise, are welcome in this palette.

Sunnier, more social rooms deserve the warmth of yellow. In the kitchen allow a clear yellow or honey to keep company with a proliferation of green plant life. Spike the color theme with cherry for a homespun look. Offices and studies also benefit from the clarity yellow brings.

If the space requires sophistication, such as in a dining room, allow neutral creams or beiges to play a larger role and spike them with a warmer green such as olive, gold, and even a hint of terra-cotta. Warm white and spring or lime green with a tinge of saffron or tangerine creates a healed and relaxed space people love to be in. The feel is clean, clear, and pure, hence peaceful.

Baths become elegant spa retreats when floored with earthy substances such as green slate or marble. They become buoyantly peaceful with sea greens and blues. A subdued pistachio combined with wedgewood or slate blue and a dollop of persimmon suggests a tamed country style.

Bedrooms spin into natural healing centers when dominated by spruce and framed by muslin. For warmth add a golden straw. A natural sisal rug mimics the texture of a forest floor. The modern naturalist might prefer periwinkle, sea green, or honey.

✿ SOUND

Voices singing together in unison epitomize harmony and invite images of a chorus of angels. Peace is unavoidable when enjoying these sounds. Gregorian chant relaxes. Church hymns and gospel music can release feelings that block inner peace and therefore restore it. Music that is simply arranged, such as guitar and vocals, can be peaceful. A single voice, perhaps yours, can caress you into peacefulness. New Age or ambient music is sometimes too formless to inspire peace. However, if you are feeling peaceful already it can stabilize that feeling. When life is frantic or we are caught in an uncontrollable and confining situation that threatens to ensnare us in its chaos, chamber music soothes. Keeping a CD of chamber music in the car for traffic snarls is an excellent idea.

Water sounds are peaceful. Think of the mesmerizing effect of ocean waves; meandering creeks; a slow, steady, drenching rain; water splashing or trickling onto metal. You can slip into unfettered peace at any time when you have a library of water music at your fingertips. Water features in your home are powerful peace inducers.

Peace precludes interruptions and noise. If a phone call would be a disturbance while you're reading, cooking, or spending time with your children, turn the ringer off if you can. Message machines can be noisy too; voicemail is often a more serene alternative. Consider not having phones in certain rooms, especially those dedicated to your health, such as bathrooms and workout rooms. Even Alexander Graham Bell would not allow a telephone to be installed in his study; he sought to avoid the interruption.

❧ AROMATHERAPY

If you're feeling argumentative, or if someone has been trying to convince you to let go of your peaceful state to become embroiled in his or her personal chaos, try cedarwood, chamomile, roman eucalyptus, frankincense, jasmine, thyme, or ylang-ylang. To unwind and relax use clary sage, geranium, lavender, marjoram, melissa, neroli, or rose in addition to chamomile and frankincense. All of these scents can be reassuring and calming.

On your way home from work, reduce stress after a busy day by means of a plug-in automobile diffuser, or at the very least as soon as you walk through the door. For the ultimate restoration of peace, take a hot bath dotted with one or a few of your favorite oils from these lists, and soak by candlelight until you're ready to nod off.

❧ FLOWER ESSENCES

Allow the wise souls of flowers to transport peace to your spirit. The Bach Five Flower Formula will bring a sense of peacefulness whenever life feels overwhelming. Use it in emergencies. If your peace is disrupted regularly because of a tendency to worry, try red chestnut. Lavender strengthens attenuated nerves. If you are highly sensitive and suffer from overstimulation, try dill.

❧ ENERGETIC DESIGN

Peacefulness is expressed within the walls of Home primarily through simplicity. Simplicity was exalted as godly by the Shakers. Their methods are tried and true. The absence of clutter and a design style that fuses serene form to simple craftsmanship produce calm. The mind can focus on what is high and holy in a Shakeresque interior.

If you are not enamored with Shaker style, the principles can be translated into many design concepts by maintaining a balance that tilts toward modesty. If you prefer ornate styles, such as Gothic, decorate with fewer objects; don't have lots of ornamental objects around. If you like plainer styles—perhaps a traditional country style pleases you—your home can accept more ornamental objects without sacrificing peace. Less means more. Rococo style is raucous compared with simple Provençal furnishings, and so not nearly as restful. Certain design periods call for louder colors too. In general, loud doesn't attract peace.

Use a light decorating touch. Avoid hardness in fabrics, design lines, and finishes. Softly flowing shapes are best. Choose draperies over blinds; in addition to fostering a soft, serene feeling, the fabric will absorb sound better too. When the windows are open, the gentle winds become tangible with the movement of the drapes. Metal blinds just bang around until you're annoyed enough to roll them up. Wood flooring is more desirable than white marble or a black and white checked pattern. Butcher-block countertops or those fashioned of matte porcelain tile have a certain softness in their appearance and feel. Wooden picture frames are more conducive to peace than high-shine metals and nervy plastics. Thick-piled rugs deaden sound and help create a feeling of peace. In some rooms, such as your bedroom, you may even choose a very large area rug. Whenever possible, choose natural fibers. The chemicals in synthetic rugs aren't restful. Peace is intolerant of rigidity, so you may find geometric patterns unrestful. Solids, florals, and flowing designs such as waves are better for an environment trying to lure and embrace peace.

In arranging furniture, leave ample room to walk around it. Nothing is quite so irritating as bumping into things day in and day out. Chi will be able to drift aimlessly, and it will be further enhanced if you balance the five elements to as great an extent as possible throughout your home. To refresh yourself about this, refer to Chapters 4 and 15.

Follow similar guidelines in choosing artwork. Muted, fuzzy images can be restful, as can tranquil subjects such as nature scenes. Lakes and forests are universally calming. Another approach to choosing artwork for your walls is to find art that illustrates activities appropriate to the room, carried out in a peaceful manner. In the kitchen, for example, a black and white print of a smiling produce merchant doting on her beautiful array of fruits and vegetables is calming. In the bedroom, a print of an unmade bed, the imprint of the being who slept in it still visible, can be relaxing. One of my best friends hung over her piano an impressionist print of a girl sitting at the piano, smiling over her shoulder at all those beholding her. These images reinforce peaceful activities in these rooms.

Architecturally, it is much more harmonious to enlist a neglected archi tectural feature in the overall design scheme rather than continue to ignore it. If, in your living room, you have an old fireplace that is oddly positioned, for the sake of peace try to arrange your furniture around it. It is, after all, the heart of your home. Disregarding it would create a con- tentious feeling.

Nature is generally peaceful, so bring it inside however you can. Use nat- ural objects to decorate your dining table. Use them for functional pur- poses. Large, flat stones make excellent platforms for pillar candles or tea lights. Interesting branches can be placed in vases for a look as stunning as a dried flower arrangement. They are especially handsome placed in large vases on the floor. When suspended from the ceiling they constitute inter- esting mobiles, the themes of which could change seasonally.

If you have a guardian tree (see Chapter 9) in your front yard, tie prayer flags requesting peace onto its branches. Each time the wind blows your prayers will be sent to heaven, where they'll be heard and responded to. If you don't have an official guardian tree, choose the tallest or healthiest one as your messenger to the gods.

Nothing is so immediately calming as kinetic light. It is indispensable to a centered home. Candles or a fire in the fireplace will melt every care away and bring you the deepest sense of peace. On tough days you might try not to use any electrical lighting at all.

Electrical conductors, such as metal furnishings and home electronics, can cause physical stress and fatigue. Shy away from metal beds, as beauti- ful as they are, especially for babies and young children.

Organization is essential to peace. I don't mean neurotic or extreme organization, but just the kind that allows you to put your finger on everything you need. Perhaps nothing is quite so distressing as not being able to find something, such as your car keys or checkbook, on your way out the door. Develop systems for keeping track of important paperwork and financial and functional items.

❧ FINISHING TOUCHES

Angels herald peace. Be sure to find places to quietly introduce angel icons. If there have been trouble spots in your home, these are excellent places to position lookout angels. Their watchful eyes will deter future disturbances.

Hang a dove or angel above your door to help ward away any influence considering wreaking havoc on your peace. This is a beautiful and subtle yet powerful message. It sets the tone for your home. Be sure to use one of the essential oils in your entryway, such that the effect starts working on all who enter straight away.

Green jade balances and strengthens earth energy within a building, making it a great house stone encouraging peace.

Evoke the power of the number six in your home. It represents harmony, beauty, and caring. If your totem animal is Deer, imagine the power of a herd of six tiny deer gracing your mantle. A cluster of six votive candles on top of your dresser or bedside table would make an excellent proponent of peace.

❧ AN AFFIRMATION FOR PEACE

Because peace resides within each of us, all we need to do is accept peace and allow it the space in our lives to blossom through the practice of being peaceful. Your serenity will attract calm, peaceful human beings into your life and will keep chaos at bay. In your practice of peace, set the tone for each day with an affirmation of peace. If you have been fighting a battle of any kind in your life, you may wish to insert a line in the affirmation that indicates your readiness to give it up. For example, "I give up trying to control my daughter's life."

I am peace.

I recognize that true peace begins in my own heart. Nothing can obstruct this peace. Any sense of doubt or fear or uncertainty is gone. I live, I rest in this peaceful moment.
Let it be.

CHAPTER TWENTY-TWO

Prosperity

*P*rosperity assumes many forms: the absence of shame in your heart, to not live hand-to-mouth, to sleep restfully at night, to feel alive, to serve others, to hike the Pacific Trail, to be able to be fully present with your children, to complete your college degree, to not struggle, to not have to hold a secular job, to have a sense of freedom, to travel the globe, to feel safe, to hold a precious life in your arms. At its core, prosperity is a deeply rooted sense that all is well, that success is yours or is imminently yours.

Prosperity consciousness cannot truly be developed without a thorough look at and, usually, purging of our existing beliefs about the nature of prosperity. However, a few basic truths hold steady for everyone, no matter their current situation or future prospects relating to comfort and freedom. One is that the universe demonstrates in every moment and in many limitless ways that life is abundant, and also that life is regenerative, even against the most highly improbable odds. The second is that it is impossible to achieve any dream, whether it be financial freedom or to be rightfully employed in a job that brings peace to the heart, if your belief system is out of alignment with that dream. The third truth is that once it is understood that all life is one, it is also understood that giving and receiving are the same act. To become part of the flow of abundance one must recognize this unity. Therefore, it is important to be generous. Giving is ultimate trust in the kindness and expansiveness of the universe. You will not be forgotten, and you'll have one more reason to love yourself.

Home can most definitely support you in your quest for prosperity, no matter what that is, as long as you can focus clearly on your objectives for prosperity while remaining detached from a specific path and from precisely how the end result will demonstrate itself. You must be able to recognize prosperity when it shows up. It is imperative to be open and ready to receive it.

Align yourself with your dream. Pursue it with every ounce of your personal integrity and with diligence, and be sure not to miss any of life's cues. It is easy to miss the cues if you are overly focused on what you perceive as the right path for achieving your goal. Life cannot be coerced or completely predicted. It often has a better and higher plan for you than you can foresee, so be open to all the possibilities. A dream of prosperity that is woven with love, empowered with faith, and driven with intent cannot help but come into being.

Make certain not to shortchange yourself by thinking yourself undeserving. This has nothing to do with the deliverance of a dream. Feeling undeserving usually reflects a sense of victimization, no matter the frame of reference. This label defers responsibility for your thoughts, words, and actions to an external force. Instead, hold the highest, most honest vision you can for yourself. Anything less serves neither the world nor yourself. If you feel genuinely prosperous, the entire world will be that much better.

EXERCISE ONE • EXPLORING PROSPERITY

Beliefs can only be altered when they can be examined. The purpose of this exercise is to reveal to you your own beliefs about prosperity through the production of a prosperity-consciousness autobiography. This exercise is designed to allow you to come face to face with those beliefs so that you can adjust them to align with your objectives. I assure you, you are bound to marvel at some of the beliefs you hold about prosperity.

For this exercise you need an entire notebook or composition book. Set aside thirty minutes or so each week until you believe you have uncovered your truth in connection with prosperity. Beginning with a few minutes of quiet meditation will help unfold your memories. Respond to the following list in as much detail as you can conjure. Highlight anything that is news to you. When all questions have been answered completely the result will be an autobiographical story about prosperity.

1. Describe your family's economic picture at the time of your birth. If you don't know, ask. If asking your parents is out of the question, for whatever reason, ask a close relative or family friend.

2. What overt messages pertaining to money and success did you receive throughout childhood? For example, did your parents tell you that family finances were none of your business? Did you hear phrases like "Money doesn't grow on trees"? Was success always presented as the outgrowth of hard (dissatisfying) work and constant struggle?

3. What is your earliest memory surrounding money? This could involve a lemonade stand, a baby-sitting job, an allowance, or the realization that money could buy things and that there was money in your piggy bank.

4. What is your earliest memory of economic status? This could have been the realization that the neighbor had a better job than your father had, for example. You might remember that there was no money to buy the thing you really wanted, or the moment you realized that other kids didn't have to wear hand-me-downs as you did.

5. When you were young, what were your dreams of adulthood? What did you want to do with your life? How did you want to be? Why?

6. What was your first job? How old were you? How did you view your responsibilities? What did you learn about yourself and life? How did what you learned alter your dreams of childhood?

7. Have you achieved any of the dreams you've had about yourself? Do you have the things you thought you would have by now?

8. Has money been a factor in the choices you've made in terms of livelihood or career?

9. What emotions do you attach to money now?

10. Are you comfortable in the company of people who have more money than you? Are you comfortable with those who have less? How does their status influence your actions and the way in which you relate to them?

11. Describe an instance in which you set a goal regarding money and met it.

12. Describe an instance in which you set a goal regarding money and didn't meet it. Why didn't you meet your goal? What was the impact on you emotionally and mentally? What impact did it have on your life?

13. Have you ever been in the position of borrowing money from a friend or family member? Did you honor any agreements made? How did borrowing money make you feel?

14. What do you enjoy doing with money? What are the feelings associated with how you handle money? Is there a correlation? For example, do you shop frivolously when you're bored or feeling low? Do you splurge on yourself when you've hit some kind of milestone?

15. What sorts of things do you refuse to spend money on?

16. What do you do to treat yourself well?

17. What is your prosperity outlook for two, five, and ten years? What do you see yourself doing to achieve success, however you define it, in each of those time frames?

18. Describe any other important feelings or circumstances revolving around prosperity that have not yet been drawn out.
19. Describe an ideal day, from the time you awake until the time you fall asleep at night.
20. How can your home and home life support you in your dreams?

EXERCISE TWO • EXPLORING YOUR GOALS

This exercise is designed to empty from your consciousness all things relating to what you hope to achieve in life. Stating intention is powerful. It will either show something to be less important than your mind had you convinced it was, or your heart will say yes as soon as the thing you love is uttered.

Make a list of everything in life you believe you most want. These things can be spiritual, emotional, intellectual, recreational, material, or physical in nature. Leave nothing out. It could be an eclectic ensemble, such as the following:

- Learn how to in-line skate.
- Have three children.
- Buy a new car every five years.
- Hire someone to clean the house.
- Never *have* to cook again.
- Afford to take two, two-week vacations every year to wherever I'd like, having money be no issue.
- Be able to retire by age fifty.
- Be close to my children always.

Whatever comes into your head, get it out. Do not stop until you've recorded every desire on paper. Note what's at the top of the list. Those things are probably currently on your mind. Now edit the list. Review each item with your heart. If you feel unsettled or unsure about any of the items, ask yourself why. Remove anything that is on the list merely out of a sense of loyalty to that particular thing. For instance, maybe you've been saying since the age of three that you want to be a nurse, and so it's on the list. But lately you've learned a little about nursing, and you know it's really not for you. You just haven't taken the time to remove it from the mental picture you hold for yourself. By removing unimportant items, you'll free up mental space for those you truly want to have materialize.

Keep your list in a place where you encounter it daily, such as inside your appointment book, on the refrigerator door, or in the map pocket in your car door. Each time you confront the list you'll come face to face with your dreams—and they'll stay energized and current.

❧ SPACE CLEARING FOR PROSPERITY

In the decluttering process that should take place prior to any effective first-time space clearing, it is important to rid yourself of anything that makes you feel poor, disempowered, uncomfortable, or ashamed. Also discard anything you dislike but are hanging onto because you believe you can't afford to purchase the thing you really love. Even if these things are highly functional, they do not serve you in manifesting your dreams. In fact, they are affirmations for struggle and deprivation. Find appropriate homes for these other things. They are best given to charities or people with whom you have no direct connection. In addition to the energy these items drain away from you that could be spent accomplishing your dreams, you simply cannot receive unless you make room to receive.

For this space clearing you will need a pen and paper; a working fireplace or large, heavy-duty cast iron pot; some matches or a lighter; and some cinnamon in the form of an essential oil or an actual cinnamon stick.

Step One

Sitting on the floor in the room in the house where you are most comfortable, center yourself. Sit quietly following your breathing for a few minutes. When your mind is clear, make a list of every fear you've ever had relating to your vision of prosperity. Be very conscious and intentional in creating this list. If it feels appropriate, ask Spirit to guide you. Once you have excavated your fears, crumple up the list and place it in the fireplace or pot and burn it. As you stare into the flames feel the fears embedded within the walls of every room of your home being sucked into the fire, where they die.

Step Two

Sit in quiet meditation. See yourself living the life of your dreams within the walls of Home. Notice the absence of fear or shame or worry or uncertainty, and the presence of trust, love, and generosity in all you think and do. See yourself in each room of your house, alone and completely comfortable. Allow your essence to bubble forth in all you undertake.

Notice too how all the furnishings and finishes cradle you in comfort. The textures, colors, and artwork all exude a certain richness and quality that suits your tastes and desires perfectly. Every room feels as though it were tailored expressly for you. Everywhere you look, all your favorite things are present. Even the kitchen pantry is stocked with your favorite healthful foods. Nothing is lacking, and you feel content.

Once you feel complete in exploring a prosperous home life, envision the entire house, with you in it, engulfed in a soft, golden light. This light instills a feeling that anything is possible and that your life is truly rich and blessed. It is blessed in that there is no worry. Everything you need and want in life is provided for. You anticipate the adventure of your future rather than sit in uncertainty about it. Your rich friendships and family ties support you in feeling loved and hence prosperous. Know that all of this is true. When you are ready, return to the present moment.

Step Three

Place a few drops of cinnamon in one or more diffusers and allow the smell to circulate through your entire house. Or place the cinnamon sticks in a pot of water and allow them to simmer on the stove. Leave all doors open. Cinnamon is said to attract wealth.

❧ AN ALTAR TO PROSPERITY

Find an especially beautiful piece of fabric to cover your altar. This could be a soft floral tapestry, a sensuous velvet, or a splendid silk. Drawing from your list of the things you most want in life, find ways to represent a few that you plan to accomplish in the short term. For instance, if your desire is to purchase a beautiful home of your own, clip a photo of your favorite style of house and place it in a gilded frame upon your altar. If it's a trip to Hawaii, place a dolphin or some other affirmation for traveling there upon the altar. You might even decide to keep the list itself on your altar. Store it in a golden box and read it each time you visit.

If your altar space is large enough, gather eight purple, golden, or beeswax candles in gold candlesticks and cluster them on the back left side of the altar as you face it. According to Feng Shui, this is the area that activates wealth. Eight is the number representing abundance. If the space is small, try using tea lights. To amplify the effect, place the candles on a mirror. Sprinkle the entire altar with gold glitter.

Keep your altar alive and fresh by removing symbols of things as you accomplish them and replacing them with representations of whatever you would next like to attract into your life. Energize your altar during visits with a mister filled with spring water and a few drops of cinnamon. Be aware that divine prosperity is yours to enjoy.

❧ COLOR

Color as it relates to prosperity is highly individual. When used in combination with sumptuous fabrics it is most powerful. It is especially important to take into consideration finishes of existing flooring and furniture, or their replacements, in choosing colors to make you feel prosperous. The size and function of the room being decorated, along with your personal tastes, will dictate the amount and intensity of the colors to be used. A large, light-filled living room can take a heavier dose of color if it pleases you.

Purple has long been held as the color of wealth, luxury, and power. This is partially due to the fact that in earlier times, authentic purple was produced from the dye of a type of mollusk. It was costly to yield, and so was reserved for the garments of priests and rulers. The Romans later revered purple for this connection with opulence and status.

Related colors of similar intensity, such as cabernet and royal blue, have a similar energy. When paired with a substantial gold—also associated with wealth—the effect is dazzling. Gold can extend into other, somewhat unexpected color groups. There are golden greens and burnished browns, for example. In fairy tales, gold is often a symbol of spiritual power. The green-gold and cabernet within the intricate patterning of a chair, when paired with a solid, deep green sofa, is striking. Golden walls, wood furniture in rich finishes, and dark metal accents complete a rich palette.

A balance of royal blue and gold spiked with a deep, clear red exudes a regal air. This combination is excellent for formal areas, such as dining rooms. It becomes more casually elegant when used in bedrooms, and is countrified when fed into floral fabric designs. It has a traditional, somewhat conservative flavor.

Purple is more flamboyant, but is easy to live with, especially when used with other rich, contrasting colors. The combination of earthy purple, pale gold, and a warm brown-gold is spiritually uplifting, yet at the same time grounding. If you love the glorious feel of purple, but your physical or mental space won't allow for such intensity, explore various shades in lilac and mauve. These lighter colors have the added benefit of giving the impression of spaciousness.

If you are daring or crave intense color, pair a clear red with purple for an altogether lavish effect. Use one or the other for accent only, and add in plenty of paler or neutral shades for balance. For example, heavy wicker furniture could accept seat cushions fashioned in a very deep plum and accent pillows of a paled plum. Clear red accents, especially in the form of glass, would partner well with the other two colors. Paint the walls a neutral color, such as a warm or antique white. You'll be lapped in luxury.

Another approach to achieving an atmosphere of richness through color is to use layer upon layer of various shades of the same color. Neutrals work best, such as a warm khaki. For strength and refinement, bring into the scheme very dark metals. This could be accomplished with furniture, such as a metal and glass coffee table, or with artwork, such as bronze sculpture.

Visualize buttery gold walls, an ivory piano with a variety of black vases on top of it, sheet music open. The look is very rich. This approach works with a wide range of colors, from shades of white through quite intense shades. It is the actual layering of color that produces the effect of wealth.

SOUND

Perhaps the most luxurious sound of all is that of moving water. The Chinese associate flowing water with the building of wealth and happiness. Enjoy these sounds with indoor and outdoor water fountains or recordings of water sounds. A tabletop fountain placed in the far left-hand corner of your desk as you are sitting at it will affirm wealth, says Feng Shui.

Music that is lilting and fluid will help impress your environment with a feeling of abundance. Some forms of jazz have this capacity. The elegance of classical music will elevate the energy of your environment regardless of its decor. Light classical music helps promote accuracy in work. You may wish to consider working alongside this type of music if you mentally link the work you do with a prosperous outcome for yourself.

AROMATHERAPY

As mentioned earlier, cinnamon bark is said to attract wealth. This is a powerful scent, but if you resonate with it, use it lavishly. Ginger and patchouli are said to draw money to you, and the uplifting scent of bergamot is said to bring abundance. These scents can be used in a diffuser.

Make up a bottle of your favorite scent using spring water and a few drops of oil and mist yourself whenever your prosperity consciousness could use a lift. If you're in sales and your car is quite often your office, purchase an automobile diffuser and keep the energetic connection to prosperity alive and well during your day. If you're trying to sell your home, any of these scents, but especially cinnamon, is effective in attracting buyers.

❧ FLOWER ESSENCES

The wisdom of flowers can speak to the soul's need for abundance. The basis of prosperity is really trust, whether that be trust in a loving universe or God, or trust in yourself to heed the wisdom of your inner voice in pursuing your bliss.

To move into a greater experience of prosperity, cerato can help by encouraging reliance on your intuition, especially during times of uncertainty. Cherry plum facilitates surrender to intuitive guidance. To help you learn to detach yourself from a specific outcome, try using filaree. Its gentle support will help free you from common worries so that a greater perspective can be revealed. Trillium can keep you balanced in your view of wealth, such that it does not become important in and of itself. Blackberry provides strength of will in manifesting objectives. It helps overcome inertia.

❧ ENERGETIC DESIGN

The goal of energetic design for prosperity is to create a feeling of infinite possibility and also a feeling that the universe conspires to provide for you abundantly. Arranging Home, whether Home is a modest apartment or prestigious manor, to accommodate the expansive potential living inside of you is rudimentary to your prosperity objective.

The best way to begin defining an abundant environment is to consider the things you hold in your highest esteem, things that inspire you. These can be things that you currently love to do or, even better, long to do. For instance, if you yearn to play the flute with proficiency, but your skill ranks at the beginner's level, make the flute more permanent in your home. This could be accomplished by displaying your flute when not in use, rather than keeping it locked away. The flute then becomes part of the decor of your environment. The indulgence is worthwhile. Having it out will tempt you to practice more often, filling your home with beautiful sound and your heart with joy. Your own flute could become the centerpiece of a small collection of flutes that could embellish your walls. By the way, the flute is an uplifting symbol to the Chinese, and bamboo flutes are often used as a Feng Shui cure to raise Chi in places where it is pressurized, such as beneath an overhead beam.

For many people, art and artifacts gathered from around the globe evoke a sense of sophistication, the kind that comes from the worldliness of exposure to a variety of people, cultures, and places. Extensive travel is often associated with privilege. Additionally, a certain richness is achieved through diversity—even diversity of placed objects. It may seem pretentious to display things from around the globe as if you have been there when you haven't. However, if you love art and are, for instance, especially fond of African art, you will feel indulged being surrounded by it in your living space.

Decide what it is that would most inspire you now. Is there some way to incorporate it literally or symbolically into your decorating scheme? It is more viable to invest in things that create energetic patterns of prosperity for you personally than to acquire things the world sees as symbols of prosperity. Your environment cannot possibly feel prosperous unless it is authentically you.

The strongest testimonial to a prosperous lifestyle is a feeling of comfort and excellent support in all areas of life. This may be where Home can be of most help. To feel prosperous, buy furniture that cradles you in support. Sofas, chairs, and even the tender support of mattresses can all contribute to a feeling of prosperity if they fit your body like a glove and allow your spirit to rest comfortably in them.

Texture is an important component of feeling prosperous at Home. For above-average affluence, investigate fabrics such as velvet; fabrics incorporating highly-textured threadwork, such as patterned cotton, silk, wool damasks, tapestries, brocatelles, and brocades (some are highlighted with gold or silver thread); patterned pile fabrics such as chenille and velour crafted from silk, mohair, wool, and cotton; and heavy silk moirés. Fringe used as trim on upholstered furniture and drapes is reminiscent of decadent Victorian styling.

Also consider using fabric motifs. Motifs have been used in weaving since the Middle Ages to convey symbolic meaning. A wreath motif, for example, symbolizes sovereignty and power. Fruit motifs will always convey the feeling of plentitude. Bees became popular during Napoleon's reign as a sign of industriousness.

Never skimp on fabrics that adorn your bed—you spend almost a third of your life there. In the winter, dress your bed in heavy English flannel sheets. Wool blankets, handmade quilts, and thickly textured cotton blankets will send you off to sleep with the reassurance that all is indeed well. Mosquito netting or other sheer fabric suspended above your bed is a delicious detail.

Silken tassels used as tiebacks for draperies are an elaborate touch, and one that won't go unnoticed. Tassels are very pretty and somehow festive. Placing a different tassel around each bedroom's doorknob is a luxurious energetic distinction. Most tassels sold in stores today are very simple, but you can find unique, ornate tassels for relatively little money that would add lots of strength to a decorating theme dedicated to prosperity.

Draperies that flow onto the floor are considered by many to reflect an opulent attitude. Whether you prefer lush velvet drapes or sheer panels, allowing them to fall as they will on your floor can help unleash the energetic flow of an infinite universe.

Consider adorning your walls with breathtaking tapestries or with masterful renditions of fine art with themes corresponding to your prosperity belief system. If you equate having a beach house with prosperity, or it is on your personal wish list, illustrate that idea with artwork. Flowing water represents wealth, and art depicting it becomes an affirmation for wealth. Hang your artwork with intention.

As discussed earlier in this chapter, feeling prosperous also means allowing yourself to exist in the continuum of generosity, giving and receiving. Remembering that Home is a metaphor for our inner states and a physical affirmation of where we're heading, we need space in our interiors to symbolically state that we are open to receive. Although the tendency is to overembellish to create a feeling of luxury, keep things as clear as possible.

Some schools of Feng Shui stipulate that the positioning and use of your kitchen stove has a strong correlation to good luck. This is partially because this is where food is prepared. Having plenty of food is a sign of abundance.

So, first ensure that your stove has a commanding position. This means, primarily, that while standing at the stove it is best that your back is not to the main entrance, which would create a feeling of unease. If the position of your stove is not lucky, place a mirror above it so the cook can see everything that transpires within the kitchen. Pay tribute to the transformational process of cooking by using a sun-shaped mirror. The burners of the stove also represent abundance. Again, having the mirror behind the stove will symbolically double the number of burners—and your wealth quotient. Keep the stovetop spotless and use every burner on a regular basis for the most optimal wealth accumulation.

In the name of prosperity, create a proper office or space for handling your finances. Home offices are common now because many people work out of their homes either because of the flexibility of their employers or their own entrepreneurial spirit. Whatever this space is for, make it a powerful place.

The power spot in your home for an office, according to Feng Shui, is the far left corner of the house as you stand facing your home from the street. If your home is two or more stories, your office could be located on any floor. It's usually best to keep the office out of the basement, primarily because of the link with insignificance that basements sometimes suffer. However, if your basement is appropriately finished, clean, and well-lit with some natural light coming in, let your intuition decide. Finished basements can often be the quietest place in the house, and that alone makes them worth considering.

The standard Feng Shui rule is to make sure that, as you sit at your desk, in the position you most frequently sit, your back is not to the door or to a large window. This strong position will feel protected and commanding all at once. Needless to say, this area should always be clean and well organized.

Keep important phone numbers in a place of honor. Don't scatter them everywhere on little scraps of paper. Collect business cards from everyone important to you in your work and keep them in a file near your telephone. Keep files for existing customers away from the telephone to symbolically clear the way for new business to come in. Taping or gluing nine coins to the bottom of your phone is said to generate a glut of business. In Feng Shui, nine Chinese coins are used and are strung together with red ribbon through the holes in their centers.

You may want to emphasize the correlation between the work you do in your office space and your wealth by allowing numbers, as expressed in geometric shapes, to dominate the decorating scheme. This is a place where the accumulative power of gold should reign. Gold will also serve you well in helping to keep your mind clear and focused. As for furniture, a chair that is very supportive of all the activities you perform while sitting in it is absolutely necessary.

Place a small tabletop fountain or healthy plant on the far left corner as you face your desk while sitting at it. Amplify profits by hanging a crystal in a window in this room. Any awards associated with your work deserve to be displayed in your office space: certificates and diplomas will reinforce your ability to achieve success in all you undertake. Photographs of people you love will constantly remind you of some of the very important reasons for working so hard.

The career area of your home is the middle front section of your house as you face it from the street. If your ability to command wealth or feel prosperous is directly linked to your career, as it is for most of us, stabilize this area in your home by placing in it some large, heavy potted plants. This area could benefit from a small water fountain also, as slow-moving water symbolizes luck entering your home via this particular room.

❧ FINISHING TOUCHES

Grapevines have traditionally been viewed as a symbol of wealth and refinement. In China, the peony is thought to be a masculine flower that attracts prosperity and radiance. It was designated the flower of the royal family. In ancient Egypt, the pen was considered a tool of infinite potential. These symbols can be incorporated into your environment to bring power to your overall design. For example, peonies can be cultivated in many parts of the country and would be an excellent choice, if the growing conditions are right, to plant near the front entryway to your house.

If you love ships, you may want to incorporate a few into your decorating scheme through the use of model ships or paintings. Old-style ships, such as merchant ships, laden with gold are symbolically the best choice. Make sure the sailing is always over smooth water. And if you're using a model ship, make sure it is sailing toward the interior of your home as opposed to sailing away from it and out of your life.

Amethyst has been revered through the ages as symbolizing wealth and royalty. It is relatively inexpensive, and a large unpolished chunk of it would make a really lovely house stone for prosperity. Citrine is said to help in accumulating and retaining wealth.

In Feng Shui, a crystal or metal vase filled with auspicious things is said to help you obtain and keep wealth. This is called a wealth vase. Choose a vase with a wide mouth, preferably in the shape of an hourglass, and fill it with semiprecious stones and crystals, three Chinese coins strung on red ribbon, and colorful beads, for example. You can borrow a rich person's wealth by adding some soil to the vase from their garden if you like. It's best to keep this vase in a cabinet out of everyone else's sight.

The medicine of Buffalo is of abundance and prayer. Its message is that nothing of value is achieved without the guidance of Spirit. If you resonate with Buffalo, find ways to incorporate it into your home. Buffalo is a beautiful reminder that we must always be aware of our source, and the source of all good.

❧ AN AFFIRMATION FOR PROSPERITY

Now that you've culled the truth about yourself in relation to prosperity, consciously release the beliefs that don't serve you and affirm your divine right to prosperity. When an affirmation is born of true belief and self-knowledge, it is powerful. Otherwise, it is simply an avoidance tactic, producing few positive results. It is best if you craft your own affirmation based on the specifics of what you learned in the exercises, but here is one to inspire you or to use if it strikes a chord within you.

My experience in life is that of richness.

My heart is full with the bounty of life. I am grateful for all the love, acceptance, compassion, kindness, and generosity I am daily shown. I give all that I am generously without seeking praise, for I know the source of all good is Spirit. I give thanks that I can participate in the abundant flow of life.
Amen.

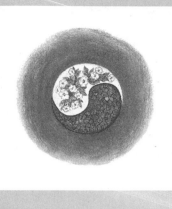

CHAPTER TWENTY-THREE

Romance

A rendezvous of magical elements: myriad stars to light a sky of the deepest midnight blue, whispered tender verses, the twelfth stroke of midnight, slow-burning allure. Romance stirs our souls in a way that makes our lives surreal, each moment synchronistic. Perhaps in no other segment of our life is vulnerability so powerful. Honor yourself for opening to such aliveness in your life now.

Examining Your Beliefs About Romantic Love

Attracting romantic love or the right relationship is deeply connected to your ability to share yourself with another as the individual you truly are. You must trust that the person you are meant to live life with exists and will love you unconditionally. Unconditional love does not require clever strategies or manipulative game playing; it does not need you to be anything other than your true, loving self.

As a prerequisite to creating a home vibrantly aligned with your dream of romantic love, you must first clarify what romantic love means to you. Following are two exercises to help you with this. Creating romantic love can be a complex process and may invoke feelings of discomfort. Pay close attention to your feelings, and if you encounter blockages or pain, you may want to consider seeking the guidance of a therapist.

EXERCISE ONE • WHAT DOES ROMANCE MEAN?

Following is a list of words we associate with romantic love. On a separate sheet of paper, quickly jot down whatever comes into your mind as you read each word. Do not censor your thoughts. Write in whatever form best accommodates your thoughts, whether that is single-word association or poetry or an essay. Allow complete and free expression for each word listed before moving on to the next.

Passion	Compatibility
Embrace	Openness
Caring	Respect
Integrity	Love
Soul mate	Kindness
Commitment	Balance
Bliss	Cherish
Honor	

Now that you have emptied your consciousness of some associations you have with these aspects of romantic love, move right into the following meditation. Allow yourself thirty to forty-five minutes to complete this exercise.

EXERCISE TWO • MEDITATION FOR ROMANTIC AMBIENCE

The purpose of this exercise is to set your intention. If you haven't already done so, please familiarize yourself with the basic meditation preparation techniques presented in Chapter 2. Have a pen and your journal or a sheet of paper ready. Read through the instructions for this exercise once. Then, after centering and relaxing yourself completely, ask yourself the following:

* How can my home best emulate romantic love?
* What things (colors, icons and symbols, furnishings) represent romantic love to me?

Simply be still and contemplate these questions for a few moments. When you feel ready, close your eyes and take a mental tour of your dream home beginning at your front door and moving clockwise around the floor plan. If you have a second story, move to it after you have completed your mental tour of the ground floor.

As you move through each room and hallway, take note of the lighting and time of day, the colors, artwork, sacred and special objects, the texture and color of upholstery and drapery fabric, the style and placement of furnishings, and so on. Pay special attention to the places where you will spend the most time with your partner.

After you have toured your entire house, ask yourself if there is anywhere you would like to revisit. Once you feel you have absorbed a complete mental picture of a home that optimally supports romance, gently and gradually return to the present time. Open your eyes.

Make notes of every new discovery made on your tour. Again, don't censor your thoughts. You may learn that the only thing the bedroom needs is a wash of apricot on the walls, or you may find out that you need to replace most of the furnishings in that room. Listen to yourself and honor your feelings. Keep your notes, which you can use for goal setting after you have taken in all of the information in this section.

❧ SPACE CLEARING FOR ROMANCE

Please familiarize yourself with Chapter 3 for information on how to prepare for your space clearing. You will need a pink candle for each room you plan to clear, and a crystal or metal bell (make sure its tone is crisp and pleasing to you).

Step One

Because pink represents the spirit of romantic love and fire is purifying, light a long-burning pink candle in each room you are clearing, leaving the one in the room you will begin in for last. After lighting the last candle, gaze into its flame and imagine being filled with the spirit of romance.

Next, dedicate your candles. You can use the following words or words of your own that have special meaning: "I dedicate these candles to romantic love and right relationship. May this house be filled with the aliveness, the passion, and the magic of romance." If it is meaningful to you, this is the appropriate time to ask Spirit for guidance in performing this space clearing.

Once you have completed the dedication and are ready, hold your hands above the flame, symbolically washing them in preparation for the clearing.

Step Two

Holding your bell, stand at the entrance of the room. Slowly begin ringing the bell while moving clockwise around the room. Use all of your senses to detect how much clearing to do in each area. Plan to spend more time in areas where energy tends to stagnate, such as corners and closets. If at any point your concentration lapses, take the time to refocus your intention. Slowly work through each room, allowing yourself to be guided by your senses. In the rooms where you and your partner will spend most of your time, you may wish to increase the vibration by chanting a meaning-ful word or words, such as "love," "respect," or "commitment," while ring-ing the bell.

Step Three

As you complete each room, seal it off in a manner with which you resonate. For example, you can seal off each room by visualizing it being filled with radiant pink light.

❧ AN ALTAR TO ROMANCE

Remember, there are no hard and fast rules for creating altars. But I would strongly suggest placing this particular altar in your bedroom for two rea-sons: the bedroom is the heart of romantic love within the home; and because of this, bedroom placement magnifies your intention, adding to the power of your altar. Standing at the entrance of your bedroom and facing it, the ideal position for your altar, according to Feng Shui, is in the far right corner of the room—the relationship area. Refer to the bagua map at the end of Chapter 4 for more information on placement.

Identify meaningful symbols of the magic of romantic love. Below is a list of suggestions. Your goal is to find objects that represent these symbols or romantic experiences. Because you are inviting someone into your intimate life, remember that pairs of things are especially powerful.

Roses	Cherubs	Romantic landscapes
Red	Candles	Poetry
Circles	Yin/Yang	Rubies
Aphrodite	Topaz	Garnets

Found objects and souvenirs—such as theater tickets to a romantic play, or stones found along an incredibly romantic beach—are even more empowered because a strong personal association with those items already exists.

Softly drape some beautiful floral cloth or handmade lace over your altar before placing the objects upon it. If it pleases you, infuse your altar with a romantic scent by filling a small crystal bowl with spring water and a perfume oil or essential oil that you associate with romance, such as rose, patchouli, jasmine, or lavender.

Fresh flowers are always romantic. If you choose to place them on your altar, be sure to replace them before they fade and die, otherwise the metaphor becomes that of diminishing love. The same holds true for dried flowers—avoid these completely.

A pair of candles placed side by side evoke feelings of the mystery and seduction of romance. Choose warm-colored candles such as pink, apricot, or red.

❧ COLOR

Universally, and in Feng Shui, pink represents romantic love. It is the color that feeds the heart chakra. There are many beautiful shades of pink, or red, to choose from. For passionate love, you might select something daring, such as magenta or deep cerise. These reds have blue bases, and are cooler. To strengthen a passionate color scheme and create harmony at the same time, pair one of these reds with a medium to deep blue, such as ocean or indigo, or a playful green, such as lime or emerald.

Because of the intensity of these colors, use them sparingly and discreetly in most rooms. They become much more demure when employed in delicate floral designs, for example. People who prefer solids could consider using a blue or green for larger areas, such as for the fabrics covering sofas or the paint covering the walls, and red-toned colors for accents. Variations of this color scheme work well in spaces such as living and family rooms.

Intimate dining rooms support dramatic color quite well. It is fairly common to encounter dining rooms with solid red walls. A fringe benefit, for some, is that red stimulates the appetite. If the room is too large, however, the color will overwhelm. Cool reds can be warmed with golden accents in things such as picture frames, and warm reds cooled with silver accents.

More subtle, sophisticated romantic reds include mauve or petal pink. If you find intense color irritating, these can easily be used throughout the home. Pair them with a grounding green such as malachite or sage, and romantic balance is attained. If you prefer warmer color, the same scheme can be used substituting shades of apricot for pink. Bedrooms and bathrooms receive this palette well. Bedrooms require softer reds, otherwise they are too stimulating for most people. Whatever your tolerance to red, always make sure your sheets—which rest right against your skin—are a soft, warm color. In the bathroom, green tile or slate floors and pale apricot walls are inviting. For a dramatic, art deco look in the bathroom, use a medium coral on the walls and pair it with a black vanity and black and white or marbled floors.

❧ SOUND

The very best music to set the tone for romance is, naturally enough, Romantic music, specifically that of Schubert, Schumann, Tchaikovsky, Chopin, and Liszt. Or imagine for a moment the sounds of a hot, languid summer's eve—falling to sleep with a backdrop of crickets singing would be delightful. If you live in the city, you can obtain a small electronic device that plays a variety of soothing sounds to go to sleep by, such as crickets singing, ocean waves, a thunderstorm, and so on.

❧ AROMATHERAPY

The following essential oils can be used to inspire love or augment your experience of romance: jasmine, juniper, lavender, patchouli, ylang-ylang. Always use these in small amounts. These scents are best used in a diffuser. You might also enjoy using them in your bath (use up to six drops per bath). Lavender-scented sheets are incredibly romantic. Sprinkle a few drops of essential oil onto a cotton pad and slip it between the sheets during the day while you are up and about. When you turn back the covers at night the dreamy scent will be released.

&c FLOWER ESSENCES

After reading their descriptions, select from the list below the one flower essence you resonate most with and try it for at least four weeks—two to four drops under the tongue, four times per day.

* Mariposa lily: For receptivity to human love.
* Basil: Increased ability to integrate spirituality and sexuality in relationships.
* Bleeding heart: For freedom in love; to overcome unhealthy attachments.

&c ENERGETIC DESIGN

Now that you have developed a complete backdrop for romantic ambience, you are ready to consider energetic elements and placement of objects. For continuity, please always consider your chosen color palette when making design and decorating decisions. However, the intention you hold in executing your plan is by far the most powerful energizer in creating romance. For a healthful relationship, allow balance and equality to become part of your romantic intentions as well. Throughout this section I've included tips on how to accomplish this.

If you are alone right now, the single most important thing you must do, before you do anything else, is make room for another person. Clean out everything, making sure there is ample room for your partner's personal belongings. Empty half of your dresser drawers for the other person, and half of your closet and storage space. This is both a symbolic and practical indication that you are ready for partnering. Whether or not the person actually lives with you any time soon, make room for him or her in your heart and home.

Refer to your notes from your preparatory exercises. Make good use of your ideas because these concepts are most meaningful to you and therefore the most powerful. Where intention goes, love flows!

Using the bagua map on page 56, locate the relationship area of each floor of your home. While standing on the street facing your home, this area is in the far right-hand corner. The bagua can be used as a guide for an entire floor or one room. First, make sure that the relationship area is not missing from your home. If it is, it is very important in Feng Shui to make the area landscaping as pristine as possible and to use some kind of outdoor lighting to elevate and brighten it. Examine these areas thoroughly as to function and appearance. It would not be good, metaphorically, if your trash bin or a litter box were located here. Clean up these areas; elevate their status by making them beautiful. To amplify relationship energy, hang a crystal prism on a nine-inch red ribbon in any windows located in these areas.

First impressions are critical from a Feng Shui perspective—and any other. For romance, hang a floral wreath on the front door (the circle symbolizing eternity). Flank the entryway with lavender. Hang a rustic metal heart plaque near or above the entryway.

Use romantic color palettes in every room with function always in mind. You probably wouldn't want a cerise couch trimmed with five layers of lace in your living room. Long burgundy velvet curtains in the living room, a sofa of forest green, and a chair of burgundy, green, and gold would be romantic with an air of richness or abundance, and would be completely appropriate, not to mention inviting and intimate. If you do prefer a lighter, more crisp look in any of the main rooms in your home, be sure to add elements of warmth, perhaps with accent color, such as apricot or sable. Wood and wicker furnishings also add warmth.

As stated earlier in this chapter, use a more restful palette in the bedroom. You can punctuate the room with a dramatic color in the red family for passion. Use common sense: if your vision of the ideal man or woman is very outdoorsy, white eyelet ruffles anywhere will feel uncomfortable. Stay away from crisp textures like linen in shades of white. The room will feel sterile. Try to incorporate sensual textures such as velvet wherever possible. Imagine long, flowing velvet drapes tied back with gold tassels, or velvet and satin pillows strewn across the bed or a window seat. You might try draping some sheer fabric across the headboard. Cover your nightstands with pieces of hand-crocheted lace.

Make sure there is basic equality on each side of the bed: identical night-stands, lamps, and so forth. Refer to Chapter 4 for basic information about bed placement—this is very important. Eliminate sharp angles that may point directly at you while you're laying in bed. For instance, if the corner of a dresser is pointing directly at the bed, this is believed to cut up Chi and can be damaging to your health and happiness. A cure might be to reposition the unit so it sits diagonally in the corner. If there are any dark corners in your bedroom, use a small lamp to provide soft uplighting.

Group meaningful objects in pairs or fives. Five is a sacred number representing marriage. You may wish to group a cluster of five pink, apricot, or red candles on top of the dresser. Perhaps two related pieces of artwork could hang above your bed. Make sure that the first thing you or the two of you see upon wakening in the morning is something very affirmative of romantic love. For instance, on the wall opposite the bed could hang a piece of art depicting romance. One possibility is a serene beach scene with a couple walking hand in hand. Draw ideas from your meditation exercise notes. Artwork showing peonies in a bedroom is a great attractor of passionate romance.

If you're not shy and you know someone who has been recently and very happily married, you can benefit from that person's marriage Chi by asking him or her to empower nine of your personal possessions. Choose small items you tend to use or carry with you frequently, such as special pieces of jewelry, your house or car keys, your driver's license. Wrap the items in a piece of cloth, preferably red—also a good choice for romance. Ask your friend to touch each item. Bring them into your home, then imagine these items transmitting blessings for happiness in romance directly to you as you place each of them on your altar to romance.

Living plants are good, especially to enliven the relationship area of the bedroom. However, if you are very sensitive, limit the number of plants in your bedroom to very few. The energy of plants can be quite yang, which can cause unrest for sensitive people. Plants are living things with auras of their own. At night our auras expand, and too many living things in one room can be overstimulating.

Fresh-cut flowers represent beauty in full expression. In Feng Shui there is a method for manifesting a specific desired outcome, referred to as the Fragrant Flower Method. It is inherently romantic and very effective for setting intention. Beginning on a meaningful or auspicious day (Valentine's Day, or the second or fifth day of the month, for example), arrange vases of various fragrant flowers in your bedroom—one on each side of the bed is very powerful—and in two other main rooms of your home. Set your intention by visualizing your home filled with the feeling of romance and romantic interludes as you set each arrangement in its place. Every three days for twenty-seven days, replace the flowers with fresh ones.

❧ FINISHING TOUCHES

Naming your rooms, especially the bedrooms, is a completely romantic, and slightly Victorian, touch. Use the numerology grid located on page 90 to fashion names that equate to a two vibration. The essence of two is the balance of yin and yang, of marriage and intimate sharing. Find a creative way to label the entrances to the rooms with their new names. For instance, you could make an eclectic collage door hanger, or a hand-painted plaque. My husband carved the names of our bedrooms in pieces of driftwood we found during a memorable day at the beach and hung them above each door.

Rose quartz brings love and warmth—especially to those who are a bit lonely. Also, it is easy to find larger specimens of rose quartz. If you place this stone at your home's energetic center and dedicate it to romantic love, it will serve you well as a visual affirmation for your dream. Garnets are known to inspire love and enhance all areas of passion. If you like wearing garnets, try a strand or two of garnet beads. Or place a garnet in the pot of a healthy plant. This is a lovely metaphor for relationship growth. Wearing emeralds is known to improve all heart functions, including love and kindness to other individuals. And red tourmaline has a softly passionate influence. Thulite is an exceptional stone for married couples because it opens the heart to the clarity of emotional intent.

Because of the collective consciousness surrounding images of angels, they are excellent icons to use in the home dedicated to romance. Consider bringing yourself and loved ones present and future under the watchful eyes of angels. Keep an eye out for four glass or ceramic angels of four to six inches in length, and mount them in the four corners of your bedroom such that they're peering down on the occupants of the room. Use angels in any imaginable romantic way throughout your home and let them serve as reminders that you are divinely protected.

Deer represent gentleness, softness, and love. Doves are symbolic of peace and love. If you choose one of these totems, display it prominently somewhere in your entryway and wherever else it can be a striking reminder of the love that dwells within you—the love attracting romantic love into your life now.

🌹 AFFIRMATIONS FOR ROMANTIC LOVE

If you are ready at a deep, cellular level to accept new love into your life now, use the affirmation below as a powerful step in attracting this love. Read this affirmation daily for as long as you would like, and at least until you feel a shift occurring in your life in favor of true love. The first sentence of the affirmation can be memorized and called to mind or recited several times throughout the day, thereby summoning the powerful message of the entire affirmation into your awareness.

I am guided to and accept my true love now.

My heart opens to the love of the one I was born to love. I completely trust that we are traveling along paths that soon will meet. I know when our paths intersect we will recognize each other as being our life's love. Spirit, unite our hearts and beings forever. Thank you.
And so it is.

If you are in the right relationship and it could use a little more romance, you may find the following affirmation useful.

Love flows freely through my being.

*I am aware that giving and receiving love are one and the same.
I accept my true and loving self and radiate love freely and
generously to my partner now. The universe responds
immediately, and I am lavishly loved. I thank Spirit for the laws
of attraction and this love.
And so it is.*

CHAPTER TWENTY-FOUR

Stability

To feel stable and secure is to be able to rest the mind in Spirit. It is to be able to trust, have faith, and direct our energy into allowing ourselves to be rocked in the cradle of the universe. There are many reasons for living in fear, the opponent of stability: abandonment, neglect, poverty, violence, abuse, the economic and political landscape. But love will always win. It has to. It is the movement of divine energy, and without its dominance over fear we would not exist.

Choosing to create our own safety and stability means taking complete responsibility for our entrance into and existence in this realm. It means honoring ourselves with the faith that each one of us is godlike. Whatever your situation, even if you were born into a family that didn't give you the love you needed, or your financial prospects seem dim, or your spouse is abusive toward you, it makes no difference. In this moment you can choose. Choose bravely, following the wisdom of your intuition and the plan your heart has revealed. You will generate stability for yourself. The unfolding of life is only obstructed when you stand in your own way.

Once you have charted your course of stability, allow Home to help you. This is one area of life in which Home can make an especially profound difference. A secure home environment will make great contributions to your overall sense of safety and comfort.

AN EXERCISE ABOUT STABILITY

Many things tend to make human beings feel more secure on a universal level. Creating a personal sense of stability within the walls of Home is easier when you know what makes you feel stable. This exercise is simple, and yet it can help you make a conscious connection between various aspects of stability and the components of your home.

Following is a list of words associated with aspects of stability. You'll need a notebook or paper and a pen, and a block of about thirty to forty-five minutes to complete this exercise. Taking one word at a time, journal in whatever format you choose about that word's meaning to you. Do not censor your thoughts; allow them to spill forth onto the page.

Next, write down any poignant associations that word has with your life experiences, special events and occasions, or specific childhood memories. *Fixed* might remind you of a time you were unpleasantly surprised by a birthday party in your honor and how it made you feel violated. Then write about how your home did or did not support you in that specific situation.

Now write about how you believe Home can represent this aspect of stability for you, and be very specific. If a pink wool blanket would make you feel very *secure*, write that down. If the *constancy* of a fully stocked pantry would bring peace of mind, write that down. Do not move on to the next word until you've exhausted your thoughts on the current word.

Stable	Steady
Secure	Firm
Responsible	Consistent
Fixed	Resolute
Steadfast	Constant
Unshakable	Repose
Reliable	

Keep your notes and use them as filters in making decisions about your home decor and life that will increase a feeling of stability.

❧ SPACE CLEARING FOR STABILITY

This space clearing will disintegrate negative energy and reset energy patterns to reflect an increased connection with the earth, producing a feeling of being grounded.

For this clearing you need chamomile essential oil and a diffuser. Chamomile is known for creating a sense of security, just as you find comfort by drinking the tea. You also need a bronze bell. The silken sound of bronze settles scattered energy. If you have a choice between sizes of bells, choose a larger bell for the deepest, most reverberant sound. Brownish-red pillar candles are needed, one for each room being cleared. If it is an option, choose squared rather than rounded candles. This shape will help gather energy from the four directions. As the candles burn they will diffuse the earth color and its stabilizing energy into the atmosphere. A ceramic or earthenware tile or candleholder will accentuate earth energy.

Step One

In the most central room of your home, place several drops of the essential oil in the diffuser and allow the scent to begin wandering through your house. Next, place and light the candles in each room to be cleared. As you light each candle, dedicate it to achieving a feeling of security through the nurturance of Home. For instance, in your bedroom you might say, "I dedicate this candle to the restful sleep that comes from knowing I am completely safe, secure, and stable."

Step Two

After lighting all the candles, return to your entryway. Connect with the spirit of your home as introduced in Chapter 3. Call in your angels and guides to help in clearing old energy patterns and setting new ones to cradle you in comfort and safety. Set your intention. Be very specific about how you would like that sense of stability to manifest.

Step Three

Begin clearing the space using the bronze bell. Ring the bell with one hand and with the other spread its energy throughout the room, including corners and closets. Use slow, steady, repetitive movements. Be very conscious about ensuring that every area receives equal attention. See yourself as a conduit, gathering and unifying equal amounts of energy from the four directions for dispersion into your home. As you complete each room, seal it off by making the infinity sign in the air with your hand, knowing that the energy in the room is consistent and firmly anchored to the earth.

❧ AN ALTAR TO STABILITY

A couple of areas within your home are particularly powerful for an altar to stability. The first is the marriage/relationship area of your home, which is the back right-hand corner as you face your home from the street. In Feng Shui this area is also associated with the element Earth. Earth energy is grounded, balanced, and stable. Another excellent position for your altar is at the center of your home. Consider these two areas and choose the one that feels the best or is most practical for erecting an altar.

This is a simple yet powerful altar. Consider using a perfectly square table-top for this altar because that will acknowledge the four directions equally. You need four smooth, round stones, such as river rocks. Choose stones that are as large as your altar space permits. Place one rock in each corner of the altar. In the center, place a large, square pillar candle on as heavy a candleholder as possible. If anything else is strongly symbolic of stability for you, you may place it upon the altar. Otherwise, leave it just as it is.

To consecrate your altar, smudge it with sage and dedicate it to your growth into a greater experience of authentic security. To energize your altar when visiting it, try misting it with a few drops of chamomile or bergamot in spring water.

❧ COLOR

Envision the color wheel as divided into quadrants. It appears this way in illustrations sometimes. For the ultimate in stability choose a color from each quadrant, with the dominant color being some shade of cinnamon, to pull in a little more earth energy. Directly across from cinnamon is sage. Ninety degrees to one side of cinnamon is cornflower, and ninety degrees to the other side, marigold. Keeping the amount of color in your decor fairly balanced will enhance stability. However, if you resonate with a particular color more, follow your intuition and allow it to play a larger role in your decorating scheme. Color is powerful, and you must resonate with any color you introduce.

An enlarged palette such as this affords decorating freedom. Although the colors may seem intense, they are of the earth and much easier to live with than you may imagine. Think of worn terra-cotta tiles of various shades, a warm apricot on the walls, green plants, and a touch of blue in the upholstery or in a painting that wraps all the colors together. Envision this: a cinnamon leather couch, honey pine floors, and a rug of rust, jungle green, and the slightest hint of blue that picks up the blue of the sky. Large green corn plants in blue ceramic pots balance the presence of the couch. Honey-colored tiles in the bathroom warm pale blue walls. Flowering plants add a colorful balance. In the bedroom, a floral duvet cover of persimmon-colored flowers, brick, and sage has a touch of blue in it and is complemented by warm wood floors. In the kitchen, a floor of green slate tiles, natural cherry cabinets, and warm white walls is unified by a painting of a beautiful meadow with clear blue skies.

These ideas represent a fraction of what can be done with the colors of the earth. For sophistication, use color subtly overall and accent important symbols of stability, such as a large mountain or tree found in a painting, by choosing icons with intense color. Cameo, warm peach, and nickel in the palest of shades with a striking chamois create a worldly-wise appeal when dotted with plants in pale or variegated green.

❧ SOUND

Music that is very ordered, steady, or repetitive creates a strong sense of stability. Baroque music, which typically has a slow tempo, can evoke this feeling. However, you may find its patterning too ornate or complex. If this is the case, pull musical ideas from your memory by recounting times in your life you felt afraid, uncertain, or out of balance and were uplifted by music in some way. When I'm feeling off-balance, folk music leads me back to my essence. There's something about it that draws my strength out so that it becomes visible to me again. You have most likely had similar experiences.

You may wish to avoid music that has little or no rhythmic order, such as New Age, some jazz, and impressionist music. Heavy metal is disruptive to the nervous system, and rap conjures strong images of the hardness of street life, which directly opposes a sense of security.

The sound of slow, steady rain can often induce a powerful feeling that all is well and safe. If you resonate with this sound you may want to consider installing a small skylight in your bedroom. The sound of rain on a skylight is very comforting and will lull you off to a peaceful sleep. Also have on hand a CD of rain sounds. Make sure the sounds are not of rainstorms, however, because that would be unsettling.

❧ AROMATHERAPY

To ease and comfort yourself, use chamomile or bergamot, as introduced earlier in this chapter. To promote feelings of security you may also wish to try aromatic cypress. And to induce a state of self-security, the feeling of being comfortable in your own body, use oregano. I find lavender a kind of cure-all essential oil. It seems to promote a feeling of good health and relaxation that is very comforting. This is one essential oil you might like to buy in larger bottles.

Except for the oregano, use these oils in a diffuser whenever you are home, or place a few drops of them along with spring water in a mister to refresh your environment whenever the need arises. Before making your bed, drizzle a few drops of oil onto a cotton pad and place it in a small plastic bag between your sheets. When you turn back the covers that evening, you're in for a comforting treat. Use a few drops of oregano in your bath, or keep a misting bottle of it handy to mist yourself when in need of instant grounding.

❧ FLOWER ESSENCES

Because becoming stable is really about learning to trust life, I highly recommend St.-John's-wort, which helps restore a feeling of trust in being divinely guided in the world. Angelica has a similar impact on the soul, and it is especially helpful during times of transition. If part of your perceived instability stems from being let down by others, a good choice is Oregon grape. Oregon grape fosters trust in the goodwill of others. If you have been blocked in being open enough to build trust with others, basil can help. Forget-me-not encourages knowing that you have spirit allies supporting you at all times.

❧ ENERGETIC DESIGN

Many aspects of design may be used to create a stable living environment. Perhaps the most distinct aspect is that of weight. Weighted objects and furnishings create a feeling of being grounded, of being hugged to the earth.

If you are in the market for new furnishings, carefully choose items that are solid or give the impression of being solid. A large, overstuffed chair, the kind you can throw your legs over the arms of, feels much more stable than a dainty slipper chair. A chunky sofa with large square feet is more reassuring than a Queen Anne–style loveseat with sinuous legs. An iron coffee table is much more anchored than a wicker one. A four-poster bed with a canopy honors your relationship to the four directions and is snug compared to a bed frame with no headboard at all.

For decoration, gravitate toward heavy objects such as large potted plants, statuary, and substantial picture frames. Stay away from fragility in all its forms. No delicate glass or porcelain figurines.

Give preference to opaque over transparent. Shy away from glass tabletops and reflective surfaces. In tableware, for example, splurge on a set of earthy ceramic dishes as opposed to clear or colored glass. If you choose crystal stemware, make sure it feels heavy and doesn't give the impression it would easily break. Use mirrors with discretion, only where functionally necessary or in tight areas that make you feel claustrophobic. Framed mirrors, rather than unframed, add a sense of security.

Square shapes gather in earth energy from the four directions and are representative of the element Earth in Feng Shui. Square tables, square tiles, and squarish design style all provide more stability. Unlike sofas and chairs sporting rounded arms and features, those with squared arms contribute more to an environment dedicated to feeling safe.

In fabrics, choose solids or patterns suggesting squareness, such as plaids. Stay away from free-form or flowing patterns and shapes. Rather than gauzy, see-through fabrics, choose something more substantial, such as heavy cotton and wool. For window treatments, blinds and drapes are both reassuring.

As I always advise, decorate intentionally. For stability, minimize scattering. Rather than strewing objects throughout a room, for example, concentrate their presence in a couple of areas. To avoid producing a lopsided feeling, you might wish to position these areas in two opposite corners of the room. Items placed diagonally across from one another anchor each other and the environment.

Weight and heft can be used to stabilize various aspects of your life. If, for instance, your relationships seem to be suffering in general, try placing something heavy in the relationship area of your home. This could be a heavy potted plant. A bookcase full of books on topics of spiritual and personal growth in your self knowledge or career area can symbolize your determination to know and be secure within yourself. Financial ups and downs can be leveled by placing a statue or large fish aquarium in the wealth area.

While on the subject of anchoring, it is imperative that furniture be arranged in a manner that keeps the room balanced—more from a weight-based perspective than a visual one. In other words, if you have a piano and a heavy sofa positioned on one side of the room and a little bookcase on the other, the room will feel off-kilter. If you can, position the sofa and piano across from one another.

Apply lighting principles in the same manner. Having one end of a room brightly lit while the other is dim is destabilizing to the psyche. Try to balance background lighting so that the entire room is evenly lit. This can easily be achieved by adding accent lighting, such as floor or table lamps, where necessary. Highlight your artwork with appropriate light so that it can illume your stable spirit any time you're in the room.

Artwork should be chosen carefully for stability, and there are many options. You may react more favorably to art mediums and styles that are more delineated, as opposed to the soft vagueness of watercolor and impressionistic style. Based on your notes from the exercise earlier in this chapter, select art that mirrors back to you the kind of stability you wish to attract. If a state of smooth and balanced emotions makes you feel secure, a painting of a ship sailing through smooth seas would reinforce that. You can even get more specific by placing the painting in the career area of your home if you believe this quality would most benefit you in your work. If family support brings safety, then find art that depicts familial love. Accentuate the role of family in your process by placing such artwork in the family area of your home. If being in nature makes you feel comforted, your choices are almost endless.

There is a direct link between natural objects and earth. If you find nature reassuring, exploit this direct link by bringing natural objects into your home environment. I've had several people comment on how beautiful the river rocks are that I have stacked on top of my kitchen counter. A basket full of pinecones next to the fireplace and lush green houseplants bring the outdoors in, as does a vase of flowers. Symbolically, chrysanthemums are said to provide grounding. In your garden you might want to include marigolds, which help release phobias and fear, or foxglove, said to stabilize emotions. Rosemary has long been held as a guardian or protector. This is a wonderful plant with which to flank the outside of your main entrance.

Upstairs rooms or finished attic spaces commonly have ceilings that slope in one direction. While these ceilings can feel cozy, they can also disrupt the equilibrium. Try painting the lower wall the same color as the ceiling and the remaining walls one contrasting color. Or try placing opposing forms on the walls for balance. One large piece of artwork on the low wall and two medium-sized pieces of artwork on the opposite wall, all carrying the same theme, will help to unify the space. Sometimes uplighting can be used to symbolically lift the sloping ceiling. Sleeping under a sloping ceiling is not conducive to good health and comfort, according to Feng Shui. If at all possible, try not to position a bed in such an area.

The structural stability of your home must be examined and addressed. Make sure your home is prepared for whatever acts of God are prevalent in your area. This will make you feel secure. If you live in an earthquake-prone area, for instance, ensure your home is anchored securely to its foundation and that all structural members are tied together.

If repairs need to be made to increase safety, give them immediate consideration. Unsafe electrical work should be corrected. Items such as loose floorboards should be fixed. Objects that can tip over easily should be affixed.

Things that might not actually be dangerous can give the impression of being dangerous. This is especially true with things hanging from the wall at the head of your bed. Be very cautious about what you place here. Things that protrude out from the wall can make you feel uneasy while you sleep— even if you are not conscious of it.

To illustrate how effective energetic design geared to stability can be, imagine in your entryway a striking painting of a canyon. Its intense earthy reds are set against sunny skies, and a deep blue river cuts steadily through it. It's taken millions of years of slow, steady movement to carve this canyon, and the end product is breathtaking. Such a painting would set the tone for your entire home, and it would add tremendous depth to a space that is, for most of us, somewhat small. A handcrafted tribal rug and something to anchor each corner of the room—some heavy potted plants or large vases filled with tree branches—immediately reassure. A strong sense of stability is created through heft, balance, color, and decorating theme.

With all this emphasis on stability, you could easily create an environment so heavy and grounded that it made you overly serious, overly responsible, unchangeable. To avoid this, make sure all five elements, according to Feng Shui, are present in each room. Create an immediate balance with Wood, the element that controls Earth. Wooden objects and furniture, plants, cotton fabrics, floral arrangements, and greens and blues—already established as beneficial for this environment—all represent the element of Wood. With enough Wood a healthful state of balance will be achieved. Use your intuition in making further refinements using the other elements.

❧ FINISHING TOUCHES

Reassurance is often attained through the help of family, friends, community. This feeling of interconnectedness can be emphasized by placing a family heirloom or collection of heirlooms in the family area of your home. This could be as simple as a small table that has long been in the family adorned with photos of family and others we deem stabilizing influences. This idea can be copied in the helpful people area of your house. A small shelf on the wall dedicated to special and helpful friends and guides can bring comfort in times when you feel fearful.

Things to hold on to are often comforting. As long as you are not completely dependent on those things to feel safe, it's okay. Pillows on the sofa are convenient to grab and hold when alone or when discussing something uncomfortable with another. A soft throw brings a sense of well-being while reading or listening to music.

If you resonate with a totem animal that represents stability to you, place a representation of the animal in your self-knowledge area to help draw out and build on those qualities that already exist within you. Turtle provides a strong connection with the earth and is a powerful teacher of the art of grounding. Hanging a square mirror in this area could symbolically reflect your inner strength and safety in the world.

Anchor your decorating scheme for stability by grouping objects in fours, which is symbolic of grounding earth energy and the four directions. A ticking or chiming clock creates a steady rhythm and sense of order. If you find these sounds comforting, place clocks in areas where you spend a lot of time alone. Jade attracts and strengthens earth energy within a dwelling, making it the ideal house stone for an environment dedicated to feeling secure.

❧ AN AFFIRMATION FOR STABILITY

Whenever it feels as though a situation threatens your newborn sense of security, whenever it's tempting to retreat to a comfortable old habit that no longer serves you, or whenever the challenge seems to require a stretch you're not sure you're capable of performing, recite this affirmation to bring a profound feeling of safety.

**The universe honors my faith in it by cradling me
in love and safety.**

*As I advance along my journey in becoming anchored I am
tightly hugged by the love of others and Spirit. I find comfort in
many places. I am increasingly able to feel protected and looked
after as I move through life. I am grateful for this new feeling.
Amen.*

Bibliography

Becker, Udo, *The Continuum Encyclopedia of Symbols*. New York, NY: The Continuum Publishing Co., 1997.

Campbell, Don, *The Mozart Effect*. New York, NY: Avon Books, 1997.

Collins, Terah Kathryn, *The Western Guide to Feng Shui*. Carlsbad, CA: Hay House, 1996.

Higley, Connie and Alan, and Letham, Pat, *Aromatherapy A–Z*. Carlsbad, CA: Hay House, 1998.

Kaminski, Patricia, and Katz, Richard, *Flower Essence Repertory*. Nevada City, NV: The Flower Essence Society, 1994.

Lin, Jami, *The Feng Shui Anthology*. Miami Shores, FL: Earth Design, Inc., 1997.

Linn, Denise, *The Hidden Power of Dreams*. New York, NY: Ballantine Books, 1988.

Post, Steven, *The Modern Book of Feng Shui*. New York, NY: Dell Publishing, 1998.

Richardson, Wally and Jenny, *The Spiritual Value of Gemstones*. Marina del Rey, CA: DeVorss & Company, 1980.

Sams, Jamie, and Carson, David, *Medicine Cards*. Santa Fe, NM: Bear & Co., 1988.

Steiger, Brad, *Totems: The Transformative Power of Your Personal Animal Totem*. New York, NY: HarperCollins: 1997.

Streep, Meg, *Altars Made Easy*. New York, NY: HarperCollins Publishers, 1997.

For More Information

For further information or a consultation, please contact Nicole Marcelis, 2212 Queen Anne Avenue N. #261, Seattle, WA 98109.